Wild
ABOUT TEXAS

Wild
ABOUT TEXAS

A Bouquet of Recipes,
Wildflowers and Wines

A COOKBOOK BY THE CYPRESS-WOODLANDS JUNIOR FORUM

Publisher
Cypress-Woodlands Junior Forum

•

First Edition
First Printing April 1989, 10,000
Second Printing May 1990, 15,000
Library of Congress Catalog Card Number 89-090738
ISBN 0-9622009-0-5

•

•

Printed by
Hart Graphics, Inc.
Austin, Texas

The Cypress-Woodlands Junior Forum is a Texas based, non-profit volunteer service organization. Founded in 1982, it is the ninth chapter of Junior Forum, Incorporated, which originated in Houston in 1946. Its purpose is to stimulate greater interest among women in civic, educational and philanthropic fields through a variety of programs that support and enrich our community:

Elementary School-Aged Children, through *Birds and Mammals* presentations from the prized McElroy collection, shown in four school districts.

Handicapped Children and Adults, through *KEEP PACE I, II and III*, playgroups offering specialized care to children from birth to three years of age who may be developmentally delayed, in conjunction with Klein Independent School District; *Petticoats, Parasols and Paraphernalia*, the heirloom fashion show benefitting Goodwill Industries of Houston.

Senior Citizens, through *Forum Friends I and II*, monthly gatherings which offer companionship, activities and luncheons; *Heritage Manor Nursing Home*, birthday celebrations for its residents.

People in Crisis, through *Northwest Assistance Ministries*, providing help to persons who need food, clothing, financial assistance, job leads, and counseling; *Interfaith* in the Woodlands, through assistance in the thrift shop.

The Chapter's founder, Peggy Jo Coker, was honored with the prestigious Jefferson Award in 1988 for her dedication in establishing the first women's service organization in the Cypress-Woodlands area. Membership has grown from 11 to over 200, with volunteer hours given to our community presently exceeding 40,000.

Proceeds from the sale of *Wild About Texas* will be returned to our community. Your support means so much to us and to the community we serve daily.

INTRODUCTION

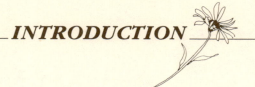

Wild About Texas is a keepsake bouquet, picked from a varietal garden of delicious recipes, wildflowers and Texas wines.

Savor the recipes, certain to tempt even the most discerning of gourmets. Capture the color of a Texas spring in the wildflower botanicals by Austin artist, Rosario Baxter. Learn about Texas wines in the exclusive section by author and award-winning wine expert, Sarah Jane English. Take pleasure in the knowledge shared by noted botanists from the National Wildflower Research Center. As a special treat, we are pleased to include a favorite recipe from Lady Bird Johnson.

A lot of love and time have been given to this very special cookbook. Each recipe has been carefully tested two or more times. Whether you selected Wild About Texas for your own collection or as a gift, we hope you enjoy it as much as we have enjoyed putting it together for you.

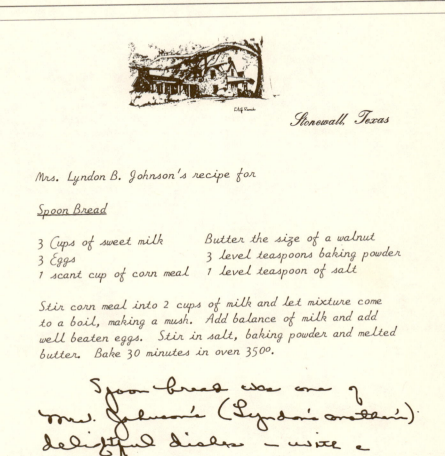

Stonewall, Texas

Mrs. Lyndon B. Johnson's recipe for

<u>Spoon Bread</u>

3 Cups of sweet milk   Butter the size of a walnut
3 Eggs   3 level teaspoons baking powder
1 scant cup of corn meal   1 level teaspoon of salt

Stir corn meal into 2 cups of milk and let mixture come
to a boil, making a mush. Add balance of milk and add
well beaten eggs. Stir in salt, baking powder and melted
butter. Bake 30 minutes in oven 350°.

Spoon bread was one of
Mrs. Johnson's (Lyndon's mother's)
delightful dishes — with a
salad (fruit or green) and meat
it makes a perfect lunch —
Lady Bird Johnson

COOKBOOK COMMITTEE

Martha Ann Kappel
Publishing Chairman

Dena Britton—Leslie Hix
Interim Chairman

Vicki Villarreal
Founding Chairman

Margaret Dunagan • *Editor*
Sherry Lindley • *Co Editor, Recipe File, Indexer*
Sherri Lowe • *Creative Writer*
Dawn McNeill • *Art Design Chairman*
Suzanne Hill • *Recipe Collection, Recipe Distribution*
Karen Braden and Connie Dyer • *Business Operations Coordinators*
Peggy Jo Coker and Karen Donelson • *Financial Chairmen*
Kitty Watkins • *Marketing—Distribution Chairman*
Irene Skor and Daisy White • *Category Chairman Coordinators*
Kathy Carson • *WILD ABOUT TEXAS Gala Chairman*
Sheryn Jones • *Cookbook Consultant*

Steering Committee:	*Proofers:*	*Typists:*	*Advisors:*
Susan Biggs	Lynn Bacon	Karen Braden	Daisy White
Kathy Carson	Sharon Brandt	Patsy Fielder	Georgan Reitmeier
Peggy Jo Coker	Alana Glass	Virginia Medford	Peggy Jo Coker
Margaret Dunagan	Sandy Williams	Lorene Servos	Nancy Cook
Connie Dyer		Mimi Walsh	Margaret Dunagan
Suzanne Hill			Connie Dyer
Martha Ann Kappel			
Sherry Lindley			
Sherri Lowe			
Dawn McNeill			
Irene Skor			
Daisy White			

Category Chairman:

Denise Alford • *Pork, Veal*
Caroline Anderson • *Desserts*
Gerry Christensen • *Pies*
Peggy Jo Coker • *Breads*
Nancy Cook • *Cookies*
Margie Crump • *Eggs, Cheese, Potpourri*
Suzanne Hill • *Poultry*

Judy Hillegeist • *Cakes*
Leslie Hix • *Salads*
Martha Ann Kappel • *Vegetables*
Sherry Lindley • *Soups*
Susanne O'Connell • *Beverages*
Lorene Servos • *Beef*
Irene Skor • *Seafood*
Daisy White • *Appetizers*

CONTENTS

ACKNOWLEDGEMENTS

About the Art . . .

The book design and illustrations are the work of free-lance artist Rosario Mercado Baxter. She is listed in *Who's Who of American Women* for her fashion illustration, design and art direction. In 1984, Rose was asked to do an invitation and later commissioned to design a poster for the *National Wildflower Research Center,* which sparked an interest in Texas flora. Her original watercolor renderings of wildflowers hang in both corporate and private collections.

About the Texas Wines . . .

The section on Texas wines is presented by the "foremost wine writer in the Southwest," Sarah Jane English. One of two books she has written, *The Wines of Texas,* was cited as a definitive source on the state's wines by the Library of Congress. She is a free-lance writer for over sixteen publications, a spokesperson for the American wine industry and a noted connoisseur of wines. Her works have brought national attention to the importance of Texas wines, earning her a place in *Who's Who in Food and Wine in Texas.* This native Texan is a member of a number of food and wine organizations, including *Confrerie des Chevaliers du Tastevin.*

About the Wildflowers . . .

The information about wildflowers has been compiled by the *National Wildflower Research Center* in Austin, under the direction of Dr. David Northington. The Center features a clearinghouse, which serves as a nationwide network to disseminate information about wildflowers and native plants, and assists individuals and organizations working toward similar goals. In addition, the Center maintains an extensive slide collection and reference library. A portion of the proceeds from the sale of *Wild About Texas* will benefit the work of the *National Wildflower Research Center.*

NATIONAL WILDFLOWER RESEARCH CENTER

In December of 1982, Lady Bird Johnson ceremonially sowed the first wildflower seeds on a parcel of land near Austin, Texas, to dedicate the newly established National Wildflower Research Center. Although the Wildflower Center officially began operation on that wintry day, the idea for such a Center had been in Mrs. Johnson's mind for many years.

Upon returning to Texas after her years as First Lady in Washington, D.C., Mrs. Johnson noticed with alarm the disappearance of the vast expanses of wildflower fields that had been so common in her childhood. She dreamed of creating a place where information about wildflowers could be gathered and disseminated nationwide. "I want to unlock some of their (wildflowers') secrets in my lifetime," said Mrs. Johnson. "Wildflowers are survivors, and they may be problem solvers for our future." The creation of the Wildflower Center is the culmination of Lady Bird Johnson's lifelong efforts to protect the environment.

Wildflowers, with their vivid arrays of color and texture, evoke myriad images. We now know that these plants which provide so much beauty can also benefit the nation's economy and improve our environment.

The purpose of the National Wildflower Research Center is to promote the conservation, preservation, and increased use of native plants in planned landscapes. We accomplish this through research and education. Through experimental research on native plants, here at the Center and in cooperative research projects across the country, a database of information about the cultivation and management of plants native to North America is being established. By studying the growth habits and requirements of our native plants, we can begin to learn how to incorporate them into commercial and residential landscapes.

Using native plants helps to restore some of the species lost through land development, provides food and cover for wildlife, and ensures the continuity of genetic material for future study. Many of these native plants may have untapped medicinal potential, and preserving these plants will give researchers the opportunity to study their properties. With the increasing occurrence of droughts throughout the country, there is a crucial need for plants such as our hardy natives, many of which have low water requirements.

The Wildflower Center Clearinghouse has been set up to provide information fact sheets on commercial sources of wildflower seeds and native plants, recommended species, related interest groups and resource people, regional bibliographies, and appropriate planting procedures for different regions in the country. Twice a year, the Center publishes a full color non-technical journal which allows professionals in diverse fields of interests an avenue for sharing information with each other and the general public.

All this and other benefits are available to members of the National Wildflower Research Center. A membership program which began in 1984, has generated over

14,000 members from all across the country. For membership information, contact the National Wildflower Research Center, 2600 FM 973 North, Austin, Texas 78725-4201. Please enclose a self-addressed 9" x 12" envelope with 75 cents postage.

How You Can Use Native Plants in Planned Landscapes

Recent trends in gardening and landscaping indicate a growing interest in lower maintenance, more ecologically-balanced designs. Incorporating native plants into your landscape can be as simple as replacing more traditional ornamentals with species native to your area, or as complex as recreating a whole natural community with its associated plants.

No matter which level of complexity you choose, the first step in planning a native plant garden is to assess your site and determine your expectations and needs. How do you use your yard? What kind of look do you hope to achieve? Will it be water efficient? Observe indigenous species in the wild to learn about their growth habits and needs. For best results, match the species you select with your site conditions.

In selecting native species, choose ones that will bloom successively in order to achieve color year round. The NWRC provides lists of recommended species and seed source lists as guidelines for each state. A mixture of annuals and perennials will ensure some greenery or flowers for each season. Annuals grow quickly and flower the first year; some perennials may take two years or more before they bloom.

If you choose to buy a commercial mix rather than mixing your own, be aware of the advantages and disadvantages of mixes. Most mixes are promoted as giving color the first year. Buying pre-mixed seed may seem more time-saving.

Many seed mixes that are on the market, however, are designed for a wide geographical region. A certain percentage of the species will not grow in your area, or if they do, they may not reseed for the next year. Some mixes have non-natives or filler seed. Be sure you know what the mix contains, and determine which species are native to your area, and what percentage of each species is in the mix. Some of the smaller, local seed companies are developing mixes for more restricted areas which contain primarily indigenous species.

For most areas, early fall is usually the best time of year to plant. Seed may need pretreatment in order to germinate. Some seeds need a period of cold stratification; others (such as the bluebonnet) have a hard seed coat which must be scarified or nicked to allow the absorption of water which initiates germination. (At the Wildflower Center, we do not recommend scarifying bluebonnet seed unless you plan to water the area.) In the South, many annuals overwinter as seedlings, so they need fall rains to germinate and establish a good root system. By planting in the fall, many of these criteria will be fulfilled.

The amount of preparation you need to do to your ground depends upon the area to be planted. The goal in ground preparation is to optimize conditions for good seed/soil contact. If you have vegetation on the area to be planted, you will need to remove them either by herbicides or mowing. Mow the weeds to an inch or less, then lightly rake the ground to expose the soil. Do not rototill the ground, as that will bring up possibly undesirable weed seeds.

Seeding can be done by hand broadcasting for small areas. Follow recommended seeding rates as listed on seed packages. When planting seed as a mix, cut the suggested rate of each speecies by ½ to ⅔. Before broadcasting the seed, mix it with damp sand to ensure even seed distribution. Rake over or tamp down the area planted to ensure good contact with the soil. Another option to seeding outdoors is to plant the seed in pots and transplant them. Seedlings can be transplanted in either the spring or fall. All plants need water to germinate. If rainfall is minimal, try to water if possible.

Like any planned landscape, a native plant area requires several years to become established. Until that time you will have to take care of it in much the same way that you would tend any garden: pruning, weeding, watering. Wildflowers and native plants often thrive in poor soils, so you won't need to fertilize them. Fertilizing them tends to increase foliage at the expense of flowers. Because these indigenous species have natural predators for their pests, they shouldn't need pesticides either.

By working with nature instead of against it, you create an ecologically-balanced landscape. Native plant gardens capture the regional beauty of an area, provide food and shelter for wildlife, and ensure the continued existence of our native vegetation for future enjoyment and study.

Wildflowers and Food Sources

In today's fast-paced world of convenience stores, mega-supermarkets, and a host of ready-made meals, it is difficult to imagine a time when hunting and gathering food encompassed a significant portion of each day and each season. Every culture throughout history has relied on the indigenous plants around them, not only for food, but for medicines, dyes, fuels, shelter, clothing, tools, and toys. In our marriage with technology it is easy to forget our connections with the past.

Today, 85% of the food we eat is derived directly or indirectly from only 20 plant species, and of that amount, 60% comes from only three species: corn, wheat and rice. Yet many wild plants have as much or more nutritional value as the foods we commonly eat. Dandelion leaves, for instance, contain more nutrients than spinach, while violet leaves have more vitamin C, proportionally, than oranges.

With the loss of our native flora, there is a real threat to future sources for food. As history has shown, in the potato blight and other monoculture failures, relying on a single or limited number of crops invites disaster. In the Southwest, many native crops which are more drought and pest resistant could provide supplements or solutions to increase food production. The mesquite, often considered to be weedy by ranchers or homeowners, has long been a staple crop for many Southwestern cultures.

In short, wildflowers and native plants have properties beyond just aesthetics to offer to future generations. As part of the biological world, we must not let ourselves become too separated from our natural connections and overlook the potential around us.

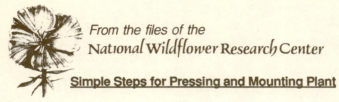

From the files of the
National Wildflower Research Center

Simple Steps for Pressing and Mounting Plant

Materials:

-white paper (typing or computer paper)
-newspaper
-corrugated cardboard (all channels
 should run the width of the
 boards to aid ventilation)
-heavy paper on which to mount plants
 (i.e. construction paper, light weight
  crescent board or cardboard)

-heavy boxes, books
 or bricks to weight
 the specimens
-Elmer's glue
-Scotch tape
-paper towels (untextured)
-toothpicks

Pressing:

1. Always use plant material that is fresh and not wilted or dry.

2. Spread out typing paper or computer paper (do not use newspaper because the ink will come off on the plant) and lay the plant down, arranging the leaves and petals so that they lie flat and unwrinkled, removing any that are dead or wilted.

3. It may be necessary to secure some plant parts
in the desired position. Do this by covering
them with strips of paper towel
and then securing them with tape,
being careful not to touch the
tape to the plant material.

4. When arranging the petals of the flower,
it may be necessary to pad around thick stems
and flower centers with folded layers of paper
towels to insure that even pressure is applied
to all flower parts. Thick parts such as bulbs
and stems may be cut in half longitudinally
or whittled down to reduce their bulkiness.

5. Fold the white paper around the plant
and sandwich it between two pieces
of corrugated cardboard. Additional
layers of newspaper may be added above
and below the plant to give extra
padding and absorbency. If there
are several specimens to be pressed,
you may continue adding a layer of
plant material then cardboard, forming a stack.

6. Weight the specimens down with heavy boxes or books. It is important to apply firm, even pressure to prevent the plant parts from curling and wrinkling before they dry.

7. Place the specimens in a well ventilated area to dry. It is not recommended to place the plants in an oven, even at low temperatures. Drying them too quickly can cause them to turn brown and become brittle. If the plants are not too thick or high in water content, they should dry in three to four days. More succulent plants, such as lilies and spiderworts, may take longer.

Mounting:

8. When dry, gently remove the pressed plant from the paper. To glue it in place, lay it face down on the paper. Hold your bottle of glue about 12" above the plant and gently squeeze producing a thin, even "thread" of glue. Cover the plant lightly but thoroughly in a fan-like pattern being careful to wipe up any large drops of glue on the plant, especially on delicate petals. **Using too much glue is more often a problem than using too little - Go Lightly.**

9. Lay a piece of mounting paper on a sheet of corrugated cardboard. Carefully lift the plant and lay it in the desired position on the mounting paper. Dab away any excess glue with paper towels. Reinforce thick roots or stems with an extra dab of glue and secure any unglued leaves or petals with a toothpick dipped in glue. You may also sew thick parts on with a needle and thread.

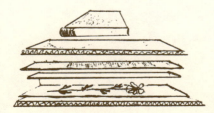

10. Cover with a sheet of wax paper to prevent the plant from sticking to over-lying paper, follow with a layer of folded newspaper for padding, then with a sheet of corrugated cardboard. If there are several specimens to be mounted, you may continue adding a layer of plant material then cardboard, forming a stack. Add weight to insure that the plants do not curl before the glue dries. Allow a few hours for drying.

Lupinus texensis

Bluebonnet - *Lupinus texensis*

The much-acclaimed bluebonnet is one of the earliest species to bloom in the spring. Visitors come from all over to pay tribute to fields of bluebonnets along roadsides. These hardy legumes prefer rocky well-drained soils of the Hill Country. All six species of Lupinus in Texas are considered to be the state flower.

Gaillardia pulchella

Indian blanket - *Gaillardia pulchella*
This familiar red flower tipped with yellow, often blankets roadsides with vivid color in late spring. Also called firewheel, Indian blanket grows on sandy soils in prairies of central and north Texas. Like many of our Texas annuals, Indian blanket adapts readily to garden conditions.

Helianthus maximiliani

Maximilian sunflower - *Helianthus maximiliani*
This attractive sunflower, with flowerheads arranged alternately along the stem, adds graceful sprays of gold to fence rows. A prairie species found throughout the Plains states, it can reach heights of 6 to 10 feet! A perennial, Maximilian sunflower blooms with a burst of color from late summer to fall. The sunflower gets its name from Prince Maximilian, a German naturalist who visited Texas in the 1830's.

Ratibida columnaris

Mexican hat - *Ratibida columnaris*
*Mexican hat is an easily-recognized perennial, with its elongated cone
and drooping rust and yellow petals. It reaches heights of 1 to 4 feet tall,
and prefers dry, calcareous soils in the western two-thirds of Texas. Look
for the flowers of Mexican hat in late spring to early summer.*

Pâté de la Maison

½ pound bacon
1 tablespoon butter
1 onion, chopped
1 pound lean ground pork
½ pound lean ground veal
½ pound chopped chicken
  livers
2 cloves garlic, finely chopped
¼ teaspoon allspice
⅛ teaspoon ground ginger
⅛ teaspoon ground cloves
2 eggs, beaten
2 tablespoons brandy
2 teaspoons salt
1 teaspoon ground pepper
½ cup pistachio nuts
1 slice cooked ham, cut in
  strips
1 bay leaf
1 sprig thyme
Cumberland Sauce (see
  page 218)
Gherkin pickles

Preheat oven to 350°. Line a 2 quart casserole or terrine with bacon, reserving a few slices for the top. Melt butter and sauté onion until soft. Mix butter and onion with pork, veal, chicken livers, garlic, spices, eggs, brandy, salt and pepper. Blend well. Add pistachio nuts and beat. Spread a third of the meat mixture in the terrine. Add a layer of ham strips and top with another third of the meat mixture. Add the remainder of the ham and cover with the remaining meat mixture. Top with bacon slices. Set the bay leaf and thyme sprig on the bacon and cover. Set the terrine in a water bath for 1½ hours. Remove the lid and press the pâté with a weight until cold. May be refrigerated for 1 week or frozen up to 3 months. Serve unmolded or slice out of terrine. Serve with a Cumberland Sauce and gherkin pickles.
Yield: 8-12 servings.

Chili Peanuts

6 cups raw peanuts, deep-
  fried until lightly browned
  and drained on paper
  towels
4 tablespoons salt
2 teaspoons chili powder
1 teaspoon cayenne pepper
1 teaspoon garlic powder
2 teaspoons onion powder

Mix dry ingredients thoroughly and toss with warm peanuts.
Yield: 6 cups.

Great for snacking.

Baked Pecan Halves

4 tablespoons butter
4 cups pecan halves
Salt to taste

Preheat oven to 300°. Melt butter in a 13x9 inch baking dish in the oven. Add pecan halves and stir to coat pecans with butter. Cook for 15 minutes. Stir again. Cook for 10 more minutes. Drain on paper towels. Salt lightly. Cool before serving.
Yield: 12-14 servings.

Crab-Stuffed Mushrooms

12 large, fresh mushrooms
  (about 1 pound)
Vegetable cooking spray
1 (6½ ounce) can lump
  crabmeat, rinsed, drained
  and flaked
¼ cup grated Parmesan
  cheese
¼ cup thinly sliced green
  onions
2 tablespoons mayonnaise
1 teaspoon worcestershire
  sauce
1 teaspoon spicy mustard
¼ teaspoon white pepper

Clean mushrooms with damp paper towels. Remove mushroom stems and chop enough to measure 1 cup. Set mushroom caps aside. Coat a small skillet with cooking spray. Place over medium heat until hot. Add 1 cup chopped mushroom stems to skillet. Cover and cook 5 minutes until tender, stirring occasionally. Combine cooked mushroom stems and remaining ingredients in a small bowl, excluding mushroom caps. Mix well. Spoon mixture into mushroom caps. Arrange in a baking dish coated with cooking spray. Bake at 350° for 15 minutes until lightly browned.
Yield: 6 servings.

Cypripedium calceolus

Stuffed Cherry Tomatoes

4½-5 dozen cherry tomatoes
2 (8 ounce) packages cream
   cheese
¼ cup mayonnaise
2 tablespoons half and half
   cream
2 tablespoons finely chopped
   onion
2 tablespoons finely chopped
   green pepper
½ teaspoon pepper sauce
⅛ teaspoon garlic salt
½ teaspoon worcestershire
   sauce
1½ tablespoons seasoned salt
1 (3 ounce) jar capers, whole
   and drained

Slice off a small part of the top of each tomato. Remove the pulp. Invert the tomatoes on paper towels to drain. Mix cream cheese, mayonnaise, and half and half. Stir in the remaining ingredients, excluding capers. (Test the saltiness before adding seasoned salt.) Stuff each tomato with the mixture and top with a caper.
Yield: 54-60 appetizers.

Cheese Petit Fours

This dish must be made ahead of time and frozen.

1 pound margarine, softened
4 (5 ounce) jars Old English
   cheese
1 teaspoon pepper sauce
1 teaspoon onion powder
1½ teaspoons worcestershire
   sauce
Dash cayenne pepper
1 teaspoon flavor enhancer
2 tablespoons dillweed
2 loaves of sandwich bread,
   crust removed

Cream all the above ingredients together except bread. Put three slices of bread together and cut into fourths. Ice with the above mixture between the layers, sparingly. Ice sides and tops of each fourth. (If too much cheese mixture is used between the layers, they tend to slide while baking.) Place on cookie sheet and freeze completely. (This freezing step may not be eliminated.) Bag petit fours and store in freezer. To cook, place frozen petit fours on cookie sheet and bake at 375° for 15-20 minutes until lightly brown. Serve hot.
Yield: 64 servings.

Brie Vivienne

Filling:
1 (12 ounce) package dried
 apricots
1 cup water
½ cup honey
½ cup pine nuts or toasted
 sliced almonds

Cheese:
1 (2 pound) wheel of Brie
 cheese
1 egg
1 (17.5 ounce) package fro-
 zen puff pastry
Crackers

Mix apricots, water and honey in a saucepan. Simmer 8 minutes until apricots are soft but not mushy. Evaporate liquid over high heat stirring constantly. Toast nuts 10 minutes at 300° until golden, stirring occasionally so they brown evenly.

Preheat oven to 400°. Cut top mold only off Brie. (Sides feel very thick, but leave them intact.) Top Brie with apricot filling and sprinkle with nuts. Roll a sheet of pastry lightly with as few strokes as possible to fit the bottom and sides and cut to overlap ½ inch on top of Brie. Brush ½ inch rim of pastry with water. Roll second sheet of pastry very lightly. Use top of Brie box to cut dough to exactly fit top of cheese. Place dough circle on top using a fork to press down and seal edges. Decorate top with flowers, leaves, or other shapes cut from leftover dough. Mix egg with a little water and brush top. Bake 25 minutes or until crust is golden brown. Let stand 45 minutes before serving. Cut into thin wedges. Serve surrounded with fancy crackers.
Yield: 40 servings.

Caviar Pie

2-3 ripe avocados
½ teaspoon lemon juice
6 boiled eggs
½ red onion, finely chopped
⅓-½ cup mayonnaise
2 (4 ounce) jars whitefish
 caviar
Crackers

Mash avocados and spread over bottom of a quiche dish. Sprinkle lemon juice over avocados. Chop eggs. Add chopped onion and mayonnaise. Spread over avocados. Top with caviar. Serve with crackers.
Yield: 10 servings.

Tyropita (Greek Cheese Pie)

1 pound filo
6 eggs
1 pound ricotta cheese
½ cup grated mozzarella
cheese
½ cup grated feta cheese
½ cup grated Parmesan
cheese
1 cup sweet butter, melted

Layer 15 sheets of filo in a 13x9 inch baking dish, buttering each sheet. Beat eggs and cheeses with an electric mixer until well mixed. Add a little milk if mixture is too thick. (Mixture should be a good consistency for pouring.) Pour mixture over filo. Layer about 15 sheets of filo, buttering each layer, over cheese mixture. Pour any remaining butter over top of filo layer. Score into diamond or square shapes. Bake at 350° for 1 hour. Yield: 30 servings.

This dish may be made ahead and frozen.

Ham and Poppy Seed Delights

1 pound butter (not marga-
rine)
3 tablespoons poppy seeds
3 tablespoons mustard
3 tablespoons horseradish
2 pounds ham, thinly sliced
2 pounds Swiss cheese, sliced
24 party rolls

Melt butter. Add poppy seeds, mustard, and horseradish. Simmer 15-20 minutes. Cool in freezer until butter forms a hard crust on top of other ingredients. Whip mixture to a soft butter consistency. Spread mixture on both sides of rolls. Add ham and Swiss cheese, sandwich style. (Use as much ham and cheese as you prefer.)

Conventional oven method: Wrap in foil. Bake at 350° for 30 minutes or until cheese is melted.

Microwave method: Wrap in plastic wrap. Bake on high until heated throughout.

Yield: 24 delights.

Delights may be frozen after wrapping. Heat straight from freezer until warm throughout.

Pineapple-Horseradish Spread

1 (16 ounce) jar pineapple
  preserves
1 (16 ounce) jar apple jelly
1 (1.12 ounce) can dry mustard
1 (5 ounce) jar horseradish
1 (8 ounce) package cream
  cheese
Crackers

Mix pineapple preserves, apple jelly, dry mustard, and horseradish. Spread over cream cheese. Serve with crackers.
Yield: Enough topping for 3 packages of cream cheese.

Excellent sauce for ham and roasts.

Layered Mexican Fiesta

1 (16 ounce) can refried
  beans
½ package taco seasoning
  mix
1 (8 ounce) carton hot avocado dip
1 (8 ounce) carton sour
  cream
1 small onion, chopped
1 (4½ ounce) can sliced black
  olives
2 large tomatoes, chopped
1 (4 ounce) can chopped
  green chilies
1½ cups shredded Monterey
  Jack cheese
Tortilla chips

Layer ingredients as listed with refried beans on the bottom of an 8-9 inch dish. Serve with tortilla chips. Best when chilled. Keeps in refrigerator 2-3 days.
Yield: 10 servings.

Tortilla Snacks

*1 (8 ounce) package cream
cheese*
*1 (4½ ounce) can chopped
black olives*
*1 (4 ounce) can chopped
green chilies, rinsed and
drained*
3-4 chopped green onions
12-24 flour tortillas

Beat cream cheese with an electric mixer until smooth. Stir in black olives, chilies, and onions. Spread flour tortillas with mixture. Roll up, chill, and slice. Serve at room temperature.
Yield: 10-12 servings.

Crab Triangles

½ cup butter, softened
*1 (5 ounce) jar sharp proc-
essed cheese spread*
1½ teaspoons mayonnaise
*8 ounces fresh lump crabmeat
(quality canned crabmeat
could be used in an emer-
gency)*
½ teaspoon garlic powder
½ teaspoon salt
6 English muffins, split

Combine butter, cheese spread, and mayonnaise. Mix in remaining ingredients to make a spread. Place a heaping tablespoon on each English muffin half and spread. Place muffins on cookie sheet and freeze for about 10 minutes. Remove from freezer and cut into quarters. Bag and freeze to use later or bake at 350° for 15-20 minutes.
Yield: 48 triangles.

May be made ahead of time and frozen.

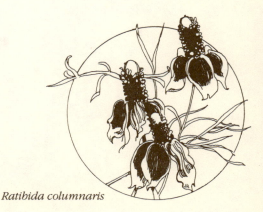

Ratibida columnaris

Artichoke Squares

2 (6 ounce) jars marinated
  artichoke hearts
1 small onion, finely chopped
1 clove garlic, minced
4 eggs
¼ cup dry breadcrumbs
¼ teaspoon salt
⅛ teaspoon pepper
⅛ teaspoon oregano
⅛ teaspoon pepper sauce
½ pound Cheddar cheese,
  shredded
2 tablespoons parsley, minced

Drain juice from one jar of artichoke hearts into a skillet. Discard juice from second jar. Chop artichoke hearts. Set aside. Sauté onion and garlic in artichoke liquid until onion is transparent. Beat eggs in a small bowl until frothy. Add bread crumbs, salt, pepper, oregano, and pepper sauce. Stir in cheese, parsley, chopped artichoke hearts, and onion mixture. Turn into a buttered 11x7 inch baking dish. Bake at 350° for 30 minutes. Let cool in pan. Cut into 1 inch squares. Serve cold or re-heat at 325° for 10-12 minutes.
Yield: 20 servings.

Artichokes with Basil Dip

4 artichokes
¼ cup salad oil
Salt to taste
Garlic clove
2 teaspoons dried basil
1 clove garlic, pressed
1 teaspoon salt
1 cup mayonnaise
1 cup lemon juice

Trim artichokes with a sharp knife, cutting off one inch of the top. Trim stems almost flat to base. Remove outside lower leaves if necessary and thorny leaf tips. Tie leaves with string to hold shape while cooking. Boil 20-45 minutes or until leaf pulls away easily. (Water should be to the top of the artichokes.) Add salad oil, salt, and garlic clove to the boiling water. Drain and remove chokes. Blend basil, garlic, and salt in juice. Add mayonnaise and mix well. Pour sauce into cooked artichokes and chill before serving. (May be made several hours ahead.)
Yield: 4 servings.

Serve as a first course for a dinner party or on a cocktail table. To eat, pull leaves away starting from the inside as the artichoke acts as a bowl to hold the sauce. When all leaves are consumed, savor the wonderful heart.

Caviar Cream Cheese Appetizer

2 (8 ounce) packages cream
  cheese
1 (3 ounce) package cream
  cheese
1 cup mayonnaise
1 small onion, grated
1 tablespoon worcestershire
  sauce
2 tablespoons lemon juice
1 dash pepper sauce
4 hard-boiled eggs, finely
  chopped
1 (3½ ounce) jar black caviar
1 cup finely chopped parsley
Party crackers

Beat cream cheese with an electric mixer until smooth. Add mayonnaise, onion, worcestershire sauce, lemon juice, and pepper sauce. Beat well. Place in a shallow serving dish. Top with eggs, caviar, and parsley (layered in this order). Serve with party crackers. Yield: 24-30 servings.

Bacon and Cheese Spread

2 (4 ounce) packages shredded Cheddar cheese
10 slices bacon, fried and
  crumbled
1 onion, finely chopped
Mayonnaise to make a
  spreadable consistency
Parsley to taste
Salt and pepper to taste
Party size pumpernickel
  bread

Combine Cheddar cheese, bacon, and onion. Add mayonnaise to a spreadable consistency. Add parsley and salt and pepper to taste. Spread on party size pumpernickel bread slices. Broil 8-10 minutes, watching carefully. Remove from oven when cheese mixture is bubbly. Cut each bread slice into 4 triangles. Yield: 40 servings.

May be frozen and thawed before broiling.

Garlic Cheese Log

2 cups (½ pound) shredded
    Cheddar cheese
1 (8 ounce) package cream
    cheese, softened
1 small clove garlic, minced
½ teaspoon salt
Poppy seed

Combine cheeses until smooth. Add garlic and salt. Mix thoroughly. Shape into two logs. Roll in enough poppy seed to coat. Chill and serve.
Yield: 20 servings.

Maui Grab

Super for a party, making the dressing and marinating the mushrooms the day before. May be refrigerated up to 6 hours before serving with no flavor loss.

Dressing:
2 cups salad dressing
1⅓ cups plain yogurt
1 tablespoon horseradish
2 tablespoons dry mustard
2 tablespoons lemon juice
¾ teaspoon Beau Monde
½ teaspoon dill
½ teaspoon garlic powder

Mix dressing ingredients.

Combine vegetables and shrimp in a 4 quart bowl. Pour dressing over and toss gently. Refrigerate at least an hour before serving. Serve with cocktail forks.
Yield: 12-14 servings.

Appetizers:
2 (8 ounce) cans water chest-
    nuts, drained
2 avocados, peeled and
    chopped
2 green peppers, sliced
1 pint cherry tomatoes
2 cucumbers, thickly sliced
1 pound mushrooms, mari-
    nated 24 hours in a light
    Italian salad dressing
1 pound medium shrimp,
    cooked and peeled

Lake Charles Dip

1 pint sour cream
1 large avocado, chopped
1 large tomato, peeled and
  chopped
1 (1.3 ounce) package Italian
  dressing mix
1 tablespoon mayonnaise
1½-2 tablespoons lemon juice
Chips

Combine all ingredients. Chill well. Stir before serving. Serve with chips.
Yield: 8 servings.

Texas Crabgrass

½ cup butter
½ medium onion, chopped
1 (10 ounce) package frozen
  spinach, cooked and
  drained
1 (7 ounce) can crabmeat
¾ cup Parmesan cheese
Melba rounds

Melt butter and sauté onions. Add spinach, crabmeat, and cheese. Serve in a chafing dish with Melba rounds.
Yield: 24 servings.

May be frozen.

Crab and Shrimp Dip

1 (8 ounce) package cream
  cheese
½ cup cooked shrimp,
  chopped
1 tablespoon worcestershire
  sauce
1 (6 ounce) can crabmeat,
  drained
1 teaspoon lemon juice
Salt and pepper to taste
⅛ teaspoon cayenne pepper
1 teaspoon horseradish,
  optional
1 (8 ounce) bottle chili sauce
Crackers

Mix all ingredients except chili sauce. Put mixture in a dip bowl and top with chili sauce. Serve with crackers.
Yield: 8 servings.

May be made ahead except for topping with chili sauce.

Mexican Dip

1 (4 ounce) can chopped
  green chilies
1 (4 ounce) can chopped ripe
  olives
3 scallions, diced
1 medium tomato, diced
2 tablespoons wine vinegar
3 tablespoons corn oil
Salt and pepper to taste
Corn chips

Combine all ingredients. Serve with corn chips.
Yield: 6-8 servings.

Mint Tea

2 family size teabags
1 quart boiling water
¾ cup sugar
Juice of 3 lemons
1 quart ginger ale, chilled
Sprigs of mint

Steep teabags in boiling water until very strong. Add sugar and lemon juice to tea while still hot. Just before serving, add chilled ginger ale and mint sprigs. Serve over ice.
Yield: 8 servings.

Percolator Punch

2¼ cups pineapple juice
2 cups cranberry juice
1¾ cups water
½ cup brown sugar
¼ teaspoon salt
1 tablespoon whole cloves
½ tablespoon whole allspice
2 small tea bags
3 cinnamon sticks, broken

Place juices, water and sugar in bottom of percolator. Place other ingredients in coffee basket. Perk like coffee. Serve hot.
Yield: 6 servings.

Great on a cold, damp day!

Citrus Tea Punch

4 cups boiling water
2 tea bags
1 (6 ounce) can frozen lime-
    ade concentrate, thawed
1 (6 ounce) can frozen lemon-
    ade concentrate, thawed
10 cups cold water

Steep tea bags in boiling water 5-10 minutes. Add limeade, lemonade and cold water. Yield: 20-25 servings.

Homecoming Party Punch

6 cups sugar
5 quarts water
4 (3 ounce) packages lemon
    gelatin
1 (6 ounce) can frozen orange
    juice concentrate, thawed
1 (6 ounce) bottle frozen
    lemon juice, thawed
2 (46 ounce) cans pineapple
    juice
1½ ounces almond extract
4 quarts ginger ale

Combine sugar and 1 quart water. Heat until sugar is dissolved and mixture is syrupy. Add gelatin, stirring until dissolved. Add fruit juices, 4 quarts water and almond extract. Let stand until ready to serve. Pour ⅛ of the juice mixture over ice in punch bowl. Add 2 cups ginger ale. Continue adding ingredients in the same proportions as needed. Yield: 100 servings.

Fruit Delight

2½ cups sugar
4 cups water
3 large bananas
2 (6 ounce) cans frozen
    orange juice concentrate
1 (6 ounce) can frozen lemon-
    ade concentrate
3 quarts lemon-lime carbon-
    ated beverage, chilled
1 (46 ounce) can unsweetened
    pineapple juice, chilled

Mix sugar with water and heat until sugar is dissolved. Combine bananas, orange juice concentrate and lemonade concentrate in blender. Combine blended mixture with sugar mixture and freeze. Before serving, defrost for 20-30 minutes. Pour lemon-lime carbonated beverage and pineapple juice over frozen mixture and serve. Yield: 24 servings.

Handy Daiquiris

1 (16 ounce) jar maraschino
   cherries
1 (6 ounce) can frozen limeade concentrate, partially
   thawed
1 (6 ounce) can frozen orange juice concentrate,
   partially thawed
2 (6 ounce) cans frozen pink
   lemonade concentrate,
   partially thawed
25 ounces light rum
8 (6 ounce) cans water

Chop cherries. Add with juice to remaining ingredients. Put in freezer. As mixture freezes, stir 2-3 times. Mixture will not freeze completely. Use as needed.
Yield: 15-20 servings.

Will keep 6 months in freezer.

Ladies' Favorite Punch

2 (6 ounce) cans frozen
   orange juice concentrate,
   thawed
1 (6 ounce) can frozen lemonade concentrate, thawed
6 cups cold water
2½ cups ginger ale, chilled
1 (10 ounce) package frozen
   sliced strawberries, partially thawed
Whole strawberries, optional
Sliced peaches, optional
Mint leaves, optional

Combine first 5 ingredients in punch bowl. A fruit ring may be made of the strawberries, peaches and mint leaves frozen in water. Float in punch bowl.
Yield: 24 servings.

Pineapple-Orange Punch

½ *gallon orange sherbet*
1 (46 ounce) can pineapple
 juice, chilled
1 (33.8 ounce) bottle ginger
 ale, chilled
3 cups orange-flavored drink,
 chilled
3 cups lemon-lime carbonated
 beverage, chilled

Place sherbet in a large punch bowl. Add remaining ingredients. Stir well.
Yield: 40 servings.

This is wonderful for Halloween!

Strawberry Party Punch

4 (10 ounce) packages frozen
 sliced strawberries, par-
 tially thawed
1 cup sugar
½ *gallon Rosé wine (for non-*
 alcoholic punch, use straw-
 berry soda)
1 (6 ounce) can frozen pink
 lemonade concentrate,
 thawed
2 quarts club soda

Combine strawberries and sugar. Add 1 quart wine and let stand at room temperature one hour. Add lemonade concentrate to mixture. Refrigerate until ready to serve. To serve, add remainder wine and club soda.
Yield: 25 servings.

Pretty when served over ice ring in punch bowl.

Holiday Simmer

2 quarts apple cider
2 cups orange juice
1 cup lemon juice
2 (46 ounce) cans pineapple
 juice
1 cinnamon stick
1 teaspoon whole cloves

Combine all ingredients in a large pot. Stir until well blended. Simmer over low heat 20 minutes. Remove spices. Serve hot.
Yield: 25 cups.

Wassail

1 (6 ounce) can frozen orange
juice concentrate
1 (6 ounce) can frozen lemon-
ade concentrate
1 ¼ cups sugar
1 teaspoon vanilla
1 teaspoon almond extract
2½ quarts water
⅛ teaspoon red food coloring
1 cinnamon stick
Orange slices

Combine ingredients (excluding orange slices) in a large saucepan and heat. Serve garnished with orange slices.
Yield: 15 servings.

Kahlua

Notice the month "setting time" and plan ahead.

1 quart vodka
3½ cups sugar
1 cup hot water
1 cup instant coffee
1 vanilla bean, split

Mix vodka and sugar. Stir until sugar dissolves. Mix hot water and coffee. Add to vodka mixture. Stir in the vanilla bean. Set for 30 days. Shake occasionally.
Yield: 1 decanter.

Makes a lovely holiday gift.

Creamy and Good Hot Chocolate Mix

1 (2 pound) box hot chocolate
mix
1 (22 ounce) jar creamer
8 quarts non-fat powdered
milk
1½ cups powdered sugar

Combine all ingredients. Store in a tightly covered container. To serve, place ⅓-½ cup of mix in cup. Add boiling water and stir.
Yield: 50 servings.

Makes a wonderful holiday gift children can make. Pour in mason jars with a colorful bit of calico tied with a ribbon. Super to give with a set of Santa mugs.

Malvaviscus drummondii

Turk's cap - *Malvaviscus drummondii*
Turk's cap thrives in sandy soils near stream sides in central and east Texas. It makes a good shrub (usually 4 to 5 feet tall) for landscaping in shady areas. The bright red flowers, whorled into turban shapes, bloom intermittently throughout summer. The red fruit of Turk's cap provides good forage for wildlife.

Great Gazpacho

6 large ripe tomatoes, peeled, seeded, and chopped
1 cup tomato juice
½ cup chopped cucumber
½ cup chopped avocado
½ cup chopped red bell pepper
2 teaspoons finely chopped jalapeño pepper
¼ cup finely chopped white onion
½ cup chopped fresh cilantro
Juice of 1 lime
3-5 drops hot pepper sauce
1 garlic clove, chopped fine
Fresh cilantro sprigs, optional

Blend the tomatoes with the tomato juice in a food processor until just combined. Add cucumber, avocado, red bell and jalapeño peppers, onion and cilantro. Process just enough to mix thoroughly. Pour into a large pitcher. Stir in lime juice, hot pepper sauce and garlic. Cover and refrigerate 2-4 hours. Pour stirred soup into individual cups and float a cilantro sprig on top.
Yield: 6-8 servings.

Fresh cilantro can be found in Asian and Hispanic markets.

Creamy-Cold Cucumber Soup

2 large cucumbers, peeled and diced
1 medium onion, chopped
¼ cup butter, melted
1½ cups chicken stock
1 tablespoon lemon juice
¾ teaspoon dillweed
Salt to taste
1 cup sour cream
Fresh dill

Sauté cucumbers and onion in butter until tender. Blend in a food processor and return to saucepan. Add chicken stock, lemon juice, dillweed, and salt. Simmer 5 minutes. Stir in sour cream. Chill 6 hours.
Yield: 4 servings.

This is a refreshing soup for a ladies' luncheon.

Chilled Cream of Avocado Soup

3 avocados, peeled and
   seeded
1½ cups chicken broth
1½ cups light cream
1½ teaspoons salt
¼ teaspoon onion salt
⅛ teaspoon white pepper
2 teaspoons lemon juice
Choice of garnish: lemon,
   lime, or oranges (grated or
   sliced in fans or wedges);
   salted or minted whipped
   cream; sour cream with
   fresh mint or dillweed;
   plain, garlic, or onion
   croutons

Purée avocados with broth. Combine with cream, salt, onion salt, and white pepper. Chill thoroughly. Stir in lemon juice. Garnish just before serving.
Yield: 6-8 servings.

Pretty summer soup for ladies' luncheon served in clear, glass cups.

Tortilla Soup

1 medium onion, chopped
2 cloves garlic, chopped
2 tablespoons vegetable oil
2 (10½ ounce) cans beef broth
2 (10½ ounce) cans chicken
   broth
½ cup tomato juice
1 teaspoon ground cumin
1 teaspoon chili powder
1 jalapeño, chopped
1 teaspoon salt
1 teaspoon worcestershire
   sauce
1 cup cooked, diced chicken
1 large tomato, peeled and
   diced
Corn tortillas, fried crisp, cut
   in strips
Avocado, sliced
Monterey Jack cheese, grated

Sauté onion and garlic in oil. Add beef broth, chicken broth, tomato juice, cumin, chili powder, jalapeño, salt and worcestershire sauce. Bring to a boil. Cover and simmer one hour. Add chicken and tomato. Place tortilla strips in bowls. Fill bowls with hot soup. Garnish with more tortilla strips, avocado slices and cheese.
Yield: 8-10 servings.

Buddy's Split Pea Soup

1 (16 ounce) package split
  peas, soaked overnight in 6
  cups water
12 cups water
1 turkey carcass, cut up; or 1
  hambone
½ cup chopped onion
½ cup chopped celery leaves
½ cup chopped carrots
2 tablespoons butter, melted
2 tablespoons flour
Salt and pepper to taste
Paprika

Drain peas and put in large Dutch oven. Add water and turkey carcass. Cover and simmer for 3 hours. Add onion, carrots, and celery leaves. Simmer covered, 1 hour. Remove carcass. Strain soup, chill, and skim off fat. Blend butter and flour. Add to reheated soup. Cook, stirring until soup boils. Add seasonings to taste.
Yield: 8 servings.

This soup freezes well after cooking.

Easy Cheese Broccoli Soup

1 medium onion, finely
  chopped
4 tablespoons margarine,
  melted
1 (10 ounce) package frozen
  chopped broccoli, defrosted
  and drained
1 (10¾ ounce) can cream of
  mushroom soup
1 (10¾ ounce) can cream of
  celery soup
1 (10¾ ounce) can chicken
  broth
1 can milk, using a soup can
  to measure
¼ teaspoon pepper
1 (10 ounce) package grated,
  medium Cheddar cheese

Sauté onion in margarine. Add soups and milk. Heat until warm. Add broccoli, pepper and cheese. Cook until cheese is thoroughly melted and soup is hot.
Yield: 8 servings.

This soup is better if made the day before and allowed to season. May be doubled easily for a large group.

Cheddar Cheese Soup

⅓ cup grated cheese
⅓ cup finely chopped celery
1 cup finely chopped green onion
2 cups water
1 medium white onion, chopped
½ cup butter
1 cup flour
4 cups milk
4 cups chicken broth
1 (16 ounce) jar processed cheese spread
¼ teaspoon cayenne pepper
1 tablespoon prepared mustard
Salt and pepper to taste
Parsley, chopped

Boil carrots, celery and green onion in water. Set aside. Sauté white onion in butter. Add flour and blend. Combine milk and chicken broth. Heat to boiling. Using wire whisk, stir broth mixture into flour mixture. Add cheese, salt and pepper. Add the vegetables and water. Stir in cayenne pepper and mustard. Heat thoroughly, stirring often. Garnish with chopped parsley.
Yield: 10 servings.

This soup may be refrigerated for several days, heating only amount needed. Add a few tablespoons of milk if soup has thickened.

Canadian Cream Cheese Soup

¼ cup melted butter
½ cup finely chopped onions
½ cup chopped celery
½ cup grated carrots
2 tablespoons flour
2 teaspoons cornstarch
2 (10¾ ounce) cans chicken broth
1 quart milk
⅛ teaspoon baking soda
2 pounds processed cheese, cut into 2 inch squares
Salt and pepper to taste
Sour cream, optional
Croutons, optional

In a large Dutch oven, sauté onions, celery, and carrots in butter until opaque. Add flour, cornstarch, broth, and milk making a smooth sauce. Add remaining ingredients. Cook 45 minutes over low heat. Garnish with a dollop of sour cream or croutons.
Yield: 12 servings.

May be frozen after cooking.

Harvest Pumpkin Soup

2 tablespoons butter or margarine
1 large onion, chopped
1 large potato, pared and diced
3 cups homemade or canned chicken broth
1 (16 ounce) can pumpkin or 2 cups fresh pumpkin purée
½ teaspoon salt
¼ teaspoon nutmeg
⅛ teaspoon ground cloves
⅛ teaspoon ground ginger
⅛ teaspoon cinnamon
⅛ teaspoon white pepper
1 cup heavy or whipping cream
White or wheat croutons

In a 3 quart saucepan over medium heat, cook onion and potato in hot butter for 5 minutes, stirring occasionally. Add chicken broth. Heat to boiling. Cover and cook over low heat until vegetables are tender. Ladle half of vegetable mixture into blender container. Blend until smooth. Return mixture to saucepan. Add pumpkin, salt, nutmeg, pepper, cloves, ginger, and cinnamon. Heat to boiling. Cover, reducing heat to low. Cook 10 minutes. Stir in cream. Heat. Garnish with croutons just before serving.
Yield: 6-8 servings.

A pretty addition to a fall party table. Use 1 whole pumpkin, seeded and cleaned thoroughly, for serving instead of a soup tureen.

Cream of Broccoli Soup

2 cups chopped fresh broccoli
1½ cups chicken broth
1 teaspoon thyme
2 tablespoons flour
2 tablespoons butter
1½ cups milk
Salt and pepper to taste
½ cup grated American cheese

Cook broccoli in chicken broth and thyme until tender. Purée in food processor or blender. Set aside. In a separate saucepan, make a roux of flour and butter, stirring constantly. Add milk and cheese. Cook slowly until the mixture thickens. Add broccoli mixture and heat thoroughly over medium heat. Salt and pepper to taste. Garnish each bowl with small amount of grated cheese prior to serving.
Yield: 4 servings.

Cauliflower Soup

¼ cup melted butter
1 large onion, sliced
1 clove garlic, crushed
1 medium cauliflower, cut in
   pieces
4½ cups chicken stock
Salt and pepper to taste
5 tablespoons coffee cream
2 slices French bread, cubed
   and toasted
1½ tablespoons chopped
   parsley

Sauté onion and garlic in a Dutch oven. Add cauliflower and chicken stock. Cook over low heat 1 hour. Strain liquid and purée cauliflower in blender. Return liquid and cauliflower to Dutch oven. Salt and pepper to taste. Stir in cream and heat short of boiling point. Add cubed French bread and parsley before serving..
Yield: 6 servings.

This soup may be made in advance. Prior to serving, add the coffee cream and heat.

Zucchini Soup

1½ pounds zucchini, cut into
   1 inch chunks
2 slices bacon, cooked crisp
   and crumbled
3 tablespoons margarine,
   melted
1 small onion, chopped
2 cups chicken stock
½ teaspoon basil
1 clove garlic
2 tablespoons parsley
1 teaspoon sugar
Salt and pepper to taste
1 cup cream, or half and half
Croutons

Sauté onion in margarine. Add all ingredients (except cream and croutons). Microwave, covered 15 minutes. Purée in food processor or blender. At serving time, reheat but do not boil. Stir in cream. Sprinkle a few croutons on top.
Yield: 24 small cups.

This recipe may be made ahead of time, reheated, and the cream added prior to serving. It is a pretty soup served in demitasse cups for a first course, hot or cold.

Potage Cressoniere - Watercress Soup

¼ cup melted butter
1 clove garlic, minced
2 cups chopped onion
4 cups thinly sliced raw
  potatoes
1 tablespoon salt
¼ teaspoon freshly ground
  black pepper
¾ cup water
1 bunch watercress
1½ cups milk
1½ cups water
2 egg yolks
½ cup light cream

Sauté garlic and onions until tender in a large saucepan. Add potatoes, seasonings, and ¾ cup water. Cover and bring to boil. Reduce heat and simmer 15 minutes until potatoes are almost tender. Cut watercress stems into ⅛ inch lengths. Coarsely chop leaves. Add stems, half the leaves, milk, and water to potato mixture. Cook 15 minutes. Purée in blender. Return mixture to saucepan and reheat. Blend egg yolks and cream. Gradually stir into soup. Cook, stirring constantly, until slightly thickened. Garnish with remaining watercress leaves and serve immediately.
Yield: 8 servings.

Asparagus-Buttermilk Soup

2 pounds asparagus
1 tablespoon lemon juice
3 cups water
4 tablespoons unsalted butter,
  melted
½ cup chopped onion
3 cups chicken stock
Salt and pepper
1 cup buttermilk
Chives or croutons

Remove tough part of asparagus. Pare tough skin from stalks leaving tips intact. Separate stalks and tips. Cut stalks into 1½ inch pieces. Heat water in small saucepan to boiling. Add tips and lemon juice. Cook until tips are tender-crisp (2-3 minutes). Transfer tips to a small bowl. Set aside. Reserve 1 cup of cooking liquid. Sauté onion until softened. Add stalks, chicken stock, reserved liquid, and salt and pepper. Heat to boiling. Reduce heat. Simmer covered until stalks are tender. Pour through a sieve. Transfer solids to a food processor or blender with 1 cup of liquid. Process to a thick purée and return to saucepan. Stir in buttermilk and asparagus tips. Heat (do not boil). Garnish with chives or croutons.
Yield: 6 servings.

Corn Chowder

¾ pound bacon
1 cup chopped onion
3 (17 ounce) cans cream-style
 corn
3 cups light cream
3 cups milk
1 tablespoon salt
¼ teaspoon white pepper
3 cups shredded Cheddar
 cheese

Fry bacon in a Dutch oven until crisp. Drain and crumble. Sauté onion until tender using 2 tablespoons bacon grease. Stir in remaining ingredients excluding cheese. Heat to boiling. Reduce heat to low. Stir in crumbled bacon and cheese until melted.
Yield: 12 servings.

Paul's Potato Soup

2 medium onions, sliced
1 tablespoon butter
3 medium potatoes, thinly
 sliced
½ cup chopped celery
2 cups chicken stock
Salt
1 cup milk, scalded
1 cup half and half
⅛ teaspoon white pepper
Nutmeg, optional
Croutons, optional
Parsley, optional

Cook onions in butter until tender. Add potatoes, celery, stock and salt. Cover and simmer 30 minutes or until potatoes and onions are soft. Press through a fine sieve or purée in a blender. Return to soup kettle and stir in milk, half and half, pepper, and a little more salt if necessary. Bring to a boil. If desired, add a sprinkling of nutmeg. Ladle into warmed soup bowls and garnish with croutons and parsley.
Yield: 6-8 servings.

This recipe is a favorite of Paul Strobel's. He is a very special person to our Junior Forum.

Of the lower 48 states, Texas is second only to California in plant species diversity.

No (4)

Cream of Vegetable Soup

¾ *cup melted butter*
1 *cup diced onion*
1½ *cup diced potatoes*
1 *cup diced carrots*
1 *cup diced green beans*
1 *cup coarsely chopped*
   broccoli
1 *cup minced leek*
1 *cup minced zuccini*
1 *clove garlic, minced*
1½ *teaspoons sugar*
1½ *quarts chicken stock*
½ *cup whipping cream*
Salt and pepper to taste
1 *tablespoon chopped parsley*

In a large pot, sauté onion over medium heat. Reduce heat to low and add remaining ingredients except chicken stock, cream, and parsley. Cook 20-25 minutes until vegetables are soft but not browned. Add stock, bringing to boil over medium-high heat. Reduce heat and simmer for 10 minutes. Cool slightly. Transfer to blender or food processor in batches. Purée until smooth. Taste, adjusting seasonings. Return to pot. Place over medium heat and gradually stir in cream. Heat, but do not boil. Garnish with parsley and serve.
Yield: 6-8 servings.

This rich soup makes a nice first course. Small portions are in order. May be frozen after cooking.

Black Bean Soup - "Frijoles Negro"

1 *(16 ounce) package black*
   beans, rinsed and soaked
   overnight
1 *bay leaf*
1 *teaspoon oregano*
1 *ham bone*
4 *cups water*
Salt and pepper to taste
½ *teaspoon sugar*
1 *tablespoon white vinegar*
2 *garlic cloves, minced*
1 *green pepper, chopped*
1 *tablespoon oil*
¼ *cup sherry*
1 *jalapeño pepper, seeded*
   and chopped
Cooked rice
1 *onion, chopped*

Place beans, bay leaf, oregano, and ham bone in pressure cooker with 4 cups water. Cook 1 hour. (In a covered pot, 2 hours.) Add salt and pepper, sugar, and white vinegar. Sauté garlic and green pepper in oil. Add to beans with sherry and jalapeño pepper. Cook ½ hour more. Serve with hot rice and chopped onions.
Yield: 8-10 servings.

Hillbilly Bean Soup

1 pound dried black beans
1 pound dried kidney beans
1 pound dried lentils
1 pound dried baby limas
1 pound dried great northern
  beans
1 pound dried navy beans
1 pound dried split peas
1 pound dried brown rice
1 pound dried barley
2 pounds black-eyed peas
4 pounds pinto beans
1 (10-ounce) can diced tomatoes with green chilies
1 onion, chopped
1 ham bone
1 clove garlic, minced
Salt and Pepper to taste

Mix first 12 ingredients together and store in airtight containers. To cook, wash and soak 2 cups of mix overnight in water to cover. In the morning drain off soaking water and add fresh water to cover. Cook slowly 3 hours in a covered pot. Add tomatoes, onion, ham bone, garlic, salt and pepper. Cook another 2 hours or until done.
Yield: A ton!

A nice gift! Give dried bean mixture with cooking instructions.

Sopa de Lima - Chicken Soup

1 chicken, stewed and boned
2 tablespoons oil
1 onion, chopped
3 fresh tomatoes, chopped
1 green pepper, seeded and
  chopped
8 cups chicken stock
1 fresh lime
3 cups cooked rice
Authentic tortilla chips
1 lime, thinly sliced

Chop chicken meat into small pieces. Sauté onion in oil. Add tomatoes and green pepper. Sauté for 3 minutes. In a large pot, combine chicken stock and juice of 1 lime. Bring to boil. Reduce to medium heat and add lime shell. Cook 5 minutes. Remove lime shell. Add rice, chicken, and onion mixture. Heat 5 minutes. Place several tortilla chips in individual soup bowls. Pour soup on top of chips. Garnish with a lime slice.
Yield: 8-10 servings.

This recipe is from the Yucatan and is delicious on cold nights. Extra spice, such as red pepper sauce, may be added.

Ron Stone's Memorial Day Chicken Soup

1 stalk of celery, chopped
1 carrot, grated
8 peppercorns
1 medium onion, quartered
4 quarts of water
1 large (3-4 pound) chicken
1 (12 ounce) package wide
egg noodles
2 chicken bouillon cubes
4 (10¾ ounce) cans con-
densed cream of chicken
soup
Parsley flakes
Salt and pepper to taste

Put celery, carrot, peppercorns, and onion in water. Add chicken, stewing until it falls off the bone. Bone chicken, tearing meat into bite-size pieces. Strain broth. Bring to boil. Add noodles, and cook 6 minutes. Add bouillon cubes and chicken soup. Stir gently so noodles do not break. Add chicken, parsley flakes, salt and pepper to taste.
Yield: 20-25 servings.

This recipe will serve a crowd. Serve with cornbread or blueberry muffins. May be frozen after cooking.

Spinach-Garlic Soup

¼ cup olive oil
6 large cloves garlic, sliced
1 medium onion, thinly sliced
2 medium stalks of celery,
chopped
1 medium carrot, grated
1 quart chicken or vegetable
broth
1½ cups (3 ounces) whole
wheat breadcrumbs
3 cups finely chopped fresh
spinach leaves
Salt and pepper to taste
Hard-boiled egg, chopped,
optional
Toasted sesame seeds, op-
tional

Heat oil in a large saucepan over medium heat. Add garlic, sautéing until lightly browned. Stir in onion, celery, and carrots, sautéing until softened. Add broth and breadcrumbs. Cover partially. Bring to simmer. Reduce heat to low. Simmer 20 minutes, stirring occasionally. Transfer mixture to food processor or blender and purée until smooth. Return to saucepan and add spinach. Simmer over medium heat several minutes to blend flavors. Season with salt and pepper. Garnish with egg or sesame seeds.
Yield: 4-6 servings.

This hearty soup makes an excellent winter meal with cheese and crusty French bread.

Meaty Minestrone

1 cup chopped celery
1 medium onion, finely
  chopped
1 clove garlic, minced
2 tablespoons olive oil
1 (16 ounce) can tomatoes
1 (6 ounce) can tomato paste
4 quarts water
1 tablespoon salt
1 teaspoon oregano
½ teaspoon basil
3½ pounds ground chuck
¾ cup breadcrumbs
½ cup Parmesan cheese
2 tablespoons minced parsley
1 egg, lightly whipped
1 small onion, minced
2 teaspoons salt
½ teaspoon pepper
1 (16 ounce) can baked beans
1 (16 ounce) can kidney
  beans
1 (16 ounce) can chickpeas
  (garbanzos)
1 (16 ounce) can spinach
1 carrot, sliced in rings
2 teaspoons minced parsley
1 (7 ounce) package spa-
  ghetti, broken into 2 inch
  pieces, cooked until al denté

Sauté celery, onion, and garlic in olive oil in a large kettle. Add tomatoes, tomato paste, water, 1 tablespoon salt, oregano, and basil. Cook to boiling. In a separate large bowl, mix ground chuck, breadcrumbs, Parmesan cheese, parsley, egg, onion, garlic, 2 teaspoons salt, and pepper. Shape into 1 inch balls. Add to boiling soup. Lower heat and simmer for 30 minutes. Add undrained canned vegetables, carrot, and parsley. Cover and simmer 30 minutes longer. Add hot, drained spaghetti to soup and serve.
Yield: 8 quarts.

This soup is a complete meal served with hard rolls or French bread. It freezes well. Use fresh herbs if available. May be garnished with Pesto.

Balkan Goulash Soup

For the best flavor, allow this soup to set several hours or overnight in refrigerator before serving. Reheat to piping hot, and add garnish.

2 tablespoons vegetable oil
1½ pounds beef chuck, cubed
4 ounces salt pork, rinsed and diced
2 cups coarsely chopped onions
1 cup coarsely chopped celery root
2 large cloves garlic, minced
3 tablespoons paprika
2 tablespoons brown sugar
1 teaspoon dried thyme, optional
1½ teaspoons caraway seeds
1 (28 ounce) can tomato purée
6 cups beef broth
1 (16 ounce) can sauerkraut, drained
3 cups peeled and diced potatoes
1 pound Polish-style Kielbasa, cut into ¼ inch slices
Plain yogurt, optional
Fresh parsley, chopped, optional

Heat oil over medium heat in a large Dutch oven. Add beef, increasing heat to medium-high and brown quickly on all sides. Remove beef with slotted spoon and set aside. Sauté salt pork in remaining drippings until golden brown. Add onions, celery root, garlic. Continue to sauté until tender. Return beef to mixture. Over medium heat, add paprika, brown sugar, thyme, and caraway. Toss to coat mixture for 2-3 minutes. Add tomato purée, beef broth, and sauerkraut. Simmer over low heat. Partially cover pot. Cook for 2 hours. Add potatoes to soup. Cook additional 30 minutes, partially covered. Add sliced sausage. Heat 15 minutes, uncovered. Garnish with dollop of yogurt and sprinkling of parsley.
Yield: 6-8 servings.

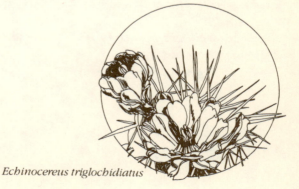

Echinocereus triglochidiatus

Red Crab Soup

2 tablespoons melted butter
¾ cup sliced onion
1 (16 ounce) can tomatoes,
  undrained
2 cups clam or chicken broth
1 tablespoon lemon juice
½ teaspoon red pepper sauce
¼ teaspoon crumbled dried
  thyme
1 (6½ ounce) can white crab
  meat, flaked
½ cup whipping cream
Fish-shaped crackers, op-
  tional
Croutons, optional
Parsley, chopped, optional

Sauté onion in butter. Add tomatoes, broth, lemon juice, red pepper sauce and thyme. Simmer 10 minutes. Purée mixture in blender and return to saucepan. Add crab meat and cream. Mix well and heat. Serve hot or cold. Garnish with crackers, croutons, or parsley. Yield: 4-6 servings.

Shrimp Bisque

1 cup water
1 cup chopped celery
1 cup diced potatoes
¼ cup chopped onion
½ teaspoon salt
Dash pepper
2 tablespoons flour
2 cups milk
1 cup cooked, cut up shrimp
2 tablespoons butter
1 tablespoon chopped parsley

Combine water, celery, potatoes, onions, salt and pepper in a large saucepan. Bring to boil. Reduce heat and cover. Simmer for 15 minutes, stirring constantly. Combine flour and milk in a separate dish until smooth. Stir into potato mixture. Add shrimp and butter to soup. Cook stirring until thick and bubbly. Garnish with parsley.
Yield: 6 servings.

Creole Shrimp Gumbo

1 ham hock
2-3 quarts of water, ham or chicken stock
4 tablespoons bacon drippings
1 stalk celery, chopped
4 large green peppers, chopped
4 large onions, chopped
4 cloves garlic, minced
2 pounds cut okra (fresh or frozen)
½ bunch parsley, chopped
2-3 (14½ ounce) cans tomatoes
1½ tablespoon salt
2 tablespoons worcestershire sauce
1 tablespoon paprika
3 bay leaves
1 (6 ounce) can tomato paste
½ teaspoon black pepper
1 tablespoon sugar
Red pepper sauce to taste
¾ tablespoon thyme
2 pounds fresh shrimp, cooked and peeled
1 tablespoon gumbo filé
Cooked rice

Place ham hock and water in a very large pot. Simmer 30 minutes. Heat bacon drippings in heavy skillet. Add celery, green pepper, onion, garlic, okra, and parsley. Cook slowly for 20 minutes. Add to ham. Add tomatoes, salt, worcestershire, paprika, bay leaves, tomato paste, black pepper, sugar, red pepper sauce, and thyme to ham. Simmer 3 hours. Remove meat from ham bone. Add meat to liquid. Remove bay leaves. Add cooked shrimp. Cook slowly until heated. Just before serving, stir in gumbo filé. Serve in bowls over cooked rice.
Yield: 12-20 servings.

This recipe freezes well. One alternative is to freeze the completed gumbo except for shrimp and gumbo filé, adding them after taking out of freezer and reheating. It feeds an army and is a wonderful way to use a leftover honey-baked ham bone and trimmings.

Arisaema quinatum

Pesto

¼ cup butter
¼ cup grated Parmesan
 cheese
¼ cup olive oil
¼ cup walnuts or pine nuts
4-5 sprigs parsley
1 clove garlic
1 teaspoon basil

Combine all ingredients in a food processor and blend until finely chopped.
Yield: 1 cup.

Italian topping for hearty soups.

Toasted Sesame Seeds

Sesame seeds

Spread sesame seeds on a cookie sheet. Toast at 350° for 15 minutes, stirring often. (Toasting brings out the nut-like flavor of the seeds.)

Garlic Croutons

1 clove garlic, crushed
¼ teaspoon salt
4 tablespoons olive oil
1 loaf French bread
½ cup Parmesan cheese

Mix garlic, salt, and olive oil. Slice bread into ¾ inch rounds and dip in the oil mixture. Sprinkle with the cheese. Toast until dry at 350°. Cut into cubes, ½ inch or larger. Omit garlic for plain croutons.

Cirsium texanum

Verbena bipinnatifida

Prairie verbena - *Verbena bipinnatifida*
Prairie verbena is a low-growing perennial found on dry plains and prairies throughout much of Texas. The lavendar or pink flowers color the landscape from spring to fall. Verbena is widely available commercially, and makes an ideal ground cover for sunny landscapes.

Lemony Fruit Dressing

1/3 cup sugar
1 tablespoon flour
1/2 teaspoon shredded lemon
   peel
1/4 cup lemon juice
1 egg
1 cup miniature marshmal-
   lows
1 cup mayonnaise

Combine sugar and flour. Stir in lemon peel, juice, egg and marshmallows. Cook, stirring over low heat until mixture thickens slightly and marshmallows melt. Cool slightly. Fold in mayonnaise. Cover and chill.
Yield: 2 cups.

Heavenly Fruit Dressing

1/2 cup sugar
2 tablespoons flour
1 cup pineapple juice
1 egg, beaten
1 tablespoon butter or margarine
1 cup whipping cream,
   whipped

Combine first 5 ingredients in heavy sauce-pan. Cook over medium heat, stirring constantly, until smooth and thickened. Let cool completely. Fold in whipped cream.
Yield: 2 cups.

Serve with fresh fruit salad or fresh pineapple chunks and strawberries as dip.

French Dressing

1 cup salad oil
1/4 cup vinegar
1 1/2 teaspoons salt
1/8 teaspoon pepper
1/4 teaspoon paprika
3/4 teaspoon sugar
1 tablespoon lemon juice
1 teaspoon worcestershire
   sauce
1 large clove garlic, minced

Combine ingredients thoroughly and chill.
Yield: 8-10 servings.

Soy Sauce Salad Dressing

⅔ cup oil
¼ cup vinegar
¼ cup ketchup
1 teaspoon dry mustard
1½ teaspoons garlic salt
2 tablespoons soy sauce
2 tablespoons sesame seeds,
  lightly toasted
Few drops hot red pepper
  sauce

Combine ingredients thoroughly and chill.
Yield: 8 servings.

Thousand Island Salad Dressing

3 eggs, hard boiled
6 stuffed green olives
1 small green pepper, cut into
  pieces
2 tablespoons onion
2 tablespoons American
  cheese
1 cup salad dressing
½ cup ketchup

Blend first 5 ingredients in blender or food
processor. Mix with salad dressing and ketchup.
Chill.
Yield: 8-10 servings.

"Geed's" Salad Dressing

1 tablespoon salt
2 large cloves garlic, minced
1 cup lemon juice, freshly
  squeezed
1 cup corn oil
¼ teaspoon cayenne pepper
½ -¾ teaspoon paprika

Place salt and minced garlic in a 2 cup
measure. Mash together with a fork. Add
lemon juice and oil. Stir until blended. Add
cayenne and paprika, mixing again. Pour into
2 salad dressing containers. Store in refrigerator until ready to use.
Yield: 2 cups.

Colorful Hazelnut Salad

Dressing:
1 cup hazelnuts
1 cup red wine vinegar
2 tablespoons honey
¾ cup olive oil
¼ cup water
1 teaspoon pepper
1 teaspoon salt

Salad:
2 red peppers, cored, seeded, and cut into 1 inch squares
¼ pound fresh mushrooms, thinly sliced
8 cups mixed greens (red-tip lettuce, Boston lettuce, escarole, etc.)

Preheat oven to 350°. Toast nuts in shallow baking pan, shaking occasionally until skins are well browned and nutmeats are pale brown (12 minutes or less). Do not over bake! All skins should be off. Grind nuts in food processor until fine. Combine vinegar, salt and pepper. Add oil, half the hazelnuts, honey and water.

At serving time, place torn and washed greens in large bowl. Whisk dressing. Pour ¼ cup dressing over red peppers and mushrooms, tossing to coat each piece. Pour remaining dressing over greens, tossing to mix well. Divide greens evenly among 6 plates. Spoon peppers and mushrooms over greens. Top each serving with remaining nuts.
Yield: 6 servings.

Spinach Salad Scull

1 pound spinach, torn
¼ pound mushrooms, sliced
¼ cup white wine vinegar
2 tablespoons dry white wine
2 teaspoons soy sauce
1 teaspoon sugar
1 teaspoon dry mustard
½ teaspoon curry powder
½ teaspoon salt
½ teaspoon pepper
¼ teaspoon minced garlic
⅔ cup salad oil
5 slices bacon, cooked and crumbled
2 eggs, hard-boiled and sliced

Combine spinach with mushrooms in a salad bowl. Mix vinegar, wine, soy sauce, sugar, dry mustard, curry powder, salt, pepper and garlic in blender. Add salad oil in stream, blending until well combined. Toss salad with dressing. Top with bacon and eggs.
Yield: 4-6 servings.

Carol's Romaine Lettuce Salad

Salad:
¼ cup slivered almonds
2 tablespoons sugar
1 bunch romaine lettuce
1 cup chopped celery
3 green onions and tops,
chopped
1 (11 ounce) can mandarin
oranges, drained

Dressing:
¼ cup oil
2 tablespoons wine vinegar
2 tablespoons sugar
¼ teaspoon salt
Few dashes hot sauce
Pepper to taste

Melt sugar with almonds-over low heat stirring until almonds are coated. Turn out and separate on greased cookie sheet. Cool. Wash, drain and tear lettuce into bite size pieces. Layer lettuce, celery, onions and oranges. Combine dressing ingredients. Pour over greens and toss at serving time. Top with almonds. Yield: 8 servings.

Almonds may be caramelized and stored in refrigerator. Dressing may be made the day before and refrigerated.

Romaine and Mandarin Orange Salad

1 head romaine lettuce, torn
2 (11 ounce) cans mandarin
oranges, drained
½ pound bacon, fried and
crumbled
1 bunch green onions,
chopped
1 (8 ounce) bottle poppy seed
dressing

Combine all ingredients. Pour dressing over prior to serving.
Yield: 4-6 servings.

The latest rage in haute cuisine is flower-tossed salads. So next time you want to add a taste of Texas to your table, throw a few flowers of Turk's cap in with your greens!

Deluxe Layered Salad

Must be made ahead.

Salad:
1 (10 ounce) package fresh
 spinach, torn
1 head lettuce, torn
6 eggs, hard-boiled and sliced
1 pound bacon, fried and
 crumbled
1 (8 ounce) can sliced water
 chestnuts, drained
1 (16 ounce) package frozen
 peas, thawed and drained

Topping:
1 cup mayonnaise
½ cup sour cream
½ (0.7 ounce) package ranch
 style dry dressing mix
¼ cup Parmesan cheese

Layer first six ingredients in large glass bowl. Mix topping ingredients in small bowl. Spread over top of salad. Top with Parmesan cheese. Cover and refrigerate overnight.
Yield: 8-10 servings.

Spinach Salad with Red Wine Dressing

1 cup salad oil
⅓ cup red wine vinegar
¼ cup sour cream
½ teaspoon dry mustard
2 tablespoons sugar
¼ cup chopped parsley
2 cloves garlic, minced
1½ teaspoons salt
2 (10 ounce) packages spin-
 ach, torn
8 slices bacon, cooked crisp
 and crumbled
4 eggs, hard-boiled and sliced
½ pound mushrooms, sliced

Mix oil, vinegar, sour cream, mustard, sugar, parsley, garlic and salt. Toss spinach with dressing to coat. Top with bacon, eggs and mushrooms.
Yield: 10 servings.

Party Spinach Salad

Salad:
1 (10 ounce) package spinach, torn
½ head red cabbage, shredded
1 medium red onion, thinly sliced
½ pound bacon, cooked crisp and crumbled
2 eggs, hard-boiled and sliced

Dressing:
5 tablespoons sugar
½ tablespoon salt
¼ cup oil
¼ cup vinegar
1 clove garlic, minced
1-2 teaspoons oregano

Layer all ingredients for salad. Spoon dressing over salad and toss 10 minutes before serving. Yield: 10-12 servings.

Spinach Salad

Salad:
1 (10 ounce) package spinach, torn
2 cups cherry tomatoes, halved
3 eggs, hard-boiled and chopped
7 slices bacon, cooked crisp and crumbled
1 cup seasoned croutons

Dressing:
2 tablespoons lemon juice
6 tablespoons oil
1 teaspoon garlic powder
¼ teaspoon pepper
1 teaspoon salt
Parmesan cheese

Combine salad ingredients. Mix dressing ingredients, leaving Parmesan cheese for topping. Pour over salad, tossing thoroughly. Yield: 8-10 servings.

Sweet Spinach Salad

Salad:
2 (10 ounce) packages spin-
* ach, torn*
2 (8 ounce) cans sliced water
* chestnuts, drained*
1 (14 ounce) can bean
* sprouts, drained*
4 eggs, hard-boiled and
* chopped*
¼ medium onion, sliced and
* separated into rings*

Dressing:
1 cup salad oil
¾ cup sugar
⅓ cup ketchup
¼ cup vinegar
1 tablespoon worcestershire
* sauce*
1 medium onion, quartered
2 teaspoons salt
½ pound bacon, cooked crisp
* and crumbled*

Toss spinach, water chestnuts, bean sprouts, eggs and onion in a large bowl.

Combine dressing ingredients, except bacon, in blender. Pour over salad. Top with bacon. Yield: 14 servings.

Mandarin Salad

1 head bibb or red-tipped
* lettuce (or a combination)*
2 (11 ounce) cans mandarin
* oranges, drained*
2 avocados, peeled and diced
1 small red onion, sliced
Poppy seed dressing

Toss ingredients with poppy seed dressing before serving.
Yield: 8 servings.

This salad is simple, colorful and delicious. It always draws raves.

Twenty-Four Hour Salad

Must be made ahead.

2 cups white cherries,
   drained, halved and pitted
2 cups pineapple tidbits,
   drained
2 cups mandarin oranges,
   drained
2 cups miniature marshmallows
2 eggs
4 tablespoons sugar
4 tablespoons vinegar
2 tablespoons butter
1 pint whipping cream,
   whipped softly

Combine fruit and marshmallows. Set aside. Beat eggs until light. Add sugar and vinegar. Cook in double boiler until smooth and thick (whisking frequently). Remove from heat. Add butter. Cool. Fold in whipped cream. Pour over fruit mixture. Mix lightly. Refrigerate 24 hours.
Yield: 10-12 servings.

Curried Fruit

1 (29 ounce) can pear halves,
   drained, liquid reserved
1 (20 ounce) can pineapple
   chunks, drained, liquid
   reserved
1 (17 ounce) can apricot
   halves, drained, liquid
   reserved
1 (29 ounce) can peach
   halves, drained, liquid
   reserved
1 (10 ounce) jar maraschino
   cherries, drained, liquid
   reserved
1 cup brown sugar, packed
1 teaspoon curry powder
½ cup butter
¼ teaspoon cinnamon
¼ teaspoon nutmeg

Mix reserved fruit juices. Pour one cup mixture into 3 quart baking dish. Add fruits. Melt butter in saucepan. Stir in remaining ingredients. Pour over fruit. Bake at 325° for 1 hour.
Yield: 8-12 servings.

Pretty to serve in a chafing dish for holiday luncheons or buffets.

Cantaloupe Balls

1 (6 ounce) can frozen orange
   juice, thawed
1 (6 ounce) can frozen lemonade, thawed
1 cup water
2 cantaloupes, cut into balls

Combine first three ingredients. Pour over cantaloupe balls. Refrigerate.
Yield: 8-10 servings.

Cold Fruit Compote

Must be made ahead.

1 (16 ounce) can dark, pitted
   sweet cherries
1 (16 ounce) can sliced
   peaches, drained
1 (12 ounce) package dried
   apricots
½ cup orange juice
¼ cup lemon juice
1 tablespoon grated orange
   peel
1 tablespoon grated lemon
   peel
¾ cup light brown sugar,
   packed

Preheat oven to 350°. Turn cherries and juice into 1½ quart baking dish. Add peaches, apricots, orange juice, lemon juice and grated peels. Top with brown sugar. Bake covered 1½ hours. Cool slightly. Refrigerate over-night.
Yield: 10 servings.

Lithospermum incisum

Grandma's Congealed Salad

*1 (6 ounce) package apricot
    gelatin*
*2 (11 ounce) cans mandarin
    oranges, drained, liquid
    reserved*
*2 (20 ounce) can crushed
    pineapple, drained, liquid
    reserved*
*2 cups miniature marshmal-
    lows*
*1 (8 ounce) package cream
    cheese, softened*
2 cups milk
*1 (4 ounce) package instant
    vanilla pudding mix*

Make gelatin using juice from oranges, pine-apple and enough water to make 2 cups. Add oranges, pineapple and marshmallows. Congeal slightly. Gradually add milk and instant pudding to cream cheese. Spread mixture over congealed salad. Chill.
Yield: 10-12 servings.

Raspberry Gelatin Salad

*2 (14 ounce) cans crushed,
    sweetened pineapple*
*1 (6 ounce) package and 1 (3
    ounce) package raspberry
    gelatin*
*2 (10 ounce) packages frozen
    raspberries, thawed*
4 bananas, sliced
*1 (16 ounce) carton sour
    cream*

Heat pineapple and its juice, slowly. Add raspberry gelatin, stirring until dissolved. Add raspberries and juice. Pour half of mixture into 3 quart dish. Slice two bananas. Distribute them throughout the pineapple-raspberry mixture so they are covered. Chill mixture until firm. Cover remaining mixture. (Do not refrigerate.) Ice chilled mixture with sour cream. Pour unchilled mixture on top, distributing bananas as before. Chill salad until firm.
Yield: 12 servings.

Strawberry-Lemon Congealed Salad

1 (3 ounce) package strawberry gelatin
1 cup boiling water
1 (16 ounce) can strawberry
  pie filling
1 (3 ounce) package lemon
  gelatin
1 cup boiling water
⅓ cup mayonnaise
1 (3 ounce) package cream
  cheese, softened
1 (8¾ ounce) can crushed
  pineapple, drained
½ cup heavy cream, whipped

Dissolve strawberry gelatin in 1 cup boiling water. Stir in pie filling. Pour into 9x9 inch dish. Chill until partially set. Dissolve lemon gelatin in 1 cup boiling water. Beat mayonnaise and cream cheese with mixer. Beat in lemon gelatin. Fold in pineapple and whipped cream. Spread on strawberry layer. Chill. Cut in squares to serve.
Yield: 8-10 servings.

Blueberry Salad

Filling:
2 (3 ounce) packages black
  cherry gelatin
1 (15 ounce) can blueberries,
  drained, liquid reserved
1 (20 ounce) can crushed
  pineapple, drained, liquid
  reserved
2 cups boiling water

Topping:
8 ounces cream cheese, softened
½ cup sugar
8 ounces sour cream
Nuts, chopped (optional)

Dissolve gelatin with hot water. Mix reserved liquid and enough water to make 2 cups. Combine with gelatin. Add blueberries and pineapple. Pour into 11x8 inch dish. Refrigerate until firm.

Combine cream cheese, sugar, and sour cream. Frost salad with topping. Sprinkle with nuts.
Yield: 12-16 servings.

Pretzel Salad

2 cups crushed pretzels
1 tablespoon sugar
10 tablespoons butter, melted
1⅔ cups frozen whipped
  topping, thawed
1 cup sugar
1 (8 ounce) package cream
  cheese, softened
2 (3 ounce) packages raspberry gelatin
2 cups pineapple juice, heated
16 ounces frozen raspberries

Mix pretzels, sugar and butter together. Press into a 13x9 inch greased pan. Bake at 400° for 7-10 minutes. Cool. Blend together whipped topping, sugar and cream cheese. Spread over pretzel mix. Dissolve gelatin in hot pineapple juice. Add raspberries. Pour over cream cheese mixture. Stir when partially set. Chill.
Yield: 12-15 servings.

Gazpacho Congealed Salad with Avocado Dressing

Salad:
4½ cups tomato juice
2 (.25 ounce) envelopes unfla-
  vored gelatin
Vegetable cooking spray
¼ cup red wine vinegar
1 teaspoon minced garlic
2 teaspoons salt
¼ teaspoon pepper
Dash cayenne pepper
2 large tomatoes, peeled and
  chopped
¼ cup finely chopped onions
¾ cup finely chopped bell
  peppers
¾ cup peeled, finely chopped
  cucumber

Dressing:
1 cup mashed avocado
1 tablespoon lemon juice
1 cup sour cream
1 teaspoon salt

Pour 1 cup tomato juice in small saucepan. Sprinkle gelatin over juice. Let stand for 5 minutes. Spray a 6 cup ring mold with vegetable cooking spray. Heat juice and gelatin. Stir until mixture simmers and gelatin dissolves. Pour into medium mixing bowl. Stir in remaining tomato juice, vinegar, garlic, salt, pepper and cayenne. Refrigerate 1 hour. Stir in chopped vegetables. Spoon into mold. Refrigerate overnight.

Combine dressing ingredients and serve with Gazpacho salad.
Yield: 12-15 servings.

Looks pretty with dressing spooned in center of mold.

Congealed Vegetable Salad

6 tablespoons sugar
1 teaspoon salt
1 (6 ounce) package lime
  gelatin
3¼ cups boiling water
¼ cup vinegar
2 cups shredded cabbage
1 cup shredded carrot

Combine sugar, salt and gelatin. Add boiling water, stirring until gelatin dissolves. Stir in vinegar. Chill until partially set. Fold in cabbage and carrots. Spoon into an 8 cup ring mold. Chill until firm.
Yield: 8-10 servings.

Snowball Salad

1½ cups sugar
1 cup sour cream
2 tablespoons lemon juice
1 (8 ounce) carton whipped
  topping, thawed
1 (14 ounce) can of crushed
  pineapple, drained
½ cup maraschino cherries
1 cup chopped pecans
3 bananas, mashed

Mix all together and freeze.
Yield: 8-10 servings.

Pistachio Salad

1 (4 ounce) package pistachio instant pudding
½ cup chopped pecans
1 cup miniature marshmal-
  lows
1 (20 ounce) can crushed
  pineapple
1 (9 ounce) carton whipped
  topping, thawed
1 banana, sliced

Combine all ingredients, except banana. Chill. Stir in banana before serving.
Yield: 6 servings.

Heavenly Salad

1 cup mandarin oranges
1 cup crushed pineapple
1 cup sour cream
1 cup chopped pecans
1 cup miniature marshmal-
  lows
1 cup coconut, optional

Mix all ingredients together. Chill overnight. Yield: 8 servings.

West Coast Onion Salad

2 cups thinly sliced onions
½ cup vinegar
1 cup water
Salt and pepper to taste
½ cup mayonnaise
1 tablespoon celery seed

Mix first four ingredients. Refrigerate over-night (at least four hours). Drain liquid from mixture 30 minutes before serving. Add mayonnaise and celery seed. Toss. Serve. Yield: 6 servings.

Broccoli-Cauliflower Salad

Must be made ahead.

Salad:
1 head cauliflower, separated
  into flowerettes
1 bunch broccoli, separated
  into flowerettes
2 bunches green onions,
  chopped
½ pound bacon, cooked crisp
  and crumbled

Mix dressing ingredients. Pour over cauli-flower, broccoli, and onion. Marinate 24 hours. Top salad with bacon before serving. Yield: 8 servings.

Dressing:
½ cup mayonnaise
¼ cup sugar
⅓ cup salad oil
½ teaspoon salt
¼ teaspoon pepper
¼ cup vinegar

Cauliflower Salad

Salad:
**2 cups thinly sliced cauli-
flower**
**½ cup pitted, chopped ripe
olives**
**½ cup pimiento-stuffed green
olives**
½ cup thinly sliced celery
¼ onion, chopped
½ cup chopped green pepper

Dressing:
**6 tablespoons olive oil or
salad oil**
2 tablespoons lemon juice
2 tablespoons wine vinegar
1 teaspoon salt
¼ teaspoon sugar
¼ teaspoon black pepper

Combine vegetables. Mix dressing ingredients in blender for 1 minute. Pour dressing over vegetables. Marinate at least 1 hour in refrigerator.
Yield: 8-10 servings.

Italian Salad

½ head cauliflower
1 bunch broccoli
2 large carrots
1 large cucumber
1 cup green olives
1 cup black olives
1 (2 ounce) jar pimientos
**Italian salad dressing to coat
well**

Chop fresh vegetables into bite size pieces. Mix with drained and chopped green olives, black olives, and pimientos. Pour salad dressing over mixture. Marinate overnight in refrigerator.
Yield: 8-10 servings.

Good for dieters when made with diet dressing.

Spicy Slaw

Slaw:
2 tablespoons salt
1 head cabbage, shredded
 fine
2 large green peppers,
 chopped
1 large red pepper, chopped,
 or 1 jar pimientos
1 bunch celery, chopped

Dressing:
2 cups sugar
½ cup water
1 cup vinegar
1 teaspoon mustard seed
1 teaspoon celery seed

Sprinkle 2 tablespoons salt over cabbage. Let stand 2 hours. Squeeze moisture out. Add chopped vegetables. Pack in 3 one quart jars. Bring dressing ingredients to a boil. Pour over vegetables. Screw on tops. Refrigerate. Yield: 3 quarts.

Creamy Cabbage Slaw

Dressing:
1 (5 ounce) can evaporated
 milk
¼ cup apple cider vinegar
2 tablespoons sugar
1 teaspoon salt
¼ teaspoon celery seed
⅛ teaspoon pepper
½ cup mayonnaise

Slaw:
4 cups shredded cabbage
1 carrot, shredded
1 stalk celery, chopped

Stir together dressing ingredients. Chill until ready to serve.

Combine slaw ingredients. Chill. Pour dressing over cabbage mixture. Toss to coat. Serve immediately. Yield: 6 servings.

Green Bean Salad

Salad:
**2 (1 pound) cans whole green
beans, drained**
1 purple onion, sliced
1 tablespoon vinegar
1 tablespoon salt
1 tablespoon salad oil

Sauce:
½ cup sour cream
1 tablespoon lemon juice
½ cup mayonnaise
1½ teaspoons dry mustard
1 tablespoon horseradish

Marinate green beans and onion in vinegar, salt, and oil mixture for 1 hour. Drain. Combine sauce ingredients. Toss with green beans and onion.
Yield: 4 servings.

Perfect Pea Salad

Dressing:
½ cup vegetable oil
¾ cup sugar
⅓ cup white vinegar
1 teaspoon salt

Salad:
**1 (16 ounce) can petite peas,
drained**
**1 (16 ounce) can whole green
beans, drained**
**1 (2 ounce) jar pimientos,
drained**
**1 (15 ounce) can white on-
ions, chopped**
**1 small green pepper,
chopped**
4 stalks celery, chopped
**1 (8 ounce) can sliced water
chestnuts, chopped**

Combine dressing ingredients.

Toss salad ingredients. Add dressing. Refrigerate overnight.
Yield: 12 servings.

Marinated Mushroom and Avocado Salad

Marinade:
½ cup salad oil
3 tablespoons tarragon
vinegar
3 tablespoons lemon juice
2 tablespoons water
4 tablespoons minced parsley
1 clove garlic, minced
¾ teaspoon salt
Dash of pepper

Salad:
2 large avocados, peeled,
sliced and cut in large
pieces
1 (8 ounce) package mush-
rooms, sliced
6 lettuce leaves

Combine marinade ingredients.

Pour marinade over avocados and mush-rooms. Chill several hours. Drain. Serve on lettuce leaves.
Yield: 6 servings.

Avocado Bacon Boats

12 slices bacon, cooked crisp
and crumbled (set aside one
slice, crumbled)
½ cup sour cream
2 tomatoes, peeled, seeded
and chopped
2 tablespoons chopped green
onion
1 tablespoon lemon juice
¼ teaspoon salt
3 avocados, halved and pitted

Combine bacon, sour cream, tomato, onion, lemon juice and salt. Carefully scoop out avocado, leaving firm shell. Dice avocado. Fold into sour cream mixture. Fill avocado halves. Top with reserved bacon bits.
Yield: 6 servings.

Million Dollar Salad

Dressing:
1 tablespoon salt
1 cup sugar
½ cup salad oil
1 cup vinegar
1 teaspoon paprika

Salad:
1 (1 pound) can sweet peas,
_   drained_
1 (1 pound) can French style
_   green beans, drained_
1 (4 ounce) jar pimientos
6 stalks celery, chopped
1 bunch green onions,
_   chopped_
1 large green pepper,
_   chopped_

Combine dressing ingredients.

Toss salad ingredients. Add dressing. Refrigerate overnight.
Yield: 12 servings.

Lentil and Rice Salad

1 cup lentils
2 tablespoons lemon juice
3 tablespoons olive oil
½ cup chopped scallions
1 cup cooked rice
¼ cup chopped coriander
_   leaves_
½ cup yogurt
Salt and pepper to taste
Tomato wedges

Cook lentils until tender. Drain. Toss with lemon juice, oil and scallions. Cool. Add rice. Chill. Add coriander, yogurt, salt and pepper just before serving. Garnish with tomato wedges.
Yield: 4-6 servings.

Marinated Bean Salad

Must be made ahead.

Salad:
1 (16 ounce) can green beans
1 (16 ounce) can small green peas
1 (16 ounce) can kidney beans
1 (14 ounce) can bean sprouts
1 (4 ounce) can pitted olives
1 (6 ounce) can artichoke hearts, halved
1 (5 ounce) can sliced water chestnuts
1 (4 ounce) jar sliced mushrooms
1 (4 ounce) jar chopped pimientos
3 stalks celery, sliced diagonally
3-4 green onions, chopped
1 medium green pepper, sliced

Marinade:
¾ cup sugar
⅓ cup salad oil
⅔ cup white vinegar
½ teaspoon pepper
Celery seed

Combine drained salad ingredients. Prepare marinade. Pour over vegetables. Marinate overnight. Drain off liquid. Serve.
Yield: 12-20 servings.

'Xeriscape' is a new concept in landscaping which emphasizes water conservation. Many of our native plants have low water requirements, and make good choices for xeriscapes.

Cold Vegetable Salad

1 (10 ounce) package frozen
    chopped broccoli
1 (10 ounce) package frozen
    French green beans
1 (10 ounce) package frozen
    cut asparagus
1 bell pepper, chopped
1 cucumber, sliced
1 (6 ounce) can artichoke
    hearts, drained

Dressing:
½ cup half and half
2 tablespoons lemon juice
2 tablespoons garlic vinegar
2 tablespoons anchovy paste
1 cup mayonnaise
¾ cup chopped parsley
¼ cup chopped onions

Microwave instructions: Poke holes in frozen vegetable boxes. Place one box at a time in microwave. Cook on high for 2½-3 minutes. Break into bite-size pieces and chill. Add peppers, cucumber and artichokes. Chill again. Combine dressing ingredients. Pour over vegetable combination.
Yield: 10-12 servings.

Hargrave Potato Salad

6 medium-large potatoes
2 tablespoons mustard
2 tablespoons vinegar
5-6 slices bacon, cooked crisp
    and crumbled
1 bunch green onions,
    chopped
1 tablespoon bacon drippings
Salt and pepper to taste

Cook potatoes until done. Mash until lumpy. Add other ingredients in order given. Mix well. May be served warm or chilled.
Yield: 10-12 servings.

Macaroni Antipasto

1 (12 ounce) package swirl
   macaroni
3 tablespoons walnut oil
2 (4.5 ounce) jars marinated
   artichoke hearts, drained
1 (9.5 ounce) jar pepper
   salad, drained
1 (6 ounce) can pitted ripe
   olives, sliced
1 (7.75 ounce) jar green
   olives, sliced
½ cup grated fresh Parmesan
   cheese
¼ cup grated Romano cheese
1 cup Danish hard salami, cut
   in chunks
¼-½ pound Pepperoni, cut in
   chunks (quantity to your
   taste)

Cook macaroni as package directs. Drain. Coat macaroni with walnut oil. Add remaining ingredients. Toss. Chill.
Yield: 6-8 servings.

Artichoke Rice Salad

Must be made ahead.

1 (6 ounce) package rice for
   chicken mix
4 green onions, thinly sliced
½ green pepper, chopped
12-24 pimento stuffed olives,
   sliced
2 (4.5 ounce) jars marinated
   artichoke hearts
¼-½ teaspoon curry powder
⅓ cup mayonnaise
2-3 cups chopped chicken,
   ham or turkey

Cook rice as directed on package, omitting butter. Cool. Add onions, pepper and olives. Drain artichoke hearts, reserving liquid. Cut artichoke hearts in half. Combine reserved artichoke liquid, a little at a time, with curry powder and mayonnaise. Use only enough liquid to thin. Add meat to rice mixture and artichokes. Add mayonnaise mixture and marinate several hours or overnight in the refrigerator.
Yield: 6-8 servings.

Colorful Rice Salad

1 (10 ounce) package frozen
   English peas
3 cups cooked rice
1 (4 ounce) jar chopped
   pimientos
1 cup diced, cooked ham
6 green onions, chopped
¾ cup sliced stuffed olives
½ cup chopped celery
⅓ cup sweet pickle relish
2 cups (8 ounces) shredded
   Cheddar cheese
¼ cup mayonnaise
Lettuce leaves, optional
Cherry tomatoes, optional

Cook peas according to package directions. Drain. Cool. Combine peas with remaining ingredients. Toss until well mixed. Chill thoroughly. Serve on lettuce leaves, if desired. Garnish with cherry tomatoes.
Yield: 6-8 servings.

Curried Rice Salad

1 (6 ounce) package long
   grained and wild rice
¾ cup mayonnaise
1 (11 ounce) can mandarin
   oranges, drained
½ cup finely chopped pecans
1 teaspoon sugar
¾ teaspoon curry
Salt and pepper to taste

Cook rice according to package directions. Cool. Add remaining ingredients. Chill.
Yield: 6 servings.

Viola pedata

Kay's Spinach Chicken Salad

Salad:
1 pound spinach
2 cups cooked, cubed chicken
2 cups broccoli flowerettes
1 (8 ounce) can sliced water
  chestnuts, drained
4 slices bacon, cooked crisp
  and crumbled
Sliced, toasted almonds (optional)
¼ cup Parmesan cheese
½ cup Chinese noodles

Dressing:
3 tablespoons soy sauce
3 tablespoons wine vinegar
3 tablespoons vegetable oil
1 teaspoon minced onion
1 teaspoon sugar
Pepper to taste

Combine all salad ingredients excluding Parmesan cheese and Chinese noodles. Shake
dressing in jar. Pour over salad. Sprinkle salad
with Parmesan cheese and Chinese noodles
prior to serving.
Yield: 6 servings.

Curried Chicken Salad

Salad:
2 cups cooked, cubed chicken
1½ cups diced celery
1½ cups crushed pineapple,
  drained or white, seedless
  grapes
¼ cup coarsely grated carrots
½ cup almond slices, toasted

Dressing:
½ cup mayonnaise
¼ cup sour cream
1 teaspoon curry powder
1 teaspoon fresh lemon juice
½ teaspoon salt

Combine salad ingredients in large bowl. Mix
dressing ingredients. Add to chicken mixture
prior to serving.
Yield: 6 servings.

Hot Chicken Salad Casserole

2 cups diced, cooked chicken
2 cups diced celery
½ cup blanched, slivered almonds
½ teaspoon salt
½ teaspoon grated onion
2 tablespoons lemon juice, freshly squeezed
1 cup mayonnaise
½ cup shredded medium-sharp yellow cheese
⅔ cup crushed potato chips

Mix first 7 ingredients. Pour into shallow, buttered 8x8 inch baking dish. Top with cheese and potato chips. Bake uncovered at 375° for 20 minutes.
Yield: 6 servings.

Oriental Chicken Salad

Salad:
4 cups cooked, cubed chicken
1 (8 ounce) can sliced water chestnuts, drained
1 (14 ounce) can pineapple tidbits, drained (reserve juice)
1 cup diced celery
1 cup seedless grapes, halved
1 (11 ounce) can mandarin oranges, drained
1 (2 ounce) package almonds, toasted
1 (5 ounce) can Chinese noodles

Sauce:
1½ cups mayonnaise
½ teaspoon salt
1 tablespoon soy sauce
2 tablespoons reserved pineapple juice
1 teaspoon curry powder

Toss all salad ingredients except noodles. Combine sauce ingredients. Add sauce to chicken combination. Top with noodles prior to serving.
Yield: 6 servings.

Chicken Salad Honolulu

Salad:
1 cup cooked rice, cooled
3 cups cooked, cubed chicken
  breasts
2 cups diced celery
1 (8 ounce) can sliced water
  chestnuts, drained
2 (14 ounce) cans pineapple
  tidbits, drained
1 (3½ ounce) can flaked
  coconut

Dressing:
2 cups mayonnaise
2 tablespoons lemon juice
2 teaspoons curry powder
¼ teaspoon salt
¼ teaspoon pepper

Combine salad ingredients. Combine dressing ingredients. Mix dressing and salad. Chill several hours before serving.
Yield: 10 servings.

Hot Chicken Salad

2 cups cooked, cubed chicken
  breasts (reserve broth)
1 cup mayonnaise
1 cup finely chopped celery
2 tablespoons chopped onion
2 tablespoons lemon juice
½ cup almonds, toasted
½ pound mushrooms, sliced
1 tablespoon salt
1 cup stuffing made with 6-7
  slices of toast crumbled
  with one egg
¼ cup cheese
1¼ cup potato chips

Mix first nine ingredients. Add chicken broth to moisten. Place in greased 1½ quart baking dish. Top with cheese and potato chips. Bake at 400° for 20 minutes.
Yield: 6 servings.

Chicken Salad

2½ cups cooked, cubed
   chicken breasts
1 cup diced celery
1 cup sliced green grapes
½ cup sliced almonds
2 tablespoons minced parsley
½ teaspoon salt (optional)
1 cup mayonnaise
½ cup whipping cream,
   whipped
2 tablespoons chopped ripe
   olives
1 (8 ounce) can sliced water
   chestnuts, drained

Mix all ingredients. Refrigerate overnight or several hours.
Yield: 8 servings.

Shrimp Salad with Avocados

2 pounds shrimp, boiled,
   peeled and chopped
2 avocados, chopped
1 bunch green onions,
   chopped
2 stalks celery, chopped
2 teaspoons lemon juice
1 teaspoon garlic salt
½-¾ pint sour cream
Salt and pepper to taste
Lettuce

Mix all ingredients except lettuce. Chill. Serve on bed of lettuce.
Yield: 6-8 servings.

*Butterflies, bees and flies all feed profusely on the rich
nectar sources of milkweeds.*

Mom's Shrimp Walnut Salad

Must be made ahead.

Lemon-Herb Dressing:
½ cup lemon juice
1 tablespoon sugar
1 teaspoon seasoned salt
1 teaspoon oregano
1 teaspoon marjoram
½ teaspoon pepper
¼ teaspoon garlic powder
1 cup olive oil

Salad:
2 tablespoons butter
½ teaspoon rosemary
1 cup chopped walnuts
2 cups jumbo shrimp, cooked
2 tablespoons dried chives
1 tablespoon chopped parsley
6 pitted ripe olives, sliced
3 medium tomatoes, chopped
¾ cup shredded Monterey
   Jack cheese
½ cup small pickled onions
6 ruffly lettuce leaves
1 avocado, sliced (optional)

Combine dressing ingredients in a jar. Shake until blended.

Melt butter with rosemary in a heavy skillet over low heat. Add walnuts. Toast walnuts lightly (10 minutes). Set aside. Pour dressing over shrimp. Marinate in refrigerator several hours or overnight. One hour before serving, add all other ingredients (except lettuce leaves and avocado) to shrimp. Continue to marinate. Serve on ruffly lettuce leaves with avocado garnish.
Yield: 6 servings.

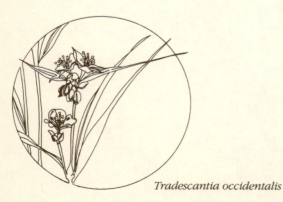

Tradescantia occidentalis

Seafood Salad

1 (6.5 ounce) can lobster
1 (6.5 ounce) can crabmeat
1 (12 ounce) bag shrimp
6 eggs, hard-boiled and
   chopped
½ cup chopped celery
½ cup ripe olives, chopped
Salt and pepper to taste
Grated onion to taste
½-¾ cup salad dressing

Combine all ingredients. Add salad dressing to desired consistency.
Yield: 8 servings.

Taco Salad

1 pound ground beef
1 (15 ounce) can ranch style
   beans
1 (1.5 ounce) package taco
   seasoning mix
1 (8 ounce) bottle thousand
   island dressing
4 ounces cheese, grated
1 large avocado, diced
1 small purple onion, sliced
   thin
1 medium head lettuce, torn
1 medium tomato, chopped
1 (8 ounce) bag corn chips,
   crushed

Brown and drain meat. Add beans and taco seasoning. Mix together cheese, avocado, onion, lettuce, and tomato. Toss with thousand island dressing. Pour hot meat and bean mixture over top of salad. Top with crushed corn chips. Serve immediately.
Yield: 6 servings.

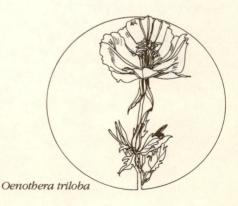

Oenothera triloba

Reunion Salad

2 (3 ounce) packages lemon
   gelatin
2 cups boiling water
1 (8 ounce) package cream
   cheese
1 cup evaporated milk
1 (20 ounce) can crushed
   pineapple
1 (2 ounce) jar chopped
   pimientoes, drained
1/2 cup chopped pecans

Dissolve gelatin in boiling water. Cream together cheese and evaporated milk. Add to gelatin. Add pineapple with juice, pimientoes and pecans. Chill, stirring occasionally until set.
Yield: 8 servings.

Dilled Cucumbers

1/3 cup vinegar
1 tablespoon sugar
1 teaspoon salt
1/2 teaspoon dried dillweed
1/8 teaspoon pepper
2 medium cucumbers, peeled
   and sliced thin
1 medium onion, sliced

Mix vinegar, sugar, salt, dillweed and pepper. Pour over cucumbers and onions. Refrigerate 1 hour.
Yield: 6 servings.

Herbed Cucumbers

2 cucumbers
4 ounces sour cream
1 teaspoon salt
1/4 teaspoon pepper
1 clove garlic, minced
1 tablespoon dill or fennel
   leaves

Peel and slice cucumbers. Combine with all other ingredients. Chill several hours.
Yield: 6 servings.

Shrimp - Avocado Salad

½ cup buttermilk
1 (3 ounce) package cream
  cheese, softened
1 small avocado, pitted,
  peeled and cubed
2 tablespoons lemon juice
1 small clove garlic
½ teaspoon salt
¼ teaspoon hot pepper sauce
6 cups torn lettuce
1 pound shrimp, peeled
18 cherry tomatoes, halved
6 slices bacon, cooked crisp
  and crumbled
4 ounces Cheddar cheese, cut
  in strips
Freshly ground pepper

Place buttermilk, cream cheese, avocado, lemon juice, garlic, salt and hot pepper sauce in blender. Blend until smooth. Place lettuce in six individual salad bowls. Arrange shrimp, cherry tomatoes, bacon and cheese strips over each serving. Sprinkle with pepper. Spoon dressing over each salad.
Yield: 6 servings.

Colorful Macaroni Salad

2 cups macaroni
½ cup mayonnaise
1 tablespoon lemon juice
1 teaspoon salt
1 teaspoon sugar
¼ teaspoon celery seed
1 tomato, diced
1 cup diced celery
3 tablespoons chopped pi-
  miento
2 tablespoons chopped green
  pepper

Cook macaroni until al dente. Drain. Rinse with cold water. Drain again. Mix mayonnaise, lemon juice, salt, sugar, and celery seed. Combine macaroni, tomato, celery, pimiento and green pepper. Add mayonnaise mixture. Chill several hours.
Yield: 6-8 servings.

Fancy Potato Salad

8-10 medium potatoes, peeled
1½ cups mayonnaise
1 cup sour cream
1½ teaspoons horseradish
1 teaspoon celery seed
1½ medium onions
½-¾ cup minced fresh pars-
    ley
1 tablespoon dill seed
Salt and pepper to taste

Boil potatoes until softened. Chop. Mix with remaining ingredients. Chill several hours. Yield: 12 servings.

P.J.'s Caesar Salad

May be prepared in front of guests.

1 clove garlic
¾ cup salad oil
2 cups white bread cubes
½ cup garlic oil
3 tablespoons lemon juice,
    freshly squeezed
2 teaspoons worcestershire
    sauce
½ teaspoon salt
¼ teaspoon pepper
8 anchovy fillets, finely
    chopped
2 heads romaine lettuce,
    chilled
2 eggs
¼ cup crumbled blue cheese
¼ cup grated Parmesan
    cheese

Crush garlic in a small bowl. Cover with salad oil. Refrigerate 30 minutes. Fry bread cubes in garlic oil until brown on all sides. Remove bread cubes from oil. Set aside. Save oil. Combine lemon juice, worcestershire, salt, pepper and anchovies. Mix well. Tear lettuce into bite-sized pieces. Place in salad bowl. Pour remaining garlic oil over lettuce. Toss to coat evenly. Break eggs over salad. Toss well. Pour lemon mixture on salad. Toss well. Add bread cubes and cheeses. Toss well. Serve at once.
Yield: 8-10 servings.

Ipomoea pes-caprae

Goat-foot morning glory - *Ipomoea pes-caprae*
This low, creeping vine is an important stabilizer of beaches and coastal dunes. Goat-foot morning glory can sprawl across distances of over thirty feet! The name goat-foot describes its unique leaf shape. The rose- or purple-colored flowers bloom from summer to late fall along warm Gulf Coast areas.

Angel Biscuits

5 cups flour
1 teaspoon salt
¼ cup sugar
1 teaspoon baking soda
3 teaspoons baking powder
4 tablespoons warm water
  (105°-115°)
1 package dry yeast
2 cups buttermilk
1 cup shortening

Preheat oven to 400°. Measure dry ingredients and sift together into large bowl. Dissolve yeast in warm water. Add buttermilk. Cut shortening into dry mixture until the texture resembles coarse cornmeal. Add buttermilk mixture gradually, stirring until the dough forms soft mass. It should handle well without being sticky. Turn dough out onto floured surface. Knead dough ten turns, or enough to smooth it. (Biscuit dough should be handled very little.) Roll out dough with floured rolling pin to ¼ inch thickness. Dip biscuit cutter into flour and cut biscuits. Dip biscuits into melted butter and fold over. Bake on cookie sheet 10 minutes.
Yield: 4-5 dozen.

Cloud Biscuits

2 cups flour
1 tablespoon sugar
4 teaspoons baking powder
½ teaspoon salt
½ cup solid shortening
1 egg, beaten
½ cup milk

Preheat oven to 400°. Combine first 4 ingredients. Cut shortening into dry ingredients until texture of small peas. Add milk and beaten egg. Stir until dry ingredients are incorporated. Turn the dough onto floured board and knead gently 20 strokes. Roll out dough to ½-¾ inch thickness. Cut with biscuit cutter. Bake for 10-14 minutes.
Yield: 18-20 biscuits.

Jam Tarts

1 (3 ounce) package cream
   cheese, softened
½ cup butter or margarine
1 cup flour
⅛ teaspoon salt
½ cup assorted preserves
   (cherry, pineapple, blueberry, etc.)

Beat cream cheese and butter in small bowl until fluffy. Stir in flour and salt. Refrigerate dough, covered, for 30 minutes. Press 1 teaspoon dough in tartlet or mini-muffin pans, keeping dough even in thickness. Place pans on cookie sheet. Spoon ½-1 teaspoon preserves into each shell. Bake at 400° for 10-12 minutes, until pastry is golden. Cool on wire rack.
Yield: 24 small tarts.

May be frozen or stored in airtight container for up to two weeks.

Blueberry Muffins

Frozen blueberries work nicely. Pat thawed blueberries dry with paper towel before adding to flour mixture.

¼ cup butter or margarine
½ cup sugar
1 egg
½ cup milk
1½ cups flour
2 teaspoons baking powder
¼ teaspoon salt
¾ cup blueberries

Preheat oven to 350°. Cream butter and sugar until light and fluffy. Beat in egg and milk. Stir in flour, baking powder and salt until moistened. (Batter will be lumpy.) Fold in blueberries. Spoon batter into 10 well-greased muffin cups, filling each about ⅔ full. Bake for 20-25 minutes.
Yield: 10 muffins.

Banana Bran Muffins

1 ¾ cups flour
1 cup all bran cereal
⅔ cup sugar
2 ¾ teaspoons baking powder
½ teaspoon salt
⅓ cup butter
1 cup mashed banana
2 eggs, beaten
¼ cup milk
½ cup chopped dates, prunes, or raisins
½ cup chopped nuts

Preheat oven to 400°. Combine flour, cereal, sugar, baking powder and salt in large bowl. Cut in butter until mixture resembles coarse oatmeal. Add banana, eggs, milk, fruits and nuts. Mix until blended. Fill greased muffin cups. Bake for 20 minutes.
Yield: 10-12 muffins.

Theese muffins freeze beautifully! Heat frozen muffins for 36 seconds in microwave oven.

May be made as a loaf. If so desired, bake in 350° oven for 50-55 minutes using a 9x5 inch loaf pan.

Orange Refrigerator Rolls

2 packages dry yeast
1 ¼ cups warm water
½ cup sugar
½ cup shortening
2 teaspoons salt
3 beaten eggs
4 ½ cups flour
Grated rind of one orange
½ cup sugar
4 tablespoons butter, softened

Soak 2 packages dry yeast in ½ cup of warm water. Add sugar, shortening, salt, remaining water, and beaten eggs. Beat in flour. (This is very soft dough.) Let rise till double in size. Mix down. Cover well and put in refrigerator. Two hours before serving, roll dough out, jelly-roll fashion, being sure to use extra flour on board. Roll ½ to 1 inch thick. Spread with mixture of orange rind, sugar and soft butter. Roll up and cut in 1 inch slices. Place in well-greased tins. Bake at 400° for 10 minutes or until brown. Remove immediately from tins. Yield: 26 rolls.

Yeast Rolls

Must be made a day ahead.

1 package dry yeast
1 tablespoon sugar
1 cup warm water
3 eggs
½ cup sugar
1 teaspoon salt
4½-5 cups flour

Dissolve yeast and 1 tablespoon sugar in water. Beat eggs, ½ cup sugar and salt in separate bowl. Add yeast mixture. In separate bowl sift flour. Gradually add liquid mixture to sifted flour, stirring until it forms soft and sticky dough. Put in refrigerator overnight in large, covered bowl. Next day, divide dough into 2 balls. Roll out on floured surface to thickness of thick pie crust. Cut pie-shape slices and roll from the large end. Brush with melted butter. Place on cookie sheet for 3 hours. Bake at 400° for 10-15 minutes. Yield: 32 servings.

Quick And Foolproof Popovers

If popovers accompany prime rib roast, use the rendered fat in place of oil. This will add flavor.

3 eggs
3 tablespoons vegetable oil
¾ cup plus 2 tablespoons milk
¾ cup plus 2 tablespoons flour

Place buttered popover tins or custard cups in 450° oven, then begin recipe. Combine eggs, oil and milk. Add flour, 2 tablespoons at a time. Do not overbeat batter! If using blender, add flour 3 different times, each for just a brief flick of the switch. Pour batter into hot pans and bake at 450° for 25 minutes or until brown and glossy. Yield: 6-8 servings.

Butterhorns

2 cups milk, scalded
2 packages dry yeast
1 cup shortening
1 cup sugar
2 teaspoons salt
6 eggs, beaten
9 cups flour
Melted butter

Add yeast to cooling milk. Combine shortening, sugar and salt with electric mixer on low speed. Add milk and yeast to the shortening, sugar and salt mixture. Add beaten eggs. Add half the flour by hand. Put soft dough on well floured board and knead lightly. Put in greased bowl, cover and let rise approximately 3 hours or until double in bulk. Divide the dough into 6 equal parts. Roll each part on lightly floured surface to 9 inch circle. Brush with melted butter and cut each circle in 16 wedge shaped pieces. Roll each wedge, starting with wide end, roll to the point. Arrange on greased cookie sheets and brush with melted butter. Cover and let rise until double in bulk or until very light. Bake at 375° for 10-12 minutes or until nicely browned.
Yield: 96 rolls.

Butterhorns freeze well. To freeze, roll each wedge, arrange on cookie sheets, and freeze. After frozen, place in plastic bags or freezer containers and store in freezer until ready to serve. To bake, place on greased cookie sheets and let rise for 3 hours or until double in bulk. Bake at 375° for 10-12 minutes.

English Scones

2 cups flour
1 tablespoon baking powder
½ teaspoon salt
1 tablespoon sugar
¾-1 cup heavy cream
4 tablespoons melted butter

Preheat oven to 450°. Sift together first four ingredients. Add cream and stir quickly until dough holds together. Turn out on floured board and pat out to ½ inch thickness. Cut in squares and dip in melted butter. Place on buttered cookie sheet or in buttered 9x9 inch baking pan. Bake for 12-15 minutes.
Yield: 7-8 scones.

Pizza Dough For Food Processor

1 package dry yeast
1 cup warm water (105°)
1 teaspoon sugar
2⅔ cups flour
1 teaspoon salt
1½ teaspoons vegetable oil

Mix yeast with warm water in 2 cup measure. Add sugar and place in warm place for 10 minutes. Add flour, salt and oil to work bowl with metal blade. Turn on machine. Slowly pour yeast mixture through feed tube. Stop machine and scrape down sides. Turn on machine. Let run 40-50 seconds until dough forms a smooth, elastic ball. (It will be sticky.) Put ball into oiled bowl, turning so all sides are oiled. Cover and place in warm place to rise until doubled (1½ hours). Divide in half and roll out. Place on 2 (11 inch) pizza pans, top with favorite sauces and toppings. Bake at 400° for 30-35 minutes or until bottom is browned.
Yield: Two 11 inch pizzas.

Oatmeal Raisin Bread

2 packages dry yeast
½ cup warm water
1 cup quick oatmeal
1¼ cups raisins
1½ cups boiling water
5 cups flour
1½ teaspoons salt
½ cup sugar
½ cup liquid shortening
2 eggs
Margarine, softened
Cinnamon

Mix yeast and water, setting aside. Put oatmeal and raisins in large bowl and pour boiling water over combination. Cool. Mix salt, sugar, liquid shortening and eggs; add to cooled oatmeal mixture. Add yeast mixture. Beat in flour to make a stiff dough. Knead until smooth. Place in greased bowl and cover. Let rise until double in size (1 hour). Roll out one half dough on floured board. Spread with margarine and sprinkle with cinnamon. Roll lengthwise and put in greased bread pan. Repeat with remaining half. Let rise again. Bake at 350° for 45 minutes.
Yield: 2 loaves.

Honey Whole Wheat Bread

4 cups whole wheat flour
½ cup non-fat dry milk
1 tablespoon salt
2 packages dry yeast
3 cups water
½ cup honey
2 tablespoons cooking oil
4-4½ cups white flour

Combine 3 cups whole wheat flour, dry milk, salt and yeast in large mixing bowl. Heat water, honey and oil over low heat until warm. Pour warm liquid over flour mixture. Blend at low speed with mixer. Stir in 1 cup additional whole wheat flour and 4-4½ cups white flour. Knead five minutes. Place dough in greased bowl. Cover. Let rise 1 hour until light and doubled in bulk. Punch down and divide in half. Shape each half into a loaf by rolling to 14x7 inch rectangle. Starting with 7 inch side, roll jelly roll fashion. Turn ends under slightly. Place in greased pan. Cover. Let rise 30-45 minutes or until light and doubled in size. Bake at 375° for 45 minutes or until loaf sounds hollow when lightly tapped.
Yield: 2 loaves.

Monkey Bread

1 cup all-bran cereal
¾ cup shortening or oil
½ cup sugar
1 cup boiling water
2 eggs, well beaten
2 teaspoons salt
2 packages dry yeast
1 cup lukewarm water
6½ cups flour
½ cup margarine, melted

Mix all-bran cereal, shortening and sugar excluding 3 teaspoons in a large bowl. Pour boiling water over this and stir. Let stand until lukewarm. Put yeast in 1 cup lukewarm water. Add the 3 teaspoons of sugar. Beat eggs and salt. Fold eggs and salt into bran mixture. Add yeast to 3½ cups flour. Blend well. Add 3 cups of flour with your hands, kneading until smooth. Roll dough out and cut into 2 inch squares. Dip each square in melted margarine. Place in two tube or bundt pans. Let rise 1½ hours. Bake at 325° for 30 minutes or until golden brown.
Yield: 2 large loaves.

Cowboy Cornbread

½ cup vegetable shortening
2 cups self-rising yellow corn meal mix
1 (8½ ounce) can cream-style corn
1 (8 ounce) carton sour cream
1 cup shredded sharp Cheddar cheese
2 eggs, beaten
1 (4 ounce) can chopped green chilies, undrained

Preheat oven to 400°. Melt shortening in a 9 inch square baking pan. Tilt pan to coat bottom evenly. Mix remaining ingredients. Add melted shortening. Mix until well blended. Pour into hot pan. Bake 30 minutes or until golden brown.
Yield: 9 servings.

Strawberry Bread

3 cups flour
4 eggs
1 teaspoon baking soda
1 teaspoon salt
2 tablespoons cinnamon
2 cups sugar
1¼ cups oil
1 cup chopped pecans
2 (10 ounce) packages frozen strawberries, thawed

Preheat oven to 350°. Sift dry ingredients together in bowl. Make a well in dry ingredients. In a separate bowl, beat eggs adding oil, strawberries and nuts. Pour liquid into well of dry ingredients and stir until mixed. Pour into two large loaf pans or four small loaf pans that have been greased and floured. Bake 45 minutes.
Yield: 2 loaves.

Rikki's Bread Sticks

1 package hot dog buns (8 buns), quartered lengthwise
1 cup butter
1 tablespoon garlic powder
1 teaspoon basil
½ teaspoon caraway seeds or sesame seeds
½ cup Parmesan cheese

Melt butter. Add garlic powder, basil and caraway seeds. Remove from heat. Add Parmesan cheese. Brush butter mixture on all areas of the bread stick with a pastry brush. Bake on a cookie sheet at 200° for 2 hours. Serve cold.
Yield: 8-12 servings.

May be frozen for several months.

Danish Coffee Cake

Dough:
1 cup flour
½ cup cold butter
1 tablespoon water

Topping:
½ cup butter
1 cup water
2 teaspoons almond flavoring
1 cup flour
3 eggs, slightly beaten

Frosting:
⅓ cup melted butter
2 cups powdered sugar
3 tablespoons water or milk
1 cup chopped almonds

Frosting Variation:
1½ ounces cream cheese, softened
1 tablespoon butter, softened
1 tablespoon cream
Powdered sugar

Preheat oven to 350°. Measure flour into bowl. Cut in butter. Sprinkle water over mixture and mix. Form into ball. Shape dough into a 12x3 inch rectangle. Place on greased cookie sheet.

Combine butter and water in saucepan and bring to boil. Add almond flavoring, remove mixture from heat. Add flour, stirring until smooth. Add eggs, again stirring until smooth. Spread mixture over dough. Bake 45-55 minutes.

Add powdered sugar to melted butter. Add liquid to desired consistency. Spread over cake and sprinkle with almonds.

Mix together cream cheese, butter and cream. Add enough powdered sugar to make a creamy consistency. Spread over cake.
Yield: 10-12 servings.

This recipe may be doubled easily.

Mrs. M's Finnish Kropsua

3 eggs, well beaten
2½ cups milk
1 cup flour
½ teaspoon salt
½ cup margarine, melted
2 tablespoons sugar
Powdered sugar

Preheat oven to 375°. Mix ingredients in order given with hand mixer or wire whisk until batter is almost smooth. Grease 13x9 inch glass dish with oil. Heat in oven until hot. Pour in Kropsua. Bake for 40 minutes. Decorate with powdered sugar. Cut in squares and serve with butter and syrup.
Yield: 8-10 servings.

Kropsua will lose some of its "puffiness" when removed from oven.

Pineapple Nut Bread

¾ cup brown sugar, packed
3 tablespoons butter or mar-
garine, softened
2 eggs
2 cups flour
2 teaspoons baking powder
½ teaspoon salt
¼ teaspoon baking soda
1 (8 ounce) can crushed
pineapple and juice
¾ cup chopped nuts
2 tablespoons sugar
½ teaspoon cinnamon
Cream cheese, whipped

Preheat oven to 350°. Cream together brown sugar and butter or margarine. Add eggs, flour, baking powder, salt, baking soda and pineapple. Mix well until all ingredients are combined. Stir in nuts. Pour into greased and floured 9x5x3 inch loaf pan. Sprinkle top with 2 tablespoons sugar and ½ teaspoon cinnamon before baking. Bake 45-50 minutes. Serve topped with whipped cream cheese. Yield: 10-12 servings.

Nut Filled Christmas Tree

Dough:
4-5 cups flour
2 packages dry yeast
1 cup milk
½ cup water
⅓ cup sugar
¼ cup butter or margarine
2 teaspoons salt
2 egg yolks, room tempera-
ture

Filling:
2 cups finely chopped nuts
⅓ cup sugar
2 tablespoons butter, melted
2 egg whites

Sift together 1½ cups flour and yeast. Heat milk, water, sugar, butter and salt over low heat until very warm (120-130°). (Butter need not be melted.) Add liquid ingredients to flour-yeast mixture. Beat with electric mixer on medium speed about 3 minutes. Add egg yolks and 1 cup flour. Continue to beat about 2 minutes. Stir in enough flour to make a moderately soft dough. Turn out onto lightly floured surface and knead until smooth and satiny (5-10 minutes). Cover dough and let rest for 45 minutes.

Stir together nuts, sugar and butter. Beat egg whites until stiff. Fold in nut mixture. Divide dough in half. Roll out ½ to a triangle 18 inches long and 15 inches at the base. Spread with ½ the filling. Roll up jelly roll fashion starting at one of the long sides to form a cone. Pinch edges to seal seam. Place seam

Continued ...

side down on large greased baking sheet. Using scissors, make cuts from top surface about ⅔ the way through the dough at 1 inch intervals, leaving last 1½ inches uncut at long end to form base of tree. Starting at the top (small end) and alternating sides, pull first piece of dough to the right and turn out; pull next piece of dough to the left and turn out. Continue to form branches, increasing the width of the tree as you proceed down the trunk. Lightly pull branches together, shortening the height of the tree. Repeat with second half of dough. Brush with oil. Let rise in place 35-45 minutes or until double in bulk. Preheat oven to 400°. Bake 10-15 minutes. For the last 5-7 minutes cover with foil to prevent excessive browning. Glaze with powdered sugar icing and decorate with candied green and red cherries. Makes 2 trees.
Yield: 12 servings per tree.

Fruit Strudel

4 ounces cream cheese, room temperature
1 cup butter, room temperature
1 cup sour cream
5 cups presifted flour
1 (14 ounce) jar strawberry preserves
1 (14 ounce) jar apricot preserves
¾ cup flaked coconut
2 cups raisins
1 cup pecans, chopped
Granulated sugar

Mix first 4 ingredients together by hand until no longer sticky. Wrap in plastic and refrigerate overnight. When ready to use, cut dough into fourths. Roll out on floured board until very thin. Spread strawberry preserves on two sections and apricot preserves on the other two sections. Sprinkle all with coconut, raisins and pecans. Roll dough tightly enclosing the sides, envelope style. Place seam down on a greased cookie sheet and sprinkle with granulated sugar. Score into 1 inch pieces before baking. Bake at 350° for 45 minutes or until brown. Cool 15 minutes then cut through and separate the strudel.
Yield: 65 one inch pieces.

May be made ahead and frozen.

Cranberry Coffee Cake

Batter:
½ cup butter or margarine
1 cup sugar
2 eggs
1 teaspoon baking powder
1 teaspoon baking soda
½ teaspoon salt
2 cups flour
1 cup sour cream
1 teaspoon almond extract
1 (14 ounce) can whole
   cranberry sauce
½ cup chopped pecans

Glaze:
¾ cup powdered sugar
½ teaspoon almond flavoring
2 tablespoons warm water or
   milk

Preheat oven to 350°. Cream butter. Add sugar gradually. Add eggs, one at a time. Stir in dry ingredients alternating with sour cream to which almond flavor has been added. Place half of batter in greased and floured tube pan. Add half of cranberry sauce. Spread evenly and then add half of the pecans. Add the other half of the batter, then add the rest of the cranberry sauce, spread evenly and then add the pecans. Bake for 50-55 minutes.

Combine ingredients and drizzle over cake while it is still warm.
Yield: 12 servings.

Garlic Bread

1 loaf French bread
4 cloves garlic
½ cup butter, melted
¼ cup grated Parmesan
   cheese
1 tablespoon minced parsley
½ teaspoon paprika

Thoroughly rub outside crust of bread with 2 slightly crushed cloves of garlic. Split loaf in half lengthwise and place each half, crust down, on cookie sheet. Put remaining 2 cloves garlic through garlic press and combine with melted butter. Brush over cut surfaces. Mix remaining ingredients. Sprinkle over buttered surface. Cut in 2 inch bias slices. Heat on cookie sheet at 350° for 5-10 minutes or until top is lightly browned.
Yield: 8-10 servings.

Hot dog buns may also be used. Slice buns in half and then in half again to make 4 sticks.

Poppy Seed Loaf

Bread is best if baked the day before. Unglazed loaves may be frozen.

Dough:
3 cups flour
1½ teaspoons salt
1½ teaspoons baking powder
3 eggs
1½ cups milk
1⅛ cups oil
2¼ cups sugar
1½-2 tablespoons poppy seeds
1½ tablespoons vanilla
1½ tablespoons almond
  extract
1½ tablespoons butter extract

Glaze (optional, but yummy!):
¼ cup orange juice
¾ cup powdered sugar
½ teaspoon butter extract
½ teaspoon vanilla
½ teaspoon almond extract

Preheat oven to 350°. Mix all ingredients 1-2 minutes. Pour into 2 large or 6 small, lightly greased loaf pans. Bake for 1 hour.

Combine ingredients. Pour mixture over hot bread.
Yield: 2 loaves.

Beer Bread

3 cups self-rising flour
½ cup sugar
12 ounces regular beer, room
  temperature
½ cup butter, melted

Preheat oven to 350°. Grease a 9x5x3 inch loaf pan. Mix flour, sugar and beer thoroughly. Spoon into greased loaf pan. Bake for 45 minutes. Punch holes in top of bread with fork. Pour melted butter over top. Bake 15 more minutes.
Yield: 8-10 servings.

Lemon Bread

Batter:
1 cup butter
2 cups sugar
4 eggs
½ teaspoon salt
½ teaspoon baking soda
3 cups flour
1 cup buttermilk
1 cup chopped pecans
Rind of 1 lemon, grated

Topping:
¾ cup sugar
Juice of 3 lemons

Preheat oven to 350°. Cream butter and sugar. Add eggs one at a time. Sift dry ingredients. Add alternately with buttermilk. Begin and end with dry ingredients. Fold in nuts and grated rind. Pour into 2 greased and floured loaf pans. Bake for 1 hour.

Combine juice and sugar. Let stand. Stir often until sugar dissolves. When bread is done, remove from pan and place on foil. Spoon juice over hot loaf.
Yield: 2 loaves.

Apricot Nut Bread

2½ cups flour
1 cup sugar
3½ teaspoons baking powder
1 teaspoon salt
3 tablespoons salad oil
½ cup milk
4 teaspoons grated orange
* peel*
¾ cup orange juice
1 cup finely chopped dried
* apricots*
1 egg
1 cup finely chopped nuts

Preheat oven to 350°. Grease and flour a 9x5x3 inch loaf pan. Measure all ingredients into large mixer bowl. Beat on medium speed ½ minute scraping sides and bottom of bowl constantly. Pour into pan and bake 55-65 minutes or until wooden pick, inserted in center, comes out clean. Remove from pan. Cool thoroughly before slicing.
Yield: 10-12 servings.

Pumpkin Bread

1 heaping cup canned
  pumpkin
½ cup vegetable oil
1½ cups sugar
⅓ cup water
2 eggs
1¾ cups flour
¾ teaspoon salt
½ teaspoon nutmeg
1 teaspoon baking soda
½ teaspoon cinnamon
¼ teaspoon cloves

Preheat oven to 350°. Grease and flour pans. Mix pumpkin, oil, sugar, eggs and water together. Add flour and stir well. Add 5 remaining ingredients and mix until creamy. Pour into well greased and floured large meatloaf pan or two 3⅝x2⅜x2¼ inch pans. Bake for 1 hour. Cool slightly before removing from pan.
Yield: 10-12 servings.

Cranberry Nut Bread

¾ cup sugar
2 cups sifted flour
1 teaspoon salt
½ teaspoon soda
1½ teaspoons baking powder
1 cup coarsely chopped
  cranberries
1 cup chopped nuts
1 teaspoon grated orange
  rind
1 egg, beaten
¾ cup orange juice
2 tablespoons oil

Preheat oven to 350°. Grease a 9x5x3 inch loaf pan. Sift first 5 ingredients together into bowl. Stir in cranberries, nuts and rind. Combine egg, orange juice and oil. Add to dry ingredients. Stir until just moistened. Turn into greased loaf pan and bake 50-60 minutes. Remove from pan after 10 minutes and cool.
Yield: 12 servings.

Erythronium rostratum

Top Hat Batter Bread

1 package dry yeast
½ cup warm water
¼ teaspoon ground ginger
3 tablespoons sugar
1 (13 ounce) can undiluted
* evaporated milk*
1 teaspoon salt
2 tablespoons salad oil
4-4½ cups unsifted flour
Melted margarine

Dissolve yeast in water in large mixing bowl. Blend in ginger and 1 tablespoon sugar. Let stand in warm place until mixture is bubbly, about 15 minutes. Stir in remaining 2 tablespoons sugar and milk, salt and salad oil. Beat in flour 1 cup at a time using low speed and beating very well after each addition. Beat in last cup of flour with a spoon. Add flour until dough is very heavy and stiff but too sticky to knead. Let rest 10 minutes. Divide dough in 2 parts and place in 2 well-greased and floured 1 pound coffee cans. Cover with well greased plastic lids to freeze. To bake, let uncovered cans stand in warm place until dough rises and makes a top hat, 45-60 minutes. (If frozen this takes 4 to 5 hours for 1 pound cans.) Bake at 350° for 45 minutes. Crust will be very brown. Brush top lightly with margarine. Let cool 5-10 minutes on cooling rack. Slide bread from can and let cool in upright position.
Yield: 2 loaves, 8 servings per loaf.

Top Hat Batter Bread Variations

Light Wheat Bread

Use 1½ cups whole wheat flour and 3 cups all-purpose flour. Replace sugar with honey.

Corn-Herb Batter Bread

To yeast bread mixture, add 2 tablespoons celery seed, 1½ teaspoons ground sage and ⅛ teaspoon marjoram. Substitute ½ cup yellow cornmeal for ½ cup of the flour.

Raisin-Nut Batter Bread

To yeast mixture, add 1 teaspoon cinnamon and ½ teaspoon walnuts into batter with final addition of flour.

Eustoma grandiflorum

Bluebells - *Eustoma grandiflorum*
One of the most beautiful Texas species, bluebells bloom in the heat of mid to late summer. An annual or weak perennial, the bluebell's lovely blue to purple flower has enticed people to overpick it in the past, which explains its current scarcity in the wild. Bluebells grow 1 to 2 feet tall in moist soils across most of Texas.

Broccoli in a Special Garlic Sauce

1 pound broccoli flowerets
2 tablespoons sunflower seed oil
2 tablespoons chopped scallions
1 tablespoon chopped ginger root
½ tablespoon chopped garlic
1 teaspoon hot chili paste
1 teaspoon wine or sherry
½ teaspoon salt
1 teaspoon sugar
1 teaspoon vinegar
4 tablespoons water
½ tablespoon cornstarch

Parboil broccoli flowers 2 minutes; drain. Run cold water over broccoli for 2-3 minutes. Heat wok and sunflower seed oil. Stir-fry scallions, ginger root, garlic and chili paste until they impart their fragrance. Add other ingredients, boil and pour over broccoli.
Yield: 4 servings.

A favorite vegetable dish enjoyed by our members at the Empress of China in Houston, Texas.

Broccoli au Gratin

2 cups milk
4 tablespoons flour
16 ounces cream cheese, softened
1 ounce Roquefort cheese, softened
1 teaspoon salt
½ teaspoon pepper
2½ pounds fresh broccoli, approximately 3 large bunches
½ stick butter
Breadcrumbs

Preheat oven to 350°. Heat milk. Blend in flour, cream cheese, Roquefort, salt and pepper. Stir constantly over low heat until smooth. Cook broccoli until barely tender. Drain and place in 3 quart casserole or 13x9 inch baking dish. Pour cheese sauce over broccoli. Bake for 30 minutes. Remove from oven, top with breadcrumbs, dot with butter and bake for 10-15 minutes, or until bubbly.
Yield: 12 servings.

May be prepared the day before.

Broccoli Stir Fry

3 tablespoons salad oil
1 bunch fresh broccoli, cut in
* 1 inch pieces*
5 stalks celery, chopped
2 small onions, sliced
½ pound fresh mushrooms,
* sliced*
¼ cup soy sauce
¼ cup water
1 tablespoon sugar
1 teaspoon cornstarch
Salt and pepper to taste

Heat oil in large skillet. Stir fry all vegetables. Cook 5-7 minutes or until desired doneness. Combine soy sauce, water, sugar, cornstarch, salt and pepper. Pour mixture over vegetables. Cover and turn off heat. Let stand 3-5 minutes. Yield: 8 servings.

Broccoli Supreme

1½ pounds fresh broccoli
1 (10¾ ounce) can cream of
* chicken soup*
1 tablespoon flour
½ cup sour cream
¼ cup grated carrot
1 tablespoon grated onion
¼ teaspoon salt
⅛ teaspoon pepper
¾ cup herb stuffing mix
2 tablespoons butter, melted

Preheat oven to 350°. Remove outer leaves and tough parts of broccoli stalks. Cut broccoli stalks into 1 inch pieces and cook in boiling, salted water for 5-8 minutes. Add flowerets and cook until tender, about 5 minutes. Blend soup and flour. Add sour cream, carrot, salt, pepper and onion. Stir in broccoli. Turn into 2 quart casserole. Combine stuffing mix and butter. Sprinkle around edge of baking dish. Bake for 30-35 minutes. Yield: 6 servings.

Peas for a Party

½ cup water
¼ cup butter
2 tablespoons sugar
2 teaspoons salt
¼ teaspoon pepper
2 (10 ounce) packages frozen
_ peas_
6 cups shredded lettuce
_ (about 1 head)_

Heat water, butter, sugar, salt and pepper in a medium-large saucepan to boiling. Stir in peas. Simmer, covered, until peas are crisp-tender, 5 minutes. Remove from heat and stir in lettuce. Steam covered for 2 minutes. Drain. Serve hot.
Yield: 12 servings.

No one can figure out what the lettuce is; guests are always curious to know what is in the peas. Looks very nice on the plate.

Carrots and Celery au Gratin

4 cups sliced carrots
2 cups sliced celery
Boiling salted water
1 (10¾ ounce) can cream of
_ mushroom soup_
⅓ cup Chablis or chicken
_ broth_
1 tablespoon minced onion
¾ cup soft breadcrumbs
2 tablespoons melted butter
_ or margarine_

Cook carrots and celery in boiling, salted water 10 minutes. Drain. Combine soup, wine and onion. Pour over vegetables. Place mixture in shallow baking dish. Toss crumbs with butter. Sprinkle over dish. Bake 30 minutes at 350°.
Yield: 6 servings.

Mustard-Glazed Carrots

2 pounds carrots, peeled and
_ cut in fourths_
1 teaspoon salt
3 tablespoons butter
3 tablespoons prepared
_ mustard_
¼ cup brown sugar
¼ cup chopped parsley

Boil carrots and salt until tender. Drain. Cook butter, mustard and brown sugar in small saucepan until syrup-like. Pour over carrots. Simmer 5 minutes. Sprinkle with parsley before serving.
Yield: 8 servings.

May be halved.

Snow Peas with Water Chestnuts

¼ *cup sliced green onions*
2 *tablespoons hot salad oil*
½ *pound fresh snow peas; or*
   1 (6 ounce) package frozen
   snow peas, thawed
1 *(8½ ounce) can sliced water*
   chestnuts, drained
1 *teaspoon sugar*
1 *teaspoon flavor enhancer*
½ *cup chicken broth, divided*
2 *teaspoons cornstarch*
1 *teaspoon salt*

Sauté onion in hot salad oil until tender. Add snow peas, water chestnuts, sugar, flavor enhancer and 6 tablespoons chicken broth. Cook over medium heat for 5 minutes. Combine cornstarch, salt, and remaining broth, stirring until cornstarch is dissolved. Add broth mixture to snow peas, stirring gently. Cook 5 minutes.
Yield: 4-6 servings.

Asparagus Casserole

2 *(15 ounce) cans asparagus,*
   drained and cut up (save 1
   or 2 spears for decoration)
3 *eggs, beaten*
1 *cup grated sharp Cheddar*
   cheese
1¼ *cups broken crackers*
1 *cup milk*
Pinch of salt
¼ *cup butter, melted*

Preheat oven to 350°. Grease an 8x8 inch baking dish. Mix all ingredients except butter. Place in dish and pour butter over all. Top with 2 asparagus spears. Bake for 30 minutes uncovered.
Yield: 6 servings.

Zucchini with Walnuts

1 *cup walnuts, divided*
6 *medium zucchini, julienned*
2 *tablespoons butter*
2 *tablespoons olive oil*
1 *teaspoon salt*
½ *teaspoon pepper, freshly*
   ground

Chop ¾ cup of the walnuts. Sauté zucchini in butter and olive oil until tender, shaking the pan and tossing zucchini to cook evenly. Pour off butter and oil. Add chopped walnuts, salt and pepper. When walnuts are well blended and heated, garnish with remaining nuts and serve.
Yield: 6 servings.

Zucchini Boats with Spinach

1 (10 ounce) package frozen, chopped spinach
4 medium zucchini
3 tablespoons finely chopped onion
3 tablespoons butter
3 tablespoons flour
1 cup half and half
½ cup milk
½ cup (2 ounces) shredded Swiss cheese
1 teaspoon salt
¼ teaspoon white pepper
5 drops hot sauce
1 tablespoon grated Parmesan cheese (optional)

Preheat oven to 350°. Cook spinach according to package directions. Drain and press dry. Set aside. Cook zucchini in boiling salted water to cover for 5 minutes. Drain and cool slightly. Cut zucchini in half lengthwise. Remove and reserve pulp, leaving ¼ inch thick shells. Drain shells and set aside. Chop pulp, drain well and set aside. Sauté onion in butter in saucepan. Reduce heat to low; add flour. Stir until smooth. Cook 1 minute, stirring constantly. Gradually add half and half and milk. Cook over medium heat, stirring constantly, until thickened and bubbly. Add spinach, zucchini pulp, Swiss cheese, salt, pepper, and hot sauce. Place zucchini shells in a 12x8 inch baking dish. Spoon spinach mixture into shells. Sprinkle with Parmesan cheese (optional). Bake, uncovered, for 15 minutes or until thoroughly heated.
Yield: 8 servings.

Tasty Italian Zucchini

2½ pounds zucchini, cut in ½ inch slices
4 tablespoons butter
½ cup chopped green pepper
½ cup chopped onion
1 (1.5 ounce) package dry spaghetti sauce mix
1 cup water
1 (3 ounce) can sliced mushrooms, drained
1 (6 ounce) can tomato paste
1 (4 ounce) package mozzarella cheese
2 tablespoons grated Parmesan cheese

Preheat oven to 350°. Cook zucchini in boiling water for 3-4 minutes or until tender-crisp. Drain well and set aside. Cook onion and green pepper in butter until tender, but not brown. Remove from heat. Stir in mushrooms, dry spaghetti mix, water and tomato paste and mix well. Gently stir in zucchini and mozzarella cheese. Turn into a 10x6 inch greased baking dish. Sprinkle with Parmesan cheese. Bake for 30 minutes.
Yield: 6-8 servings.

Escalloped Eggplant

1 medium eggplant
Salt and pepper to taste
1/4 cup butter
1 1/4-2 cups evaporated milk
1 1/2 cups cracker crumbs
2 teaspoons flavor enhancer

Preheat oven to 350°. Peel, slice and cook eggplant until easily mashed. Season with salt and pepper. Add other ingredients. Pour into a buttered baking dish (1 1/2 inches deep). Bake 20-30 minutes.
Yield: 6 servings.

Herbed Squash Casserole

2 pounds fresh or frozen
   yellow squash, sliced
1 medium onion, chopped fine
1 (10 3/4 ounce) can mushroom
   soup
1 cup sour cream
2 tablespoons diced pimiento
   (optional)
1 carrot, grated
1 (8 ounce) package herb
   stuffing mix
1/2 cup butter

Preheat oven to 375°. Boil squash in salted water for 5 minutes or until tender. Drain well. Mix onions, soup, sour cream, pimiento and carrot. Add soup mixture to squash. Toss lightly. Melt butter and mix with stuffing mix. Mix half stuffing mix with squash mixture. Pour into a greased 2 quart casserole. Sprinkle remaining stuffing mix on top of casserole. Bake uncovered for 30 minutes.
Yield: 8-10 servings.

Auntie's Stuffed Squash

5 medium sized yellow
   squash
1/2 cup minced onion
1/4 cup butter
1/4 cup breadcrumbs
1/4 cup minced celery
1 clove garlic, minced
1/2 teaspoon salt
1/4 teaspoon pepper
1 cup grated Cheddar cheese
Paprika

Preheat oven to 350°. Boil whole squash in salted water, until tender. Cool, split lengthwise and scoop out pulp. Sauté onion and celery in butter adding garlic, salt and pepper. Add squash pulp. Stuff shells with this mixture; top with grated cheese and paprika. Bake for 20-30 minutes in a greased dish.
Yield: 6-8 servings.

Meredith's Favorite Spinach

2 (10 ounce) packages frozen
  chopped spinach, cooked
  and drained
1 (1.3 ounce) package dry
  onion soup mix
1 cup sour cream
½ cup grated Monterey Jack
  cheese

Preheat oven to 350°. Combine all ingredients, except cheese. Place in a lightly buttered 2 quart baking dish. Top with cheese. Bake 20 minutes.
Yield: 4 servings.

Artichoke-Spinach Casserole

Must be made the day before.

1 (6 ounce) jar marinated artichoke hearts, drained
2 (10 ounce) packages frozen
  spinach, thawed
2 (3 ounce) packages cream
  cheese, softened
2 tablespoons butter
4 tablespoons milk
½ cup grated Parmesan
  cheese
Pepper to taste

Place artichokes in casserole. Squeeze spinach dry. Place on top of artichokes. Beat cream cheese and butter until smooth. Add milk. Spread over spinach. Top with a grind of pepper and Parmesan. Cover. Refrigerate up to 24 hours. Bake at 350° for 40 minutes, covered the first 30 minutes, then uncovered 10 minutes.
Yield: 6-8 servings.

Celery Almondine

⅓ cup slivered almonds
2 tablespoons butter
4 cups diagonally sliced
  celery
1 chicken bouillon cube,
  crumbled
1 tablespoon instant onion
1 teaspoon flavor enhancer
½ teaspoon sugar
⅛ teaspoon garlic powder
⅛ teaspoon ginger

Sauté almonds in 2 tablespoons butter until lightly browned. Remove from skillet. Set aside. In same skillet, stir fry remaining ingredients for 10 minutes. Sprinkle with almonds when ready to serve.
Yield: 6 servings.

Spinach Lasagne

6 lasagne noodles
1 (10 ounce) package frozen spinach
1 (8 ounce) carton cottage cheese
¼ cup grated Parmesan cheese
4 ounces grated mozzarella cheese
1 (15 ½ ounce) jar spaghetti sauce
½ pound bulk sausage, browned and drained, optional

Cook noodles according to package directions. Cook spinach and drain well. Mix cottage cheese, Parmesan cheese, and mozzarella cheese with spinach. Spread mixture on each individual noodle. Roll up. Put all 6 noodles in a 13x9 inch baking dish. Pour spaghetti sauce over noodles. Bake at 350° for 20-25 minutes.
Yield: 4 servings.

May be frozen and reheated.

Lasagna Roll-Ups

Sauce:
1 pound hot Italian sausage, cut in ½ inch pieces
¾ cup chopped onion
1 clove garlic, minced
1 (24 ounce) can tomato juice
1 (6 ounce) can tomato paste
½ cup water
2 teaspoons sugar
½ teaspoon salt
1 bay leaf

Filling:
2 cups creamed cottage cheese
1 egg, beaten
½ cup Parmesan cheese
2 cups mozzarella cheese, grated
¼ teaspoon salt
¼ teaspoon pepper
8 lasagna noodles, cooked and rinsed

Cook sausage in skillet until brown. Remove. Sauté onion and garlic in ¼ cup drippings. Add remaining ingredients and simmer for 1 hour. Remove bay leaf. Add sausage to sauce.

Combine cottage cheese, egg, ¼ cup Parmesan cheese, 1 cup mozzarella cheese, salt and pepper. Chill. Grease 13x9 inch baking dish. Pour 1 cup of sauce in bottom. Put ¼ cup of cheese mixture on each noodle and roll up. Place casserole with the seam down. Pour remaining sauce over noodles and top with rest of Parmesan and mozzarella cheeses. Bake, uncovered at 350° for 30 minutes.
Yield: 6-8.

Good "company dish" that may be prepared a day ahead.

Herb Linguine

1 (7 ounce) package linguine
¼ cup butter
⅓ cup chopped parsley
½ teaspoon garlic powder
½ teaspoon oregano leaves
1 tablespoon lemon juice
Parmesan cheese, optional

Cook linguine in a 3 quart saucepan according to package directions. Drain well. In same saucepan, melt butter. Stir in linguine and remaining ingredients (except Parmesan cheese). Cook over medium heat, stirring constantly until heated through (2-3 minutes). Sprinkle with Parmesan cheese, if desired.
Yield: 4 servings.

Blends nicely with a veal or chicken dish.

Linguine with Tomatoes and Basil

4 large ripe tomatoes, cut into
   ½ inch cubes
1 pound Brie, rind removed
   and cut into pieces
1 cup chopped basil
3 cloves garlic, minced
1 cup olive oil
½ teaspoon salt
½ teaspoon pepper
1½ pounds linguine
Parmesan cheese, to taste

Two hours before serving, combine tomatoes, Brie, basil, garlic, oil, salt and pepper. Set aside, covered at room temperature. When ready to serve, cook linguine according to package directions until tender but still firm. Drain linguine and immediately toss with tomato and Brie mixture. Serve at once topped with Parmesan cheese.
Yield: 4-6 main dish servings, or 8-10 side dish servings.

A flower may look completely different from an insect's point of view. Many petals have ultraviolet or infrared patterns that humans cannot see.

Linguine with Artichokes

¼ *cup olive oil*
¼ *cup butter*
1 *teaspoon flour*
1 *cup chicken stock*
½ *teaspoon garlic salt (op-*
   tional)
2 *teaspoons fresh lemon juice*
1 *teaspoon parsley, minced*
Salt and pepper to taste
1 *(6 ounce) jar marinated*
   artichoke hearts, drained
2 *tablespoons fresh grated*
   Parmesan cheese
1 *pound linguine, cooked*
2 *tablespoons olive oil*
2 *tablespoons fresh grated*
   Parmesan cheese
1 *tablespoon butter, softened*

Heat ¼ cup olive oil and ¼ cup butter in heavy skillet over moderately low heat. Add flour. Cook, stirring constantly for 3 minutes. Stir in chicken stock cooking over moderately high heat for 1 minute. Add garlic, lemon juice, parsley, salt and pepper to taste. Cook for 5 minutes over low heat, stirring occasionally. Add artichoke hearts and 2 tablespoons Parmesan cheese. Cook, covered for 8 minutes. Combine 2 tablespoons olive oil, 1 tablespoon Parmesan cheese, softened butter and ¼ teaspoon salt in large casserole. Add drained linguine, tossing with cheese mix. Divide pasta among 4 plates, top with sauce, garnishing each serving with grated Parmesan cheese.
Yield: 4 servings.

Noodle Kugel

1 *pound medium noodles*
1 *cup cottage cheese*
1 *(8 ounce) package cream*
   cheese
1 *cup butter*
1 *cup sugar*
1 *cup sour cream*
6 *eggs, beaten*
1 *tablespoon vanilla*
2¾ *cups milk*
⅔ *cup raisins*

Preheat oven to 375°. Cook noodles. Drain well but do not rinse. While noodles are hot add cheeses, butter and sugar. When mixture has cooled add sour cream and the eggs. Add vanilla to milk. Add this liquid and raisins to noodle/cheese combination. Bake in a 14x11 inch buttered baking dish for 1 hour. Serve immediately.
Yield: 35-40 servings.

Kugel may be baked in muffin tins for individual servings. (Bake for 45 minutes if prepared in muffin tins.) May be prepared in advance and reheated at serving time.

Pasta Primavera

1 (12 ounce) package pasta
2 carrots
½ cup English peas
1 cup broccoli flowerets
1 small red bell pepper
1 small green bell pepper
2 medium zucchini
3 tablespoons olive oil
½ pound asparagus tips
4 plum tomatoes, chopped
4 tablespoons chopped parsley
Salt and white pepper to taste
2-3 tablespoons lemon juice
4-6 tablespoons olive oil
½ cup Parmesan cheese

Prepare pasta according to package directions or your own pasta recipe. Peel carrots and cut into 2x¼ inch strips. Drop into boiling water and cook for 1 minute. Add peas and broccoli flowerets, continue cooking for 2 minutes. Remove from the water. Refresh under cool water and set aside while sautéing remaining vegetables. Cut the red and green peppers into 2x¼ inch strips. Cut zucchini about the same size. Heat olive oil in a skillet. Sauté peppers in oil for 1 minute. Add zucchini and asparagus tips. Continue cooking over a high flame, stirring until all vegetables are cooked but still crisp, about 2 minutes. Combine sautéd vegetables with blanched vegetables, adding chopped tomatoes. Toss into cooked pasta along with parsley, salt, pepper, lemon juice, olive oil and Parmesan cheese. Serve immediately.
Yield: 8-10 servings.

Spinach Topped Tomato Slices

1 (10 ounce) package frozen
  chopped spinach
3 beef bouillon cubes
1 small onion, chopped fine
½ cup butter, melted
2 cups soft breadcrumbs
4 eggs, beaten
½ cup grated Parmesan
  cheese
1 teaspoon minced garlic
½ teaspoon pepper
⅛-¼ teaspoon cayenne pep-
  per
12 thick slices fresh tomato

Preheat oven to 350°. Cook spinach in a small amount of water to which beef bouillon cubes have been added. Drain and set aside. Sauté chopped onion in butter. Stir in breadcrumbs, beaten eggs, Parmesan cheese, garlic, pepper, and drained spinach. Arrange sliced tomatoes in a large flat baking dish. Top each slice with mounds of the spinach mixture. Bake for 15-20 minutes.
Yield: 12 servings.

Thick and Rich Macaroni and Cheese

1 (12 ounce) package elbow
   macaroni
¾ cup finely chopped onion
1 large green pepper,
   chopped fine
½ cup butter or margarine,
   melted
2 tablespoons flour
1 (13 ounce) can evaporated
   milk
½ cup milk
4 cups (16 ounces) shredded
   sharp Cheddar cheese,
   divided
1 (8 ounce) package proc-
   essed cheese, cubed
⅛ teaspoon pepper
2 tablespoons chopped pi-
   miento (optional)
Paprika

Preheat oven to 350°. Cook macaroni accord-ing to directions and set aside after rinsing with warm water. Sauté onion and green pepper in butter in large saucepan until tender. Add flour, stirring until smooth. Cook 1 minute, stirring constantly. Gradually add milk, cook over medium heat, stirring until thick. Add 3 cups Cheddar cheese, processed cheese and pepper. Stir until smooth. Stir in macaroni. Pour into lightly greased 3 quart baking dish. Bake uncovered for 20 minutes. Sprinkle with remaining 1 cup Cheddar cheese, pimiento and paprika. Bake an additional 5 minutes.
Yield: 8-10 servings.

Not for the diet conscious.

Spanish Rice

1 cup uncooked rice
3 tablespoons bacon drip-
   pings or oil
1 medium onion, chopped
4 garlic cloves, minced
1-2 teaspoons cumin
1-2 teaspoons chili powder
1 (14½ ounce) can tomatoes
1 (14½ ounce) can chicken
   broth or water
Salt and pepper to taste
1 cup frozen peas, optional

Brown rice in bacon drippings or oil. Add next four ingredients, sautéing along with rice. Add remaining ingredients. Cover and cook slowly until all liquid is absorbed, 25-30 minutes.
Yield: 6 servings.

Green Chile Rice

1 cup sour cream
½ pound Monterey Jack
  cheese, grated
1 (4 ounce) can diced green
  chiles
1 (2 ounce) jar pimientos,
  diced
½ teaspoon minced onion
2 cups cooked white rice

Preheat oven to 350°. Mix first 5 ingredients. Let stand for 2 hours. Place cooked rice in a 9x9 inch baking dish. Pour cheese-chili combination over rice. Bake for 30 minutes. Yield: 8-10 servings.

Sue's Rice

½ cup butter
3 green onions, chopped
1 (4 ounce) can mushrooms
  or ¼ pound fresh mush-
  rooms, sliced
1 cup rice
1½ cup water
1 (14½ ounce) can beef bouillon
½ teaspoon oregano

Preheat oven to 400°. Sauté green onions and mushrooms in melted butter. Combine mixture with the remaining ingredients in a 1½ quart baking dish. Bake for 10 minutes. Reduce heat to 350°. Bake for 30 additional minutes, uncovered.
Yield: 6 servings.

Goes very well with beef and pork.

Shrimp Fried Rice

2 bell peppers, chopped
1 bunch green onions,
  chopped
⅓ cup cooking oil
2 cups cooked rice
2 eggs
1 (14 ounce) can bean
  sprouts, drained
1 pound shrimp, peeled and
  boiled
3-4 tablespoons soy sauce

Sauté lightly, bell pepper and green onions in oil. Stir in rice, then eggs. Add bean sprouts, shrimp and soy sauce. Turn fire on warm and stir until thoroughly warm. Do not overcook. Serve immediately.
Yield: 6 servings.

Mother's Scalloped Potatoes

½ cup butter
4 green onions, chopped
1 (4 ounce) can mushroom buttons
1 (10¾ ounce) can mushroom soup
1 cup half and half
Salt and pepper to taste
6 large white potatoes, peeled and sliced thin

Preheat oven to 350°. Melt butter in skillet. Sauté onions and mushrooms. Add soup, half and half, salt and pepper. Layer sliced potatoes in a 13x9 inch baking dish. Pour sauce over potatoes. Bake 40 minutes.
Yield: 6 servings.

Holiday Sweet Potatoes

Vegetables:
2½ cups canned sweet potatoes
1 tablespoon butter
½ teaspoon ground cloves
½ teaspoon nutmeg
½ teaspoon allspice
Orange juice concentrate to taste
Marshmallows

Sauce:
½ cup brown sugar
¼ cup butter
1 egg
½ cup bourbon

Preheat oven to 350°. Mash sweet potatoes with butter, cloves, nutmeg and allspice. Add orange juice concentrate to taste. Place in a round dish. Make well in center. Place marshmallows around well. Brown lightly in oven. Mix brown sugar, butter, egg and bourbon in top of double boiler, adding bourbon last. Cook and stir until slightly thickened. Pour into well of sweet potatoes. Serve immediately.
Yield: 8 servings.

Texas is so large it contains ten major vegetational zones. The extremes in temperature and rainfall create vastly different habitats from east to west and north to south.

Potato Casserole

5 medium size Idaho pota-
  toes
1 (8 ounce) carton sour
  cream
1 (8 ounce) package cream
  cheese, softened
1 ½ cups grated Cheddar
  cheese
3 tablespoons butter
½ teaspoon salt
½ teaspoon black pepper
½ teaspoon paprika (op-
  tional)

Preheat oven to 350°. Peel, pare, cook, drain and mash potatoes. Add sour cream and cream cheese. Mix well. Add 1 cup grated Cheddar cheese (reserving ½ cup for topping), butter, salt and pepper. Mix well. If too thick, add a little milk, but do not let it get too thin. Place potato mixture in greased 1½ quart casserole. Top with remaining ½ cup Cheddar cheese. Cover and bake for 30-35 minutes. Sprinkle with paprika for extra color and flavor, if desired.
Yield: 6 servings.

Potato and Broccoli Cheese Strata

Vegetables:
4 potatoes, skins on, thinly
  sliced
¼ cup margarine
1 teaspoon salt
¼ teaspoon paprika
⅛ teaspoon pepper
1 (10 ounce) package frozen
  broccoli spears, partially
  cooked

Sauce:
2 tablespoons margarine
2 tablespoons flour
1 ¼ cups milk
½ teaspoon salt
¼ teaspoon pepper
¼ cup chopped pimiento
1 cup shredded Cheddar
  cheese

Preheat oven to 425°. Place potatoes in greased 13x9 inch baking dish. Melt butter in small saucepan. Stir in salt, paprika and pepper. Brush this on potato slices. Bake uncovered for 45 minutes. Melt 2 tablespoons margarine in small saucepan. Blend in flour and stir in milk. Cook over low heat stirring constantly until mixture thickens. Stir in salt, pepper, chopped pimiento and Cheddar cheese. Stir until cheese is melted. Arrange broccoli spears over poratoes. Pour cheese sauce over all. Cover and bake 10 minutes longer or until broccoli is tender and sauce bubbles.
Yield: 4-6 servings.

Mushroom Potatoes

4-6 large potatoes
1 (10¾ ounce) can cream of
mushroom soup
¾ soup can milk
½ pound American cheese,
grated
1 cup round, butter flavored
crackers, crushed
5 tablespoons butter
Salt and pepper to taste

Preheat oven to 350°. Boil potatoes until tender. Cool. Peel, dice and place potatoes in bottom of 2 quart casserole. Salt and pepper to taste. Mix together mushroom soup and milk. Pour mixture over potatoes. Sprinkle with American cheese and crackers. Dot with butter. Bake 20 minutes or until bubbly.
Yield: 6 servings.

Easy Baked Potatoes

Best if made a day ahead. May be frozen.

2 pounds frozen hash brown
potatoes
1 (10 ounce) package frozen
onions; or 1¼ cups fresh
chopped onions
2 (10¾ ounce) cans cream of
potato soup
2 cups sour cream
1 cup Cheddar cheese
Salt and pepper to taste

Preheat oven to 350°. Thaw potatoes and onions, if frozen. Combine all ingredients. Place in a greased 13x9 inch baking dish. Cover and bake 1½ hours. Uncover the last half hour and sprinkle with extra cheese if desired.
Yield: 8 servings.

Basil Tomatoes

1 pint package cherry toma-
toes, washed and drained
1 teaspoon basil
¼-½ cup butter

Gently toss together over low heat until tomatoes are heated through.
Yield: 6 servings.

Campsis radicans

Trumpet creeper - *Campsis radicans*
This woody vine has reddish orange flowers in the shape of a trumpet. A perennial that blooms all summer, trumpet creeper grows in moist soils along streams and in thickets throughout Texas. The species name "radicans" refers to its aerial rooting habits. Though not poisonous itself, trumpet creeper is sometimes confused with poison ivy.

Roast Prime Rib

1 prime rib roast
Flour
Salt and pepper

Preheat oven to 500°. Dust roast with flour, salt and pepper. Place roast in oven for 15 minutes. Turn oven to 400°. Cook 18 minutes per pound without opening oven.
Yield: 1 medium rare Prime Rib Roast.

This is a tried and true method for medium rare, juicy meat.

Beef Rouladen mit Tunke

Top round of beef, cut into 6
   pieces measuring 4x8x½
   inch each
Salt and pepper to taste
6 teaspoons spicy mustard
½ cup finely chopped dill
   pickles
½ cup finely chopped shallots
¼ cup finely chopped parsley
16 slices bacon
Flour
Oil
1-2 medium white onions
1 (16 ounce) package carrots
1 (14-16 ounce) can of tomatoes
1 cup Burgundy
½ cup water
¼ of a (1.25 ounce) package
   onion soup mix
2 bay leaves
½ teaspoon thyme
2 cloves, minced
Flour

Pound meat pieces to ¼ inch thick. Salt and pepper slices of meat. Spread with mustard. Fill with chopped dill pickle, shallots, and parsley. Roll and wrap each with a slice of bacon. Secure with toothpicks. Dust with flour. Brown roulades in a bit of oil. Slice carrots and onions while meat is browning. Sprinkle carrots and onions over roulades. Mix tomatoes, Burgundy, water, onion soup mix, bay leaves, thyme and cloves together in a bowl. Pour over the beef in a large roasting pan. Cover. Bake at 350° for 45 minutes. Lower temperature to 300°. Bake 1 hour or until tender. Remove roulades and thicken sauce with flour. Strain and serve.
Yield: 6 servings.

This is company beef.

Beef Wellington

A true culinary masterpiece made easy with frozen pastry. Duxelles may be made in advance, frozen, and thawed to use. Sauce Chasseur may be made 2-3 days ahead. The pastry wrapped beef may be prepared 8 hours before cooking.

1 (17½ ounce) package frozen puff pastry
1 (3-4 pound) whole beef fillet, trussed
Salt and pepper
1 tablespoon vegetable oil
Duxelles (see recipe)
Egg glaze made with 1 beaten egg and 1 teaspoon salt
1½ cups Sauce Chasseur (see recipe)

Duxelles:
2 tablespoons butter
2 shallots, finely chopped
1 pound mushrooms, finely chopped
1 tablespoon chopped parsley
Salt and pepper

Sprinkle beef with salt and pepper. Heat oil in a large skillet. Brown beef on all sides over high heat, 8-10 minutes. Cool completely. Prepare duxelles. Refrigerate.

Melt butter. Add shallots. Stir until soft. Add mushrooms. Stir often until dry. Remove from heat. Add parsley. Add salt and pepper. Yield: 2 cups.

Lightly grease baking sheet. Roll out puff pastry on a cloth towel or foil to a rectangle 6 inches longer and wider than trussed beef. Spread dough with cooled duxelles, leaving a 2 inch border of dough. Remove trussing from fillets and place upside down on duxelles. Cut a 2 inch square from each corner of dough and brush edges of the rectangle with egg glaze. Lift one long edge of dough to top of fillet. Fold over the opposite edge to enclose fillet. Press gently to seal. Fold ends to make neat package. With the help of the cloth towel or foil, roll enclosed fillet over onto prepared baking sheet so seams are underneath. Brush with egg glaze. Cut leaves or other decorative shapes from leftover pastry. Attach to top of pastry with egg glaze. Brush decorations with egg glaze. Using a sharp knife, cut 3 equally spaced holes in top of dough. Insert a roll of foil in each hole to let steam escape. Cover. Refrigerate 2-3 hours until dough is firm. (May be prepared to this point 8 hours ahead, covered and refrigerated.)

Sauce Chasseur:
4 tablespoons butter
2 shallots, finely chopped
¼ pound mushrooms, thinly sliced
1 cup white wine
1 cup brown sugar, packed
1 cup brown gravy
4 tablespoons Madeira wine
2 tablespoons tomato paste
1 tablespoon chopped parsley
¾ teaspoon finely chopped tarragon
Salt and pepper
Watercress, optional

Melt 2 tablespoons butter in saucepan. Cut remaining 2 tablespoons butter in pieces. Set aside. Stir shallots into melted butter. Sauté until soft. Stir in mushrooms. Cook 2-3 minutes until tender. Pour in wine. Stir in brown gravy and tomato paste. Bring to a boil, stirring often. Immediately remove from heat. Whisk in butter pieces, parsley and tarragon. Season lightly with salt and pepper. (Sauce should not be boiled after last addition of butter.) May be made 2-3 days ahead. Add butter to reheat sauce just before serving. Yield: 1½ cups sauce.

Preheat oven to 425°. Bake beef 30 minutes, until dough is browned and beef is cooked to rare (400° on a meat thermometer). Check pastry after 15 minutes. (If pastry is becoming too brown, reduce oven to 400°.) Transfer to a large platter and keep warm 10-15 minutes. (Juices will become more evenly distributed and meat will be easier to cut.) Garnish with watercress. Serve with Sauce Chasseur. Yield: 8 servings.

Juicy Baked Tenderloin

1 whole beef tenderloin
Olive oil
Flavor enhancer

Tie tenderloin securely with string. (This is important to make perfect, tender slices.) Rub tenderloin with olive oil. Sprinkle both sides with flavor enhancer. Place on foil-lined cookie sheet. Preheat oven to 425°. Roast 15 minutes. Reduce oven to 250°. Bake 45 minutes. Adjust time for degree of doneness. The precise heating makes a lovely brown crust. Serve at room temperature. Yield: 8-10 servings.

Great recipe for a party. Flavor is fantastic.

Texas Brisket

1 brisket, lean trimmed
Meat tenderizer
Liquid smoke
Salt and pepper
Brown sugar
Celery salt
Paprika
Nutmeg
Garlic salt
Onion salt
Barbecue sauce

Cover all sides of brisket with meat tenderizer, liquid smoke, salt and pepper. Wrap in foil. Refrigerate overnight. Next day sprinkle generously with remaining ingredients, excluding barbecue sauce. Cook in aluminum foil at 300° for 2 hours. Lower heat. Bake at 200° for 5-6 hours. Let meat cool completely. Trim off fat as you slice the brisket. Pour liquid off meat and place in refrigerator until fat portion of liquid comes to top. Remove hardened fat. Spread each slice of meat with your favorite barbecue sauce. Pour fat free meat liquid over meat. Cover meat with foil. Return to oven for 1 hour.
Yield: 1 delicious brisket.

Western Grilled Steak

1 cup bacon drippings or 1
  cup oil
½ cup finely chopped onions
⅓ cup lemon juice
2 tablespoons worcestershire
  sauce
1 tablespoon horseradish
1 teaspoon paprika
½ teaspoon salt
1 large clove garlic, minced
2 bay leaves
Steaks at least 1 inch thick for
  barbecue

Heat bacon drippings or oil in saucepan. Add chopped onions, lemon juice, worcestershire sauce, horseradish, paprika, salt, garlic, and bay leaves. Stir thoroughly to make sauce. Place steaks in single layer in a shallow pan. Pour sauce over meat. Allow to stand at room temperature for 30 minutes, turning steaks once. Grill, basting with remaining marinade.
Yield: 6-8 steaks.

Carpet Bag Steak

6-8 small sirloin, fillet, or
   rump steaks
4 tablespoons butter
12-18 oysters
¼ cup chopped mushrooms
¾ cup breadcrumbs
1 tablespoon chopped parsley
Grated rind of ½ lemon
Salt and pepper
1 egg

Trim steak. Cut a pocket in it. Heat butter in saucepan. Sauté mushrooms and oysters for 5 minutes. Transfer to mixing bowl. Mix in breadcrumbs, parsley, lemon rind, and seasonings. Beat egg. Stir into mixture. Stuff dressing into pockets in meat. Skewer edges together. Roast at 375°-400° for 40-60 minutes, depending on cut of meat.
Yield: 6-8 servings.

Steak Diane

4 tenderloin steaks
Salt and pepper to taste
5 tablespoons butter
1 tablespoon oil
3 tablespoons brandy
½ cup beef stock
2 tablespoons heavy cream

Flatten steaks. Season to taste with salt and pepper. Sauté steaks on each side until tender in 3 tablespoons butter and 1 tablespoon oil. Remove from skillet. Add beef stock and brandy to skillet. Cook over high heat until stock is reduced to half. Add remaining butter and blend into sauce. Add cream, blending until sauce is smooth. Pour sauce over steaks and serve.
Yield: 4 servings.

Great for company.

Grilled Flank Steak Teriyaki

½ cup soy sauce
¼ cup vegetable oil
¼ cup honey
2 tablespoons wine vinegar
1-2 cloves garlic, sliced
1½ teaspoons minced fresh
   ginger root or ¾ teaspoon
   ground ginger
1 (1½ pound) flank steak

Combine first 6 ingredients. Pour over flank steak. Marinate at least 3-4 hours in refrigerator, turning occasionally. Remove steak from marinade. Grill over hot coals to desired doneness, about 15 minutes. Slice across grain in thin slices.
Yield: 4 servings.

Marinade may be refrigerated to use later. Meat may be cooked in iron skillet over medium heat.

Green Chili Casserole

1 pound ground beef
½ cup chopped onions
Salt and pepper to taste
2 (4 ounce) cans chopped
*   green chili peppers*
1 cup grated sharp Cheddar
*   cheese*
4 eggs
1½ cups milk
¼ cup flour
Hot sauce to taste

Brown beef and onions. Season with salt and pepper. Place 1 can green chili peppers in bottom of pan. Top with grated cheese. Add browned meat mixture. Mix eggs, milk, flour and red pepper sauce. Pour over meat. Cook at 350° for 40-50 minutes. Top with second can green chili peppers.
Yield: 6-8 servings.

Pedro's Mexican Pie

1-2 pounds ground chuck
½ cup chopped onion or 1
*   teaspoon dried onion*
1 teaspoon oregano
2 beef bouillon cubes, dis-
*   solved in 1 cup hot water*
1 (14.5 ounce) can tomatoes
1 (8 ounce) bag corn chips
1 (15 ounce) can pinto beans
1 (4 ounce) can chopped
*   green chilies*
1 cup shredded Cheddar
*   cheese*

Brown meat. Add onions and oregano. Mash tomatoes or run through blender for a few seconds. Combine with bouillon. Place a layer of corn chips in a greased 13x9 inch baking dish. Add meat, beans, chilies and cheese. Pour tomato mixture over layers. Top with layer of corn chips. Bake at 350° for 25-30 minutes.
Yield: 6-8 servings.

Indian paintbrush seed is so tiny you can plant a whole acre with several handfuls. There are 10,000,000 seeds in one pound!

Green Enchiladas

1 (10¾ ounce) can cream of
  chicken soup
½ pound processed cheese
1 (5 ounce) can evaporated
  milk
1 (4 ounce) jar chopped
  pimientos
1 (4 ounce) can chopped
  green chilies
1 pound ground beef
1 onion, chopped
½ pound Cheddar cheese,
  grated
Margarine
12 tortillas

Melt together soup, processed cheese and milk. Add chopped chilies and pimientos. Set aside. Brown meat. Remove from heat. Add onion and Cheddar cheese. Fry each tortilla quickly in small amount of melted margarine. Drain on paper towels. Spoon meat mixture onto each tortilla and roll tightly. Place seam side down in a 13x9 inch baking dish. Pour cheese sauce over. Cover with foil. Bake at 350° for 10 minutes. Remove foil. Bake uncovered 20 minutes.
Yield: 4-6 servings.

These are delicious. May be made ahead and baked later. For different flavor, fill tortillas with cheese and onion.

Fajitas

2 pounds skirt steak

Marinade:
1 (7 ounce) can Salsa Verde
1 (16 ounce) bottle Italian
  dressing
1 small onion, chopped
1 garlic clove, chopped
1 (4 ounce) can jalapeños

Flour tortillas
Guacamole
Onions
Tomatoes
Grated cheese

Cut meat into 2 inch wide strips. Combine marinade ingredients. Pour over meat. Marinate overnight. Place on skewers. Grill, basting often. Cook 30 minutes over moderate heat. Remove meat from skewers. Cut into smaller bite-sized pieces. Serve fajitas with warm flour tortillas, guacamole, onions, tomatoes and cheese.
Yield: 6-8 servings.

Picadillo

3 tablespoons olive oil
2 pounds lean ground beef
1 large onion, chopped fine
1 clove garlic, chopped fine
3 medium tomatoes, peeled
   and chopped
2 tart cooking apples, peeled,
   cored and chopped
½ cup raisins, soaked 10
   minutes in ¼ cup water
½ cup pimiento-stuffed olives,
   halved crosswise
2-3 jalapeño peppers, seeded
   and chopped
½ teaspoon oregano
½ teaspoon thyme
Salt and pepper
½ cup slivered almonds
1 tablespoon margarine
Rice

Heat oil in a large heavy skillet. Add beef and brown, stirring to break up meat. Add onion and garlic. Sauté until tender. Drain off grease. Stir in tomatoes, apples, raisins with their liquid, olives, peppers, oregano, thyme, salt and pepper. Simmer uncovered, stirring occasionally (20 minutes). Sauté almonds in margarine until golden brown. Mound beef mixture on large platter. Sprinkle with almonds. Surround with rice.
Yield: 6-8 servings.

A favorite throughout Latin America. Each country has its own version. Serve with beans, guacamole, and tortillas. The spiced beef mixture may also be used for empañadas, tacos, and green peppers.

Grilled Steak Kabobs

¾ cup dry red wine
3 tablespoons olive oil
3 tablespoons lemon juice
2 cloves garlic, minced
½ teaspoon salt
¼ teaspoon rosemary
¼ teaspoon thyme
3 pounds top sirloin steak, cut
   into 1½ inch cubes

Mix together wine, olive oil, lemon juice, garlic, salt, rosemary and thyme. Marinate meat in this mixture for several hours or overnight, turning meat occasionally. Skewer meat and cook over moderately hot coals, turning once (8 minutes for rare).
Yield: 4-6 servings.

Vegetables may be included on skewers to make full meal. Serve over rice or noodles.

Beef and Vegetable Stew

2 pounds beef round or chuck
  steak, cut into serving
  pieces
2 teaspoons salt
¼ teaspoon pepper
½ cup flour
6 tablespoons bacon drip-
  pings or oil
1 large onion, sliced
2-3 cups water
1 beef bouillon cube
1 teaspoon savory
1 teaspoon marjoram
1 teaspoon basil
1 (1 pound, 13 ounce) can
  whole tomatoes
6 carrots, peeled and sliced
6 small potatoes, pared and
  quartered

Trim any fat from beef. Mix salt and pepper with flour. Dredge meat in mixture. Heat oil in skillet. Brown beef slowly. Add onion, cooking until golden. Put meat and onion in large dutch oven. Add water and bouillon cube to drippings in skillet. Add herbs and cook a few minutes. Pour over meat. Add vegetables. Cover. Bake at 325° for 2½-3 hours. (May add additional water if necessary.)
Yield: 6-8 servings.

Savory Onion Pot Roast

3-4 pound roast (chuck,
  round, or rump)
1 (1.25 ounce) envelope dry
  onion soup mix
1 (10¾ ounce) can cream of
  mushroom soup
1 ¼ cups water
Carrots, optional
Potatoes, optional

Preheat oven to 325°. Trim most of fat from roast. Brown roast in small amount of fat in skillet. Place in roasting pan or large baking dish. Sprinkle dry onion soup mix over top. Mix mushroom soup and water together. Pour over roast. Cover pan. Bake 3½-4½ hours, depending on size of roast. If desired, add peeled carrots and potatoes during last hour of cooking. Makes a delicious gravy when cooked slowly.
Yield: 6-8 servings.

French Oven Stew

3 pounds stew meat
3 large carrots, cut in chunks
1 (16 ounce) jar small pearl
   onions, drained
1-2 (16 ounce) cans small
   potatoes, drained
1 (14-16 ounce) can stewed
   tomatoes with juice
½ can beef consommé
1 green pepper, cut in chunks
1 (4 ounce) can button mushrooms
½ cup white wine or bourbon
4 tablespoons minute tapioca
1 tablespoon brown sugar
½ cup breadcrumbs
Salt and pepper to taste

Mix all ingredients. Place in heavy roaster with lid. Stir after 4 hours. Bake at 250° for 6-7 hours.
Yield: 8-10 servings.

Great to prepare if you're going to be gone all day. Serve with salad and French bread.

Casserole For All Seasons

1 pound ground beef
1 clove garlic, crushed
1 teaspoon salt
1 teaspoon sugar
1 (16 ounce) can tomato
   sauce
1 (8 ounce) package noodles
3 green onions, chopped
3 ounces cream cheese, softened
1 cup sour cream

Brown beef and drain. Add garlic, salt, sugar, and tomato sauce. Simmer. Cook noodles according to package instructions. Mix together onions, cream cheese, and sour cream. Layer in a 2 quart baking dish, starting with small amount of meat sauce, noodles, sour cream filling, meat sauce, noodles, sour cream filling and remaining sauce on top. Bake at 350° for 20-30 minutes.
Yield: 4-6 servings.

May be frozen.

All Day Oven Bake

1 (1.25 ounce) package dry
  onion soup mix
2 (10¾ ounce) cans mush-
  room soup
1 can water
2 pounds stew meat
½ pint sour cream
Rice or noodles

Mix soups and water together. Pour around stewing meat. Cover tightly. Place in oven at 250°-300° for 6-8 hours. Remove from oven. Stir in sour cream. Return mixture to oven until heated. Serve over rice or noodles.
Yield: 6-8 servings.

Super for working moms.

Texas Beef and Zucchini Bake

1 pound lean ground beef
3 medium zucchini, thinly
  sliced
¼ cup sliced green onions
  with tops
2 teaspoons salt
¼ teaspoon garlic powder
2 teaspoons chili powder
1 (7 ounce) can chopped
  green chilies
3 cups cooked rice
1 cup sour cream
2 cups grated Monterey Jack
  cheese
1 large fresh tomato, sliced
Salt and pepper to taste

Brown beef. Drain off excess fat. Add zucchini, onion and seasonings. Sauté vegetables until tender-crisp, stirring frequently. Add green chilies, rice, sour cream and 1 cup cheese. Turn into buttered, shallow 2 quart baking dish. Arrange tomato slices on top. Season with salt and pepper. Top with remaining cheese. Bake at 350° for 20-25 minutes.
Yield: 6-8 servings.

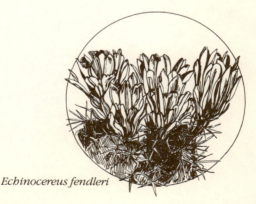

Echinocereus fendleri

Beef en Pappillote

½ teaspoon oregano
2 teaspoons parsley flakes
2 teaspoons onion flakes
2 teaspoons black pepper
2 teaspoons salt
½ teaspoon dry mustard
½ teaspoon garlic salt
Dash red pepper
2 tablespoons butter, melted
1 sirloin steak, 2 inches thick
Toasted coarse breadcrumbs

Combine spices and enough melted butter to make a paste. Rub mixture into sides of steak. Coat each side with toasted breadcrumbs. Place in paper bag and close end. Bake on rack in roasting pan at 350° for 2 hours. Yield: 4-6 servings.

Great spicy flavor.

Piquant Meatballs

Meatballs:
2 pounds ground beef
2 eggs
¼ cup water
1 cup Italian seasoned dry
   breadcrumbs
1 small onion, grated
1½ teaspoons salt
⅛ teaspoon pepper
2 teaspoons parsley
Oil
Rice

Sauce:
1 (16 ounce) can jellied
   cranberry sauce
1 (12 ounce) bottle chili sauce
2 tablespoons brown sugar
1 tablespoon lemon juice

Mix all ingredients, except oil and rice. Form into 1 inch balls. Brown in oil in large frying pan.

Combine all ingredients in saucepan. Simmer until smooth. Add meatballs. Simmer 1 hour. Serve over rice.
Yield: 6-8 servings.

May freeze after cooking.

Italian Spaghetti Sauce

1 ½ _pounds ground beef_
1 _onion, diced_
2 _tablespoons oil_
2 _(6 ounce) cans tomato paste_
2 _(8 ounce) cans tomato_
  sauce
1 _garlic clove, minced_
1 _(16 ounce) can Italian style_
  tomatoes
¼ _teaspoon pepper_
1 _teaspoon salt_
1 _bay leaf_
1 _tablespoon sugar_
1 _teaspoon oregano_
2 _teaspoons basil leaves_
½ _cup hot water_

Brown meat and onion in oil in a large skillet or dutch oven. Add all other ingredients. Stir. Cover and simmer for at least 2 hours. Yield: 6-8 servings.

Sauce tastes better next day. May be frozen.

Cabbage Rolls Lebanese Style

1 _head of cabbage_
1 ½ _pounds ground round beef_
¾ _cup uncooked rice_
Salt and pepper to taste
Garlic cloves to taste
6 _tablespoons butter, sliced_
2 _lemons_
1 _tablespoon salt_
2 _teaspoons pepper_
2 _teaspoons whole cumin seed_

Steam cabbage for 5-7 minutes, long enough to separate leaves and not let cabbage get soft. Separate the leaves and cut out the middle vein. Mix together beef, rice, salt and pepper. Put 1-2 tablespoons meat mixture on each leaf. Roll and place seam side down in cabbage lined pot adding a whole garlic clove or two between layers of rolls. Add enough water to come up halfway over rolls. Top with slices of butter, the juice of 2 lemons, salt, pepper and a sprinkle of whole cumin seed. Cover pot. Simmer slowly for 30-45 minutes. (Do not boil.)
Yield: 6-8 servings.

Serve with plain yogurt and lemon slices to squeeze on top.

Easy Stroganoff

3 tablespoons butter
1 large onion, sliced
½ pound mushrooms, sliced
½ cup water, wine or sherry
1 bouillon cube
2 tablespoons flour
2 pounds round steak, cut in
   strips
Salt and pepper to taste
1 cup sour cream
Noodles

Sauté mushrooms and onions in butter until tender. Add water or wine, bouillon cube and flour. Stir until smooth. Add meat, salt and pepper. Cover. Cook 2 hours on simmer until tender. Add more water if necessary. Add sour cream. Serve over noodles.
Yield: 6 servings.

Oriental Stroganoff

1 cup chopped onions
½ cup butter or margarine
2 pounds round steak, cut in
   strips
4 tablespoons flour
1 teaspoon pepper
1 teaspoon salt
1 teaspoon paprika
2 (10¾ ounce) cans cream of
   chicken soup
2 (4 ounce) cans sliced
   mushrooms
2 (8 ounce) cans sliced water
   chestnuts
1 cup sour cream
Rice
1 (3 ounce) can Chinese
   noodles

Sauté onions in butter. Mix meat with flour, pepper, salt, and paprika. Add to butter and onions. Cook until meat is browned. Add chicken soup, mushrooms, and chestnuts. Simmer for 30-40 minutes. Turn off heat. Stir in sour cream. Serve over rice. Top with Chinese noodles.
Yield: 8 servings.

Betty's Hamburger Stroganoff

¼ cup margarine
½ cup minced onion
1 pound ground meat
1 clove garlic, minced (op-
    tional)
2 tablespoons flour
2 teaspoons salt
¼ teaspoon pepper
¼ teaspoon paprika
1 pound mushrooms, sliced
1 (10¾ ounce) can condensed
    cream of chicken soup
1 cup sour cream
Snipped parsley, chive or
    fresh dill
Noodles or rice

Preheat electric fry pan to hamburger temperature. Melt margarine. Sauté onions until
clear and golden. Stir in meat, garlic, flour,
salt, pepper, paprika and mushrooms. Sauté 5
minutes or until hamburger is brown. Simmer. Add soup. Simmer 10 minutes. Stir in
sour cream. Sprinkle with parsley. Serve over
hot buttered noodles or rice.
Yield: 4-6 servings.

_May be frozen. Defrost. Warm until bubbly at
350° for 20-35 minutes._

Elegantly Rolled Chicken Breasts

3 large chicken breasts,
    boned, skinned, and halved
Salt
6 thin slices boiled ham
6 ounces natural Swiss
    cheese, cut into 6 sticks
¼ cup flour
2 tablespoons butter or mar-
    garine
½ cup water
1 teaspoon chicken flavor
    gravy base
1 (3 ounce) can sliced mush-
    rooms, drained
⅓ cup Sauterne
2 tablespoons flour
½ cup cold water
Toasted sliced almonds

Pound chicken lightly to make cutlets ¼ inch
thick. Sprinkle with salt. Place ham slice and
cheese stick on each cutlet. Tuck in sides of
each. Roll up as for jelly roll. Press to seal
well. Skewer or tie securely. Coat rolls with
flour. Brown in butter or margarine. Remove
chicken to 11x7 inch baking dish. In same
skillet, combine ½ cup water, gravy base,
mushrooms and wine. Heat, stirring in crusty
bits of skillet. Pour mixture over chicken.
Cover. Bake at 350° for 1¼ hours. Transfer
chicken to warmed platter. Blend 2 tablespoons flour with ½ cup cold water. Add to
gravy in baking dish. Cook, stirring until
thickened. Pour a little gravy over chicken.
Garnish with almonds. Pass remaining gravy.
Yield: 6 servings.

Chicken and Ham Crepes

Place piece of wax paper between each crepe as cooked. Leaving wax paper in place, may be frozen in freezer bags until ready to use.

Crepes:
6 eggs
2 cups milk
2 tablespoons melted unsalted
   butter
1½ cups sifted flour
½ teaspoon salt
2 tablespoons sugar

Filling:
6 tablespoons butter
3 tablespoons onion
½ cup finely chopped celery
1 carrot, finely chopped
5 tablespoons flour
1 (10 ounce) can chicken
   broth
1 (4½ ounce) jar mushroom
   pieces, reserving liquid
¼ cup Madeira or sherry
   wine
1 cup heavy cream
1 teaspoon salt
¼ teaspoon pepper
2 cups cooked cubed chicken
1 cup cooked cubed ham
2 tablespoons chopped parsley
½ teaspoon thyme
12 crepes

Beat eggs in large bowl until foamy. Stir in milk and melted butter. Sift in flour, sugar and salt. Beat until smooth. Chill 2 hours. Heat a 6-8 inch iron skillet until drops of water bounce. Butter skillet lightly with pastry brush dipped in butter. Pour small amount batter (¼ cup) into pan. Coat bottom in circular motion. Cook over medium heat until set and underside golden. Turn crepe over and brown other side. Remove to plate.
Yield: 24 crepes.

Sauté vegetables in butter 5 minutes. Stir in flour. Cook 1 minute. Gradually stir in broth and liquid from mushrooms. Cook, stirring constantly until mixture bubbles and thickens. Stir in wine. Lower heat. Simmer 10 minutes, stirring often. Stir in ½ cup cream, salt and pepper. Combine chicken, ham, mushrooms, parsley and thyme in bowl. Stir in 1½ cups of sauce.

Place ¼ cup filling on each crepe. Roll up. Place filled crepes seam side down in lightly buttered 13x9 inch baking dish. Crepes may be refrigerated or frozen at this point. Whip remaining cream until stiff. Fold into remaining sauce. Spoon over crepes. Bake at 375° for 20 minutes.
Yield: 12 crepes or 6 servings.

May be assembled and frozen to be baked at a later date.

Chicken Breasts in Phyllo

1½ cups mayonnaise
1 cup chopped green onions
⅓ cup lemon juice
2 cloves garlic, minced
2 teaspoons dry tarragon
12 chicken breast halves,
_ boned and skinned_
Salt and pepper
36 sheets Phyllo dough
1⅓ cup butter, melted
⅓ cup freshly grated Parme-
_ san cheese_

Combine first 5 ingredients to make a sauce. Flatten chicken breasts to ¼ inch thickness throughout. Lightly sprinkle chicken pieces with salt and pepper. Place sheet of Phyllo on working surface. Brush with melted butter (2 teaspoons). Place second sheet on top of first. Brush with melted butter. Repeat with third sheet. Spread 1½ tablespoons of sauce on each side of chicken breast (3 tablespoons in all). Place breast in one corner of buttered Phyllo sheets. Fold corner over breast. Fold sides over, rolling breast up in sheets to form a package. Place in an ungreased baking dish. Repeat with remaining breasts and Phyllo sheets. Brush packets with remaining butter. Sprinkle with Parmesan cheese. At this point, the dish may be tightly sealed and frozen. Thaw completely before baking. Bake at 375° for 20-25 minutes, until golden. (A large amount may take 1 hour to bake.) Serve hot. Spoon melted butter from baking dish over tops.
Yield: 9-12 servings.

May be frozen until day served. Thaw before baking.

"Simply Divine" Chicken

4 boneless chicken breasts
4 slices ham
4 slices mozzarella
1 tablespoon mayonnaise
2 teaspoons water
1 cup seasoned breadcrumbs
Chopped green chilies, op-
_ tional_

Pound chicken breasts. Place slice of ham and slice of cheese on each breast. Roll. Secure with toothpick. Mix mayonnaise and water. Coat breast with mayonnaise mixture, then roll in breadcrumbs. Place in 13x9 inch baking dish. Bake at 400° for 20-25 minutes. Top with a sprinkling of green chilies, if desired.
Yield: 4 servings.

Chicken Breast in Croute

1 (10 ounce) package frozen
   patty shells
1 tablespoon butter
3 chicken breasts, boned,
   skinned and halved
6 thin slices boiled ham
1 (14.5 ounce) can asparagus
   spears, drained
1 egg lightly beaten with 1
   tablespoon water

Sauce:
2 tablespoons butter, melted
2 tablespoons flour
1 ¼ cup chicken broth
¼ cup dry vermouth
⅓ cup shredded Swiss cheese

Defrost patty shells in refrigerator overnight or at room temperature until workable but still cold to touch. In medium skillet, melt butter. Sauté chicken breasts over medium heat, one minute on each side. Remove from skillet. Cool. Preheat oven to 400°. On lightly floured surface, roll 1 patty shell into an 8½ inch circle. Place cooled chicken breast on lower half of pastry. Fold 1 slice of ham in quarters to fit on top of chicken. Top with 3 asparagus spears trimmed to fit. Fold top half of pastry over asparagus. Press down edges and trim pastry. Crimp edges with fork to seal. Place on ungreased baking sheet. Repeat with remaining chicken and patty shells. Roll remaining pastry scraps for garnish if desired. Place on pastry. Brush with egg glaze. Bake in preheated oven for 35 minutes. If baking from frozen state, add 10 minutes to baking time. Serve at once with sauce.

In a small saucepan, over medium heat, stir flour into melted butter. With whisk, blend in broth and vermouth. Heat to boiling. Lower heat and simmer 3 minutes. Remove from heat, add cheese. Stir until melted. Makes 1¾ cups.
Yield: 6 servings.

May be prepared in advance and frozen before baking. Best to double recipe and freeze half. Time consuming but well worth it!

Phlox drummondii

Chicken and Artichoke Delight

1 (3 pound) chicken
Salt and pepper
¼ cup butter
¼ cup flour
2 cups milk
3 ounces Gruyère or Swiss
  cheese, cut into chunks
⅛ pound Cheddar cheese, cut
  into chunks
1 tablespoon flavor enhancer
2 cloves garlic, pressed
½ teaspoon red pepper
1 (4 ounce) can mushrooms,
  drained
1 (14 ounce) jar artichoke
  hearts, drained
Rice or noodles

Boil chicken in water seasoned with salt and pepper. Remove skin and bone. Cut into large pieces. Set aside. Melt butter. Stir in flour until blended. Slowly add milk, stirring until sauce is smooth. Add cheese. Add seasonings. Stir until cheese melts and sauce bubbles. Add chicken to sauce. Add mushrooms and artichoke hearts. Serve over rice or noodles. Yield: 6-8 servings.

May prepare a day ahead.

"Tis the Season" Chicken

Assemble the night before and refrigerate.

1 (6 ¼ ounce) package fast-
  cooking long grain and wild
  rice mix with herbs and
  seasonings
3 pounds chicken breast, cut
  into serving pieces
1 (16 ounce) can whole berry
  cranberry sauce
3 tablespoons butter or margarine
2 tablespoons soy sauce
1 teaspoon lemon juice
½ cup thinly sliced almonds

Preheat oven to 325°. Sprinkle rice in buttered 13x9 inch baking dish. Spread package of seasonings over rice. Arrange chicken, skin side up, on top. In sauce pan, combine cranberry sauce, butter, soy sauce and lemon juice. Heat, stirring until melted. Pour over chicken. Cover tightly with foil. Bake 1-1 ¼ hours. Uncover. Sprinkle with almonds. Bake 10 minutes more. Will stay warm for 30 minutes.
Yield: 4-6 servings.

Tastes fancy, but is easy.

Chicken á la Mayra

8 chicken breasts, skinned
  and boned
8 slices bacon
1 (12 ounce) package wafer-
  thin sliced beef or 1 (4
  ounce) jar dried beef, thinly
  sliced
1 (8 ounce) carton sour
  cream
1 (10¾ ounce) can cream of
  mushroom soup
1-2 teaspoons worcestershire
  sauce

Wrap bacon slices around chicken. Brown chicken in a hot skillet. Set aside. Line buttered 13x9 inch baking dish with sliced beef. Add chicken breasts. Mix sour cream, mushroom soup, worcestershire sauce. Pour over chicken breasts. Bake at 350° for 1½ hours, until chicken breasts are tender.
Yield: 6-8 servings.

Broccoli, Rice and Chicken Casserole

½ cup chopped celery
½ cup chopped onion
1 tablespoon diet margarine
3 cups cooked rice
1 (10 ounce) package
  chopped broccoli, cooked
8-10 ounces chicken, cooked
  and cubed
2 (4 ounce) cans sliced mushrooms, drained

Cheese Sauce:
2 teaspoons cornstarch
2 cups skim or lowfat milk
3 teaspoons chicken bouillon
  crystals
1 (8 ounce) jar of processed
  cheese

Sauté celery and onion in diet margarine. Add cooked rice, broccoli, chicken, and sliced mushrooms. Mix well. Place in 13x9 inch baking dish. Heat cornstarch, milk, chicken bouillon and processed cheese in saucepan. Stir until cheese dissolves. Pour cheese sauce over rice mixture. Bake at 350° for 30 minutes.
Yield: 6 servings.

Great for freezing.

Chicken Breasts Supreme

¼ *cup flour*
2½ *teaspoons salt*
1 *teaspoon paprika*
6 *whole chicken breasts,*
boned, skinned and halved
¼ *cup butter or margarine*
¼ *cup water*
2 *teaspoons cornstarch*
1½ *cups half and half cream*
¼ *cup cooking sherry*
1 *teaspoon lemon peel*
1 *tablespoon lemon juice*
1 *cup grated Swiss cheese*
½ *cup chopped parsley,*
optional

Combine flour, salt and paprika on waxed paper. Coat chicken with flour mixture. Melt butter in large skillet. Lightly brown chicken breasts on both sides. Add ¼ cup water. Simmer covered, 30 minutes, until chicken breasts are almost tender. Arrange chicken in 13x9 inch baking dish. Mix cornstarch with ¼ cup half and half. Stir into drippings in skillet. Cook, stirring over low heat. Gradually stir in remaining half and half, sherry, lemon peel, and lemon juice. Continue cooking, stirring until sauce is thickened. Pour over chicken. Bake chicken covered at 350° for 35-40 minutes, until sauce is bubbly hot. Remove cover. Top with Swiss cheese. Heat to melt cheese. Garnish with parsley.
Yield: 6-8 servings.

Chicken Cutlets with Lemon Sauce

4 *chicken breasts, boned,*
skinned and halved
1 *egg*
Pinch of red pepper
½ *cup wheat germ*
Vegetable shortening spray
1 *tablespoon margarine*
3 *tablespoons lemon juice*
Lemon slices
Fresh parsley, chopped

Place chicken between 2 sheets waxed paper. Flatten to ½ inch thickness, using a meat mallet or rolling pin. Combine egg and red pepper. Dip breast in mixture. Coat with wheat germ. Spray large skillet with cooking spray. Melt margarine. Add chicken. Cook over medium heat 3-4 minutes on each side. Remove to platter and keep warm. Pour lemon juice in pan. Cook on high heat 1 minute stirring constantly. Pour over chicken. Garnish with lemon slices and parsley.
Yield: 4 servings.

Light and healthy!

Lemon Baked Chicken

4-5 pieces of chicken
3 tablespoons oil
3 tablespoons fresh lemon
 juice
1 clove garlic, crushed
½ teaspoon salt
1 teaspoon lemon pepper
1 tablespoon worcestershire
 sauce
Lemon slices
Chopped parsley
Sliced toasted almonds

Arrange chicken in 13x9 inch baking dish. Combine other ingredients (excluding lemon, parsley and almonds). Pour over chicken. Cover. Bake at 350° for 1 hour. Garnish with lemon slices, parsley, and almonds before serving.
Yield: 4 servings.

Creamy Baked Chicken Breasts

4 whole chicken breasts,
 boned, skinned and halved
8 slices (6 ounces) Swiss
 cheese
1 (10¾ ounce) can cream of
 chicken soup
¼ cup dry white wine
1 cup herb seasoned stuffing
 mix
¼ cup melted margarine

Arrange chicken in lightly greased 13x9 inch baking dish. Top with cheese slices. Combine soup and wine. Spoon over chicken. Top with stuffing mix. Drizzle butter over crumbs. Bake at 350° for 45-55 minutes.
Yield: 8 servings.

Quick and easy.

Although goldenrod has been credited with causing hayfever, the real culprit is ragweed — an inconspicuous plant which blooms at the same time as goldenrod.

Baked Italian Chicken

1 cup water
1 cup chili sauce
½ teaspoon salt
½ teaspoon dried oregano
¼ teaspoon celery seed
⅛ teaspoon pepper
1 (2-3 pound) fryer, cut up
½ cup finely ground, dry
   breadcrumbs
4 tablespoons butter or margarine

Combine water, chili sauce, salt, oregano, celery seed and pepper in bowl. Dip chicken in mixture. Coat skin side with crumbs. In 13x9 inch baking dish, melt butter or margarine. Place chicken, crumb side up, in baking dish. Pour remaining chili sauce mixture over chicken. Bake at 375° for 1 hour, until chicken is tender.
Yield: 6 servings.

Marinated Chicken and Mushrooms

Marinates overnight.

4 pounds chicken, boned and
   skinned
1 pound mushrooms
1 whole clove garlic
1 (16 ounce) bottle Italian
   salad dressing
6 cups white wine
4 (10½ ounce) cans chicken
   gravy
White rice

Cut chicken into strips or bite size pieces. Trim and halve mushrooms. Combine chicken, mushrooms, garlic, dressing and wine in a 13x9 inch baking dish. Cover and marinate in refrigerator overnight. Drain chicken and mushrooms. Reserve 2 cups marinade. Arrange chicken mixture in baking dish. Mix reserved marinade with chicken gravy. Pour over chicken mixture. Bake at 325° for 1½ hours. Serve over white rice.
Yield: 10-12 servings.

Freezes well.

Breasts with Fine Herbs

2 tablespoons butter or mar-
garine
2 chicken breasts, boned,
skinned and halved
1 (6 ounce) can sliced mush-
rooms, drained
¼ cup dry white wine
½ teaspoon crushed fine
herbs (cook's choice of
paprika, oregano, sage,
dried thyme or dried rose-
mary)

Melt butter in medium skillet. Add chicken. Brown on both sides, 12-16 minutes. Add mushrooms, wine and herbs. Cook, covered over low heat 5-10 minutes, until tender. Yield: 4 servings.

Oven Barbecued Chicken

Make the night before. Cook 1 hour before serving time.

2 chickens, cut-up
1 (8 ounce) can tomato sauce
1 cup ketchup
½ cup worcestershire sauce
1½ teaspoons red pepper
sauce
½ cup melted margarine
1 teaspoon mustard
1 teaspoon chili powder
4 tablespoons vinegar
½ teaspoon pepper

Place chicken in 13x9 inch baking dish. Combine remaining ingredients as a sauce. Pour over chicken. Cook uncovered at 350° for 1 hour. Yield: 8-10 servings.

Chicken Sauté Sec

2 tablespoons flour
1 teaspoon garlic salt
¼ teaspoon pepper
½ teaspoon thyme or basil
4-5 pieces chicken
⅓ cup margarine
¾ cup Chablis or Sauterne
½ cup sliced mushrooms
¼ cup chopped green onion
2 teaspoons chopped parsley

Combine flour, garlic salt, pepper, thyme or basil in small bowl. Dust chicken with mixture. Melt margarine in skillet. Brown chicken. Add wine. Cook 15-20 minutes on low. Sauté mushrooms and onions. Add to chicken. Cook another 15-20 minutes. Sprinkle with parsley.
Yield: 4 servings.

Seasons Italian Chicken

2 chicken breasts, boned, skinned and halved
1 (10¾ ounce) can cream of mushroom soup
1 (8 ounce) carton sour cream
1 (4 ounce) jar sliced mushrooms
3 tablespoons sherry
1 (.7 ounce) envelope Italian dressing mix
Rice or noodles

Place chicken breasts in single layer in 13x9 inch baking dish. Mix other ingredients together, excluding salad dressing. Pour mixture over chicken. Sprinkle dry salad dressing mix over top. Cover. Bake at 350° for 45 minutes. Serve with rice or noodles.
Yield: 4 servings.

Rudbeckia hirta

"Panic Chicken"

3 chicken breasts, boned,
  skinned and halved
½ cup prepared breadcrumbs
½ cup Parmesan cheese
Garlic powder to taste
Salt and pepper to taste
½ cup melted butter
Herb and butter seasoned
  rice mix

Coat chicken with butter. Mix crumbs, cheese, and spices. Roll chicken in crumb-cheese mixture. Place in 13x9 inch baking dish. Bake at 350° for 45-60 minutes. Prepare seasoned rice and use as bed for chicken.
Yield: 4-6 servings.

Add a salad and supper is ready!

Chicken Sopa

½ cup chopped onion
1 (4 ounce) can diced green
  chilies
½ cup margarine
1 (10¾ ounce) can cream of
  chicken soup
1 (12 ounce) can evaporated
  milk
1 package corn tortillas
2 cups cubed cooked chicken
½ pound grated Cheddar
  cheese

Sauté onions and chilies in margarine until onions are clear. Add soup and milk. Heat slowly. Dip tortillas into soup mixture until softened. Line a buttered 13x9 inch baking dish with tortillas. Pour a layer of soup mixture over tortillas, next chicken. Continue layering. Top with cheese layer. Bake at 350° for 20-25 minutes, until brown and bubbly.
Yield: 4 servings.

Chicken Quesadillas

1 cup shredded or finely
  chopped cooked chicken
1½ cups (6 ounces) shredded
  Monterey Jack cheese
6 large flour tortillas
3-4 green onions, chopped
½ cup picante sauce
½ cup grated Parmesan
  cheese
Vegetable cooking spray
¼ cup melted butter or margarine

Guacamole:
1 ripe avocado
¼ cup grated onion
2 teaspoons lime juice
1 tomato, finely chopped
Salt and pepper to taste
1 cup chopped tomato

Arrange 2-3 tablespoons chicken and ¼ cup Jack cheese over half of each tortilla. Spread almost to the edge. Sprinkle each with onion, Parmesan cheese and picante sauce. Fold in half. Brush both sides of tortilla with butter. Place on vegetable sprayed broiler pan. (May need to use toothpick to hold tortilla together.) Broil 5-6 inches from heat until lightly browned and crisp. Turn and broil other side. Top with guacamole and chopped tomato.

Mash avocado. Mix with other ingredients excluding tomato.
Yield: 4-6 servings.

Chicken Enchiladas

2 cups cooked diced chicken
2 cups sour cream
2 (4 ounce) cans chopped
  mild green chilies
1 cup chopped green onion
½ teaspoon salt
4 cups shredded Monterey
  Jack cheese
12 flour tortillas
1 (10 ounce) can mild enchilada sauce

In large bowl, combine first 5 ingredients and 2 cups cheese. Dip tortillas in enchilada sauce. Spread chicken mixture down middle of tortilla and roll up. Place seam side down in 13x9 inch baking dish. Repeat with remaining tortillas. Top with remaining cheese. Bake uncovered at 350° 20 minutes, until cheese is melted and enchiladas are heated through.
Yield: 6-8 servings.

May be made ahead, refrigerated and baked before serving.

Chicken Enchiladas with Tomatoes

2 cups chopped cooked
  chicken
1 (8 ounce) package cream
  cheese, softened
½ cup chopped onion
½ teaspoon salt
8 tortillas
Cooking oil
1 pound jalapeño processed
  cheese
2 cups chopped fresh tomatoes
¼ cup milk

Preheat oven to 350°. Combine chicken, softened cream cheese, onion and salt. Fry tortillas in ¼ inch oil until tender. Fill tortillas with chicken mixture. Roll. Place seam side down in a 11x7 inch baking dish. Heat cheese, 1 cup tomatoes and milk over low heat. Stir until cheese is melted. Pour sauce over tortillas and place remaining tomatoes on top. Bake at 350° for 30 minutes.
Yield: 4-6 servings.

Inexpensive with company flair.

Spicy Chicken Casserole

1 package of corn tortillas,
  cut in quarters
1 chicken, cooked and cubed
1 (10¾ ounce) can cream of
  mushroom soup
1 (10¾ ounce) can cream of
  celery soup
1 (8 ounce) can tomatoes
  with chilies
½ cup chopped onion
8 ounces sour cream
1 cup grated Cheddar cheese

Line tortillas in a well greased 11x9 inch baking dish. Top with chicken. Mix together soups, tomatoes with chilies, onion and sour cream. Pour over chicken and top with grated cheese. Bake at 350° 25-30 minutes, until bubbly.
Yield: 6-8 servings.

Great for slumber parties and football weekends.

The best time of year to plant wildflower seeds is in the fall. Many of the Texas annuals overwinter as seedlings, while others need a dormant period or weathering to induce germination.

Parmesan Cheese Chicken

1 (10¾ ounce) can cream of
  chicken soup
1 (1.25 ounce) package onion
  soup mix
¼ cup melted butter or margarine
1½ cups uncooked rice
3 cups warm water
1 cup crushed packaged herb
  stuffing mix
⅔ cup grated Parmesan
  cheese
¼ cup chopped parsley
1 cup lemon juice
½ cup melted butter or margarine
5 chicken breasts, boned,
  skinned and halved

Combine chicken soup, onion soup mix, margarine, rice and warm water in a large flat 3 quart baking dish. Combine stuffing mix with Parmesan cheese and parsley. Dip chicken pieces in lemon juice, then in margarine. Roll in cheese-stuffing mix. Place chicken breasts on top of rice mixture. Bake uncovered at 375° for 1 hour.
Yield: 10 servings.

Rice mixture and chicken breasts may be prepared ahead of time, refrigerated separately and combined at the last minute. This is an excellent dinner party recipe.

Curried Chicken Casserole

6 cups cooked, cubed chicken
2 cups chopped celery
1 cup chopped onion
1 cup slivered almonds
2 teaspoons lemon juice
2 teaspoons salt
1½ cups mayonnaise
2 (10¾ ounce) cans cream of
  chicken soup
8-10 hardboiled eggs, sliced
2 (8 ounce) cans sliced water
  chestnuts, drained
½ teaspoon curry powder
Crushed potato chips (to
  cover)

Mix all ingredients together (excluding potato chips). Pour into a 13x9 inch baking dish. Top with the potato chips. Bake at 350° for 25 minutes. Lower oven temperature to 300° for an additional 25 minutes.
Yield: 8-10 servings.

Great dish for ladies luncheons.

Chicken Kiev with Mushroom Sauce

¾ *cup butter or margarine*
1 tablespoon chopped parsley
1 tablespoon chives
1 tablespoon minced green
  onion
½ *teaspoon salt*
3 chicken breasts, boned,
  skinned and halved
Salt and pepper
1 egg
1 tablespoon cold water
Flour
⅔ *cup breadcrumbs*
¼ *cup butter or margarine*

Sauce:
¼ *cup butter or margarine*
½ *cup finely minced onion*
1 pound mushrooms, thinly
  sliced
2 tablespoons lemon juice
1 teaspoon salt
Dash pepper
1 cup sour cream
1 (8 ounce) package fine
  noodles, cooked and
  drained

Mix ¾ cup softened butter or margarine, parsley, chives, green onion, salt and pepper. Shape into 6 sticks. Chill or freeze until firm. Place 1 breast between 2 pieces of wax paper. Pound slightly. Repeat with others. Place one stick of herbed butter on each breast. Roll breast so butter is completely enclosed. Close with wooden picks. Sprinkle lightly with salt and pepper. Preheat oven to 400°. Beat egg and water together. Dredge breasts in flour. Dip in egg mixture. Roll in breadcrumbs to coat well. Heat ¼ cup butter in large skillet over medium heat. Sauté until golden, turning gently with two forks. Place in 13x9 inch baking pan. Bake 15-20 minutes.

Melt butter in large skillet over medium heat. Add onion. Cook 2 minutes. Add mushrooms. Sprinkle with lemon juice, salt and pepper. Cook 5 minutes stirring occasionally. Remove from heat. Stir in sour cream. Mix half sauce with noodles. Spoon on serving platter. Remove picks from chicken. Serve with remaining sauce.
Yield: 6 servings.

Coreopsis tinctoria

Chicken Tetrazzini

¼ cup butter
¼ cup flour
1 teaspoon salt
¼ teaspoon garlic salt
⅛ teaspoon white pepper
2 cups milk
2 cups half and half cream
2 teaspoons chicken bouillon
    crystals
⅓ cup sherry wine
⅔ cup Parmesan cheese
7 ounces spaghetti, cooked
    and drained
2 cups cooked cubed chicken
5 ounces mushrooms, sliced
    and sautéed

Melt butter. Blend in flour, salt, garlic salt and pepper. Add milk, half and half, and bouillon. Cook, stirring constantly, until thick and smooth. Add sherry, ⅓ cup Parmesan cheese, spaghetti, chicken and mushrooms. Stir carefully. Pour into 2 quart baking dish. Sprinkle with remaining Parmesan cheese. Bake at 375° 20-25 minutes, until hot and bubbly.
Yield: 6-8 servings.

A classic.

Chicken Piccata

8 chicken breasts
¼ cup flour
Salt and pepper
1 tablespoon paprika
1 tablespoon olive oil
¼ cup butter
2 tablespoons Maderia wine
3 tablespoons lemon juice
1 lemon, sliced
4 tablespoons capers
¼ cup parsley

Pound breasts until ¼ inch thick. Combine flour, salt, pepper, and paprika in bag. Toss chicken breasts in mixture. Heat butter and oil in skillet. Sauté chicken 2-3 minutes on each side. Drain on paper towels. Drain off all but 2 tablespoons of oil. Stir in Maderia and lemon juice. Return chicken to skillet adding lemon slices, capers and parsley. Cook until sauce thickens.
Yield: 8 servings.

Serve with fettuccini and Caesar salad. For variety, use veal.

Chicken Paprika with Hungarian Dumplings

Chicken:
1 (2-3½ pound) chicken, cut
   in pieces
Salt
1 cup chopped onion
¼ cup corn oil
2 teaspoons flavor enhancer
   (optional)
2½-3 tablespoons Hungarian
   paprika
1 cup diced canned tomatoes
1 cup water
½ cup sour cream

Dumplings:
6 cups water
2 teaspoons salt
2 cups unsifted flour
1½ teaspoons salt
1 cup water
2 egg yolks
½ cup melted butter

Place chicken in a stewing pan. Salt to taste. Sauté onion in oil 2-3 minutes. Add flavor enhancer, paprika, tomatoes, and water. Pour mixture over chicken. Cover pan tightly. Simmer 1 hour, until tender. Add sour cream.

Put water in 4 quart saucepan. Add 2 teaspoons of salt. Bring to a boil. Mix flour, 1½ teaspoons salt, water, and egg yolks in a mixing bowl. Dough will be very sticky. Place dough on cutting board. With a sharp knife cut dough into small pieces. Drop in boiling water. When all dough has been cut, cover pan and let dumplings simmer until they come to top of water (5-10 minutes). Drain and rinse with cold water. Return to pan. Add butter and a small amount of sauce from Chicken Paprika. Serve on a platter topped with chicken and sauce.
Yield: 6-8 servings.

This is an old family recipe brought over to this country.

Chicken and Snow Peas

2 large whole chicken breasts
2 tablespoons soy sauce
2 tablespoons sherry
½ teaspoon ground ginger
1 clove garlic, crushed
1 tablespoon oil
1 cup sliced onions
1 cup sliced mushrooms
7 ounces snow peas

Cut chicken into bite-sized pieces. Blend soy sauce, sherry, ginger and garlic together. Add chicken. Marinate 30 minutes. Heat oil in large skillet. Add chicken, onions and mushrooms. Sauté 10 minutes. Add pea pods. Sauté another 5 minutes or until chicken is done.
Yield: 4 servings.

Chicken Veronique

2 large chicken breasts,
  boned, skinned and halved
2 tablespoons butter or margarine
1 cup sliced mushrooms
2 tablespoons sliced green
  onions
⅓ cup chicken broth
1 tablespoon all-purpose flour
1 cup seedless grapes, halved
¼ cup dry white wine
3 cups hot cooked rice

Cut chicken breasts into 1 inch pieces. Set aside. In wok, melt butter or margarine over medium high heat. Stir-fry mushrooms and onions in butter 2 minutes, until tender. Add chicken pieces. Stir-fry 5 minutes until chicken is done. Blend chicken broth and flour. Add to chicken mixture. Cook, stirring until thickened and bubbly. Cook and stir 1 minute longer. Add grapes and wine. Heat. Serve at once over hot cooked rice.
Yield: 4 servings.

Old Fashioned Roast Turkey

1 (14-16) pound turkey
4 teaspoons melted butter or
  margarine
1 tablespoon salt
½ teaspoon pepper
2 teaspoons seasoned salt
1 teaspoon ground poultry
  seasoning or sage
1 teaspoon garlic powder
1 teaspoon ground ginger
1 teaspoon paprika
¼ teaspoon cayenne pepper
¼ teaspoon dried basil
1 large onion, quartered
4 stalks celery with leaves
1 cup water

Clean and dry turkey. Reserve neck, giblets and liver. Brush turkey with melted butter. Mix dry seasonings. Rub thoroughly into inside and outside of bird. Put onion and celery inside cavity. Truss and tie securely. Place breast side up in roaster. Add 1 cup water. Cover. Bake at 350° until tender, 3-4 hours. Remove cover for last ½ hour and lower temperature to 300° to evenly brown.
Yield: 14 servings.

Pan juices in roaster may be combined with giblet broth to make a delicious gravy.

Apricot Herb Cornish Hens

4 (1-1½ pound) Cornish
　game hens
¾ cup butter, softened
½ teaspoon marjoram leaves
⅔ cup apricot preserves

Preheat oven to 350°. Remove giblets and rinse birds. In a small bowl stir together butter and marjoram. Place 1 tablespoon butter mixture on breast meat, directly under skin (lift up skin gently to expose pocket for butter). Tuck wings under and tie legs. Place in 13x9 inch baking dish, breast side up. In 1 quart saucepan, melt remaining butter mixture. Brush birds with some of butter mixture. Cover with foil. Bake for 1 hour 40 minutes. Add apricot preserves to remaining melted butter mixture. Heat until melted. During the last 15 minutes of baking, uncover hens, brush lightly with sauce. Continue baking until golden brown. Serve with remaining sauce.
Yield: 4 servings.

Stuffed Quail

12 quail
1 pound pure pork sausage
12 thin slices bacon
2 cups flour
Salt and pepper
1 cup margarine
3 tablespoons grape jelly
2 cups red wine

Stuff quail with sausage. Wrap strip of bacon around quail breast. Season flour with salt and pepper. Roll quail in seasoned flour. Melt margarine in large skillet. Place quail in skillet. Brown. Remove quail. Add enough seasoned flour to drippings to make brown gravy to cover birds. Add wine and grape jelly. Place quail in a large, deep baking dish. Pour gravy over quail. Cover with foil. Bake at 250° until tender (1½-2 hours).
Yield: 6 servings.

Game may be overcooked 2-3 hours with no change in quality. However, it may be ruined by undercooking as little as five minutes. Because game has a tendency to be dry, always serve with gravy or light sauce.

Quail or Dove En Creme

4-6 birds
2 tablespoons butter
½ cup finely chopped mush-
    rooms
½ cup finely chopped onion
1 tablespoon chopped parsley
½ cup white wine
½ cup heavy cream
Wild rice

Wash and dry birds. Rub with salt and flour. Sauté lightly in butter. Place birds in baking dish. Set aside. Sauté mushrooms and onions. Add parsley and white wine. Pour over birds. Bake at 350° for 45 minutes, basting once or twice. Add heavy cream. Bake additional 15 minutes. Serve with wild rice.
Yield: 4 servings.

Roast Duck

Sauce:
⅓ cup butter
½ cup orange juice
6 tablespoons orange marma-
    lade
1 cup red Burgundy wine
Cornstarch, if necessary

Ducks:
2 ducks
Salt and pepper
Garlic powder
Flavor enhancer
2 small onions
2 stalks celery

Melt butter. Add orange marmalade, orange juice and wine. Heat until all are blended. Do not boil. Thicken sauce if necessary with cornstarch.

Season ducks. Place one small onion and one stalk celery in cavity. Place each duck in a piece of heavy foil, breast side down. Spoon small amount sauce on each duck. Wrap tightly. Cook in 300° oven for 2½ hours, until tender. Open foil. Turn ducks breast side up. Baste with sauce occasionally. Cook until brown.
Yield: 4 servings.

Game may be overcooked 2-3 hours with no change in quality. However, it may be ruined by undercooking as little as five minutes. Because game has a tendency to be dry, always serve with gravy or light sauce.

Marinated Medallions of Pork Tenderloin

Must be made ahead.

Marinade:
4 (1-2 pound) pork tender-
loins
1 clove garlic, crushed
3 tablespoons soy sauce
1 tablespoon Hoisin Sauce
(Chinese)
2 teaspoons sugar
½ teaspoon Five Spice Pow-
der (Chinese)

Water
3 tablespoons peanut oil
Honey

Sweet and Sour Sauce:
½ cup water
⅓ cup sugar
⅓ cup vinegar
1 tablespoon cornstarch
1 tablespoon soy sauce

Cut each tenderloin into thirds. Mix ingredients and marinate for 36 hours.

Preheat oven to 425°. Cover bottom of roasting pan with water. Add tenderloins. Add peanut oil to marinade. Brush on meat. Roast 15 minutes. Baste tenderloins again with marinade. Reduce oven to 350°. Roast 10 minutes more. Brush tenderloins with honey. Roast 10 minutes. Slice pork into ½ inch medallions.

Combine ingredients in saucepan. Cook over high heat, stirring constantly, until thickened. Pour over medallions and serve.
Yield: 8-10 servings.

May be frozen after prepared. May be served as a main dish as stated or a wonderful, hearty hors d'oeuvre, using sauce for dipping.

Opuntia phaeacantha

Pork St. Tammany

½ cup boiling water
½ cup chopped dried apricots
2 tablespoons melted butter
2 green onions, finely chopped
½ cup chopped fresh mushrooms
¼ cup chopped green pepper
1 (6 ounce) package long grain and wild rice mix, cooked
3 tablespoons chopped pecans
1 tablespoon chopped fresh parsley
⅛ teaspoon salt
⅛ teaspoon pepper
Dash of red pepper
Dash of garlic powder
4 (1½ pound) boneless pork tenderloins
4 slices bacon
Canned apricot halves
Fresh parsley sprigs

Pour boiling water over dried apricots. Let stand 20 minutes to soften. Drain. Sauté green onions, mushrooms, and green pepper in butter until tender. Add prepared rice, apricots, pecans, parsley, and seasonings. Stir until combined. Cut lengthwise slit on top of each tenderloin, being careful not to cut through the bottom or sides. Spoon half of stuffing mixture into the opening of one tenderloin. Place cut side of second tenderloin over stuffing. Tie tenderloins together securely. Place on rack in roasting pan. Top with 2 bacon slices. Repeat procedure with remaining 2 tenderloins. Place aluminum foil tent over tenderloins. Bake at 325° for 1½-2 hours or until meat thermometer registers 170°. Remove foil last 30-40 minutes of baking. Remove from oven and let stand 5 minutes. Remove string. Slice and garnish with apricot halves and parsley sprigs.
Yield: 8-10 servings.

White prickly poppies, with their abundant pollen, provide a ready food source for honeybees. Most of the plant is mildly poisonous, and the foliage is so prickly, cattle avoid the poppy even during severe droughts. If you break a prickly poppy stem, you'll find a brightly colored yellow or orange sap.

Pork Pyrenees

2 pounds boneless lean pork,
  cut into 1 inch cubes
¼ cup flour
1 teaspoon salt
Dash pepper
3 medium onions, quartered
8 ounces French dressing
1 (16 ounce) can tiny whole
  carrots, drained
½ cup water
1 bay leaf
2 cups sliced fresh mush-
  rooms
3 cups cooked rice
Parsley

Mix salt, pepper, and flour. Coat meat. Brown onion and meat in ⅓ cup of dressing. Add carrots, water, remaining dressing, and bay leaf. Simmer covered 1 hour. Add mushrooms during the final 10 minutes. Remove bay leaf. Serve over hot rice. Garnish with parsley.
Yield: 6 servings.

Sweet Cabbage and Sausage

6 slices bacon
1 medium head of cabbage,
  cut into chunks
1 medium onion, chopped
¼ cup water
2 tablespoons brown sugar
1 clove garlic, minced
1 teaspoon seasoned salt
½ teaspoon dried, crushed
  red pepper
1 pound Polish sausage, cut
  into 1-inch slices

Cook bacon in Dutch oven until crisp. Remove bacon, crumble and set aside. Add remaining ingredients to drippings. Cover and cook over medium heat 15 minutes, stirring occasionally. Sprinkle bacon on top.
Yield: 6 servings.

This is a quick and easy Sunday night family dinner.

Ham Balls

Ham Balls:
2 pounds ground sirloin
2 pounds ground ham
2½ cups graham cracker
   crumbs
1½ cups milk

Sauce:
2 (8 ounce) cans tomato
   sauce
½ cup vinegar
1 cup brown sugar, packed
1 teaspoon dry mustard

Mix ingredients and form into balls.
Yield: 28-30 ham balls.

Mix ingredients and pour over ham balls in
large baking dish. Bake, uncovered, at 250°
for 2 hours.
Yield: 8-10 servings.

*This recipe may be used as a main dish or for
an appetizer. Ham balls may be frozen. After
defrosting, make sauce and bake.*

Broccoli-Ham Casserole

3 tablespoons butter, melted
½ cup chopped celery
½ cup chopped onion
½ cup chopped green pepper
1 (10 ounce) can cream of
   mushroom soup
½ cup water
1 (8 ounce) jar processed
   cheese spread
1 (8 ounce) jar sliced mush-
   rooms, drained
1 cup rice, cooked
2 (10 ounce) boxes frozen,
   chopped broccoli, cooked
   and drained
1 pound cooked ham, diced
Grated Cheddar cheese

Sauté celery, onion, and green pepper in
butter. Add soup, water, cheese spread, and
mushrooms. Mix well. Add rice, broccoli, and
ham. Put into 12x9 inch baking dish. Sprinkle
Cheddar cheese on top. Bake at 400° for 30
minutes.
Yield: 8 servings.

Freezes well.

Veal Parmesan

6 veal cutlets (tenderized
   round steak may be substituted)
2 eggs, slightly beaten
1 cup round butter flavored
   cracker crumbs
¼ cup Parmesan cheese
Salt
Pepper
Oil
6 slices mozzarella cheese
1 (32 ounce) jar Italian sauce
   with mushrooms

Mix cracker crumbs with Parmesan cheese, salt and pepper. Dip cutlets into beaten eggs, then into crumb mixture. Brown meat in oil. Drain. Place veal in 12x9 inch baking dish. Put one slice mozzarella cheese on each cutlet. Pour sauce over top. Bake, uncovered, at 350° for 30-40 minutes.
Yield: 4-6 servings.

Perfect Veal Cutlets

¼ cup flour
½ cup grated Parmesan
   cheese
1 teaspoon salt
⅛ teaspoon pepper
1½ pounds veal cutlets
2 tablespoons olive oil
1 clove garlic, minced
½ cup dry white wine
½ cup consommé or beef
   stock
1 tablespoon lemon juice
Fresh parsley, chopped

Combine flour, cheese, salt, and pepper. Cut cutlets into serving pieces. Wipe meat dry. Sprinkle with flour mixture and pound into meat. Sauté garlic in olive oil. Brown meat slightly. Remove garlic. Add wine, stock, and lemon juice. Cover. Simmer slowly for 30 minutes. Before serving, sprinkle with fresh parsley.
Yield: 6 servings.

Serve with your favorite pasta or new potatoes and fresh snow peas.

Texas contains over 5,000 species of flowering plants.

Veal Scaloppine with Fresh Tomatoes and Avocado

*8 thin veal scallops, dried
with paper towels
1 tablespoon butter, melted
1 tablespoon olive oil
Homemade Pesto Sauce (page
48)
2 medium tomatoes, chopped
1 medium avocado, peeled
and chopped*

Sauté veal until lightly browned in hot butter and olive oil. Place veal on serving dish. Spread sauce on top. Top with tomatoes and avocado. Serve immediately.
Yield: 4-6 servings.

Veal Scaloppine in Lemon Sauce

*1½ pounds veal, ¼ inch thick,
cut in serving pieces
Salt
Pepper
Flour
2 tablespoons butter
3 tablespoons oil
¾ cup beef stock
6 lemon slices, cut thin
1 tablespoon lemon juice
2 tablespoons butter, softened*

Season veal with salt and pepper. Coat lightly in flour. In heavy 12-inch skillet, melt butter and oil over moderate heat. When foam subsides, sauté veal, 4 or 5 scallops at a time, until golden brown, 2 minutes on each side. Remove veal. Pour off most of fat, leaving thin film. Add ½ cup of beef stock. Boil briskly for 1-2 minutes, stirring constantly and scraping browned bits from bottom. Add veal. Arrange lemon slices on top. Cover. Simmer 10-15 minutes. Remove veal to heated platter. Surround with lemon slices. Add remaining beef stock to juices in skillet. Boil briskly until stock is reduced to syrupy glaze. Add lemon juice. Cook, stirring for 1 minute. Remove skillet from heat. Swirl in 2 tablespoons of softened butter. Pour sauce over scallops.
Yield: 4 servings.

Veal Scaloppine Marsala

1½ pounds veal, trimmed,
    pounded very thin
½ cup flour
⅓ cup freshly grated Parmesan
    cheese
¼ cup butter
2 cups sliced fresh mushrooms
2 green onions, chopped
½ cup beef broth
2 tablespoons fresh lemon juice
⅓ cup Marsala wine
Parsley, chopped
Orange slices, optional

Mix flour and Parmesan. Dredge veal. Brown immediately, 30 seconds per side, in skillet with half butter. Set aside. Keep warm. Add remaining butter. Sauté mushrooms and onion. Add broth, lemon juice, and wine. Return meat to skillet simmering for 10 minutes. To serve, pour juices and mushrooms over meat. Garnish with parsley. If desired, add thin orange slices for color.
Yield: 4 servings.

Excellent served with fettuccine and fresh asparagus.

Veal Piccata

1½ pounds veal round, cut ¼
    inch thick
Salt
Pepper
Flour
3 tablespoons butter
1 tablespoon olive oil
2 cloves garlic, minced
½ pound fresh mushrooms,
    sliced
2 tablespoons lemon juice
½ cup dry white wine
3 tablespoons parsley,
    chopped
½ lemon, thinly sliced

Sprinkle veal with salt and pepper on both sides and dust lightly with flour. Heat butter and olive oil in a skillet. Add veal and brown on both sides. Remove veal. Add garlic and mushrooms to pan and cook 1 minute. Return veal to skillet. Add lemon juice and white wine. Cover. Simmer 20 minutes, or until veal is tender. Remove to a warm platter, and garnish with parsley and lemon slices.
Yield: 4 servings.

This is very good served with Fettuccine Alfredo!

Sauce Verde

⅓ cup sour cream
⅓ cup mayonnaise
1 tablespoon chopped parsley
2 teaspoons chopped green
  onion
1 teaspoon lemon juice
¼-½ teaspoon salt
¼ teaspoon dill weed
Generous dash hot pepper
  sauce

Combine ingredients. Mix thoroughly. Chill at least one hour to blend flavors.
Yield: ⅔ cup sauce.

Delicious served with hot or cold salmon.

Tangy Tartar Sauce

1 cup mayonnaise
1½ tablespoons minced sour
  pickles
1½ tablespoons minced parsley
1½ tablespoons capers
1½ tablespoons minced green
  olives
1½ tablespoons grated white
  onion

Combine all ingredients. Chill several hours.
Yield: 1 cup.

Seafood Sauce for Grilling

¼ cup butter, melted
1½ teaspoons soy sauce
1 tablespoon lemon juice
1 teaspoon worcestershire
  sauce
1 small garlic clove, crushed
Dash red pepper sauce
3-4 drops liquid smoke

Mix all ingredients in small pan and heat. Brush on seafood while grilling. Baste often.
Yield: 4 servings.

Excellent on swordfish, shrimp and salmon.

Snapper a la France

2 pounds snapper, sea bass,
   catfish or other large
   textured fish fillets, cut in 4
   pieces
1 teaspoon salt
Ground pepper to taste
¼ teaspoon paprika
2 large cloves garlic, crushed
6 tablespoons minced parsley
6 tablespoons olive oil

Preheat oven to 350°. Wipe fish dry. Season on both sides with salt and pepper. Arrange single layer of fish in greased, shallow, baking dish. Rub surface with paprika and garlic. Sprinkle with parsley and oil. Bake 15-30 minutes, basting often. Flesh should barely separate when tested with fork. Serve with juice spooned over fillets.
Yield: 4 servings.

Easy Baked Flounder

½ cup butter
1 egg
Dash salt
Dash white pepper
2 tablespoons milk
2 tablespoons lemon juice
5 fresh or frozen flounder
   fillets
3 cups finely ground round
   butter crackers
Paprika

Melt butter in 13x9 inch baking dish. Combine egg, salt, pepper, milk and lemon juice. Dip each fillet in egg mixture, then in cracker crumbs. Place in baking dish. Sprinkle leftover crumbs over fish. Top with paprika. Bake uncovered at 375° for 30-35 minutes, until brown on top.
Yield: 4 servings.

One of the most unusual plants in Texas is frostweed. When the temperatures freeze, the stem breaks open and the sap flows out to form a sparkling mass of ice crystals.

Blackened Redfish

**4 (8-10 ounce) fish fillets,
  preferably redfish or pom-
  pano**
1 cup unsalted butter, melted
2½ teaspoons salt
1 teaspoon onion powder
1 teaspoon garlic powder
1 teaspoon cayenne pepper
¾ teaspoon white pepper
¾ teaspoon black pepper
**½ teaspoon crushed thyme
  leaves**
Chopped parsley
Lemon, sliced

Dip fish fillets in ½ cup melted butter. Mix seasonings together. Season fillets with the mixture. Set aside at least 10 minutes. Heat cast iron skillet over very high heat at least 10 minutes. (The skillet cannot be too hot!) Be sure to use exhaust fan while heating and cooking. Place seasoned fillets in hot skillet. Pour 1 tablespoon butter over each fillet. (Be careful, as butter may flame.) Cook uncovered over high heat until underside looks charred (about 2 minutes). Turn fish over. Pour 1 tablespoon butter on top. Cook until fish is done (about 2 minutes). Sprinkle fillets with parsley. Adorn with sliced lemon.
Yield: 4 servings.

Friday Night Flounder

½ pound mushrooms, sliced
2 medium onions, chopped
2 cloves garlic, minced
½ teaspoon dried whole basil
2 tablespoons vegetable oil
1½ cups chopped tomato
6 tablespoons lemon juice
4 flounder fillets
Salt and pepper to taste
**1 pound fresh spinach, stems
  removed**
Lemon slices
Fresh parsley

Sauté mushrooms, onion, garlic and basil in oil until onion is tender. Remove from heat. Stir in tomato and lemon juice. Set aside. Sprinkle flounder with salt and pepper. Place in well greased 2 quart baking dish. Top with vegetable mixture. Cover. Bake at 350° for 20-25 minutes, until fish flakes easily with a fork. Place spinach in Dutch oven. (Do not add water!) Cover and cook 3-5 minutes. Drain spinach. Chop and arrange on large serving platter. Transfer fish and vegetables to the platter. Garnish with lemon slices and fresh parsley.
Yield: 4 servings.

Makes a beautiful presentation and is healthy, too.

J.B.'s Boiled Shrimp

1 large or 2 small lemons,
   quartered
½ bell pepper, quartered
1 bag crab boil
1 small white onion, quartered
1 clove garlic
1 cup plus 2 tablespoons salt
5 pounds shrimp with heads,
   rinsed several times

Boil water in 2 gallon kettle. Add all ingredients excluding shrimp. Once water is rolling, add shrimp. Cook for ONLY 3 minutes. Reduce heat. Let stand 2 minutes more. Rinse and serve.
Yield: 8 servings.

Wonderful for a summertime patio party.

Pretty Party Shrimp

½ pound mushrooms, sliced
1 tablespoon butter
Vegetable cooking spray
1 pound shrimp, cooked
1 (14 ounce) can artichoke
   hearts, cut in half
5 tablespoons flour
5 tablespoons butter
1 teaspoon salt
½ teaspoon pepper
1 cup milk
1 cup cream
2 teaspoons worcestershire
   sauce
½ cup Parmesan cheese
Paprika
Brown rice

Sauté mushrooms in 1 tablespoon butter in small skillet. Set aside. Spray 2 quart baking dish with spray. Put shrimp, artichokes and mushrooms in bottom of baking dish. Melt butter over low heat. Stir in flour until blended. Add salt and pepper. Slowly stir in milk and cream. Cook until medium thick. Remove from heat. Add worcestershire and cheese. Pour over shrimp, mushrooms and artichokes. Sprinkle with paprika. Bake at 350° for 30 minutes. Serve over brown rice.
Yield: 6 servings.

May be frozen.

*Texas Wildflower Day is always the fourth Saturday
in April.*

Empress Avocado Shrimp with Tangy & Spicy Sauce

½ pound medium-size shrimp, cleaned and peeled
2 avocados, halved lengthwise and seeded
1 tablespoon Chinese horse-radish mustard
3 teaspoons sugar
1 tablespoon olive oil
2 teaspoons vinegar
3 tablespoons lemon juice

Boil shrimp for 2 minutes. Drain. Cool shrimp in cold running water 2-3 minutes. Mix Chinese horseradish mustard, sugar, olive oil, vinegar and lemon juice. Toss with shrimp. Fill avocado with shrimp and pour remaining sauce on top. Serve cold.
Yield: 4 servings.

An Empress of China specialty Forum members enjoy.

Jambalaya

2 medium onions, chopped
½ medium green pepper, chopped
1 clove garlic, finely chopped
3 tablespoons olive or vegetable oil
1 pound fresh or frozen medium raw shrimp, peeled and deveined
1 cup uncooked rice
2 cups chicken broth
1 (16 ounce) can tomatoes
1 teaspoon salt
⅛ teaspoon pepper
⅛ teaspoon ground thyme
⅛ teaspoon red pepper sauce
1 bay leaf, crumbled
1½ cups cubed cooked ham

Cook onions, green pepper, garlic and 2 tablespoons of oil in 4 quart Dutch oven over low heat for 3 minutes. Add shrimp. Cook, stirring frequently, until shrimp are pink. Turn shrimp mixture into bowl and reserve. Cook remaining 1 tablespoon oil and rice in Dutch oven over medium high heat, stirring frequently, until rice is light brown. Stir in chicken broth, tomatoes (with liquid), salt, pepper, thyme, pepper sauce and bay leaf. Heat to boiling. Reduce heat. Cover and simmer 15 minutes. Stir in reserved shrimp mixture and ham. Cover and cook until hot.
Yield: 6 servings.

Szechwan Shrimp

2 tablespoons cornstarch
1 tablespoon sherry
3 tablespoons chicken broth
2 tablespoons soy sauce
2 tablespoons ketchup
½-1 teaspoon chili paste
1 teaspoon sugar
2 tablespoons vegetable oil
1 pound raw shrimp, peeled
  and cut in half lengthwise
1 clove garlic, minced
1 tablespoon minced ginger
  root
Scallions
Rice

Dissolve cornstarch in sherry. Mix with chicken stock, soy sauce, ketchup, chili paste and sugar. Set aside. Preheat oil in wok or skillet to 375°. Stir fry shrimp, garlic, and ginger root for 2 minutes. Add scallions. Stir fry 1 minute more. Add chicken broth mixture. Stir fry until thickened. Serve over rice.
Yield: 4 servings.

Chili paste is available at Asian markets.

Soy Barbecued Shrimp

1 pound fresh large or jumbo
  shrimp
1 clove garlic, finely chopped
¼ teaspoon salt
¼ cup soy sauce
¼ cup oil
¼ cup lemon juice
1½ tablespoons finely
  chopped parsley
1 teaspoon dehydrated onion
  flakes
¼ teaspoon pepper

Peel and clean shrimp. Combine remaining ingredients. Stir vigorously to mix oil. Pour over shrimp. Allow to marinate at least 30 minutes. Place shrimp on heated grill. (Shrimp may be skewered.) Cook over moderately low heat. Baste with sauce twice during cooking. Turn shrimp over once. Cook 5 minutes. Test for doneness by cutting shrimp in half. Shrimp are done when opaque throughout.
Yield: 4 servings.

Serve with the marinade as a dip.

Spicy Shrimp Bake

3-5 pounds medium headless
  shrimp
1½ cups margarine, melted
4 ounces Italian salad dressing
1 tablespoon worcestershire
  sauce
1 tablespoon soy sauce
3 cloves garlic, minced
2 bay leaves
3 teaspoons salt
1-2 ounces black pepper,
  coarsely ground
3 lemons, squeezed
1 tablespoon paprika

Use one or two 13x9 inch baking dishes, depending on size or amount of shrimp. Melt margarine in dish. Add shrimp and seasonings. Bake at 350° for 15-20 minutes, stirring every five minutes. (Do not overcook as shell will stick to shrimp.) Shrimp is done when it has curled up.
Yield: 6-8 servings.

Dip French bread in the butter sauce to complete the meal.

Baked Barbecued Shrimp

If cooking more than 5 pounds shrimp, double ingredients.

1 cup butter
½ teaspoon celery salt
¼ teaspoon cayenne pepper
2 bay leaves
2 teaspoons dry mustard
¼ teaspoon ginger
2 teaspoons paprika
⅛ teaspoon black pepper
3 teaspoons salt
3 cloves garlic, minced
2 lemons, squeezed
½ teaspoon rosemary
3-5 pounds shrimp in shell

Melt butter in 13x9 inch pan. Add all other ingredients. Marinate shrimp at least ½ hour. Bake in marinade at 350° for 30 minutes, stirring occasionally.
Yield: 6-8 servings.

Delicious with French bread dipped in sauce.

Barbecued Shrimp

2 pounds shrimp, unpeeled
¼ pound butter, sliced
Cayenne pepper
Sage
Garlic salt
Coarse ground pepper

Place shrimp in large baking dish. Place butter slices on top of shrimp. Cover shrimp generously with remaining ingredients. (There should be a generous layer of spices on shrimp, according to degree of spiciness you prefer.) Bake at 375° for 30-45 minutes. Stir and baste frequently with butter sauce.
Yield: 4-6 servings.

Serve over rice, with French bread and lots of napkins.

Shrimp Rockefeller

1½ pounds shrimp, cleaned
¾ cup margarine
3 tablespoons flour
2½ cups milk
¼ teaspoon worcestershire
  sauce
2 tablespoons Parmesan
  cheese
Salt
White pepper
2 tablespoons chopped green
  onions, including tops
3 tablespoons finely chopped
  celery
¼ cup chopped parsley
Garlic powder
Red pepper sauce
2 (10 ounce) packages frozen
  chopped spinach, cooked
  and drained well
Breadcrumbs
¼ cup margarine

Boil shrimp and set aside to cool. Make a thin white sauce with 3 tablespoons margarine, flour, milk, worcestershire sauce, Parmesan cheese, salt and white pepper to taste. Sauté in skillet for approximately 5 minutes, 6 tablespoons margarine, green onions, celery, parsley, garlic powder and red pepper sauce. Layer spinach mixture, shrimp and white sauce in a 13x9 inch casserole dish or individual shells. Top with breadcrumbs lightly browned in ¼ cup margarine. Bake at 350° for 20 minutes.
Yield: 6-8 servings.

May be prepared with crab, lobster or both in place of shrimp.

Shrimp with Saffron Rice

Shrimp:
½ cup butter
2 tablespoons chopped shallots
1 pound fresh shrimp, unpeeled
½ teaspoon oregano
½ cup dry white wine
Dash white pepper
Salt to taste

Rice:
3 tablespoons butter
1 medium onion, chopped
2 cups rice
2 cups fish or chicken stock
Pinch saffron
1 teaspoon salt
¼ teaspoon white pepper
½ cup toasted pine nuts

Melt butter in a frying pan. When very hot, cook shallots until translucent. Add shrimp and oregano. Cook over a high flame, stirring until shrimp becomes pink and meat is opaque. Add wine, salt and pepper. Remove shrimp. Cool enough to peel. Peel shrimp. Keep shrimp warm and return peelings to butter-wine mixture. Place mixture in a food processor and purée. Strain out shells. This gives a richly flavored butter to use in flavoring rice.

Melt butter in a saucepan. Stir in chopped onion and cook over a moderate flame until translucent. Stir in rice. When rice is completely coated with butter, add fish or chicken stock, saffron, salt and pepper. Bring to a boil. Reduce heat to lowest possible setting. Cover and cook slowly for 20 minutes. Stir in toasted pine nuts. Taste and adjust seasonings. Stir in shrimp butter. Pack into a lightly oiled mold. Invert on a serving plate and surround with shrimp.
Yield: 6 servings.

Pine nuts may be found at gourmet or Chinese stores.

Argemone albiflora ss texana

Shrimp Diablo

2 pounds large shrimp
4 tablespoons olive oil
1 green onion, chopped
    including top
1 clove garlic, minced
1 teaspoon parsley, chopped
1 teaspoon cracked black
    pepper
1/3 cup sherry
2 cups beef gravy
1 tablespoon worcestershire
    sauce
1 1/2 tablespoons lemon juice
1 teaspoon dry mustard
2 tablespoons ketchup
4 cups cooked rice

Peel and devein raw shrimp. Sauté shrimp in olive oil until red. Add onion, garlic, pepper and parsley. Cook over hot fire 3-4 minutes until shrimp is golden brown. Add sherry, beef gravy, worcestershire, lemon juice, mustard and ketchup. Cover. Simmer 20 minutes. Serve over rice.
Yield: 6 servings.

May be made the morning before serving and re-heated. Wonderful with spinach salad and dinner rolls.

"Best Ever" Fried Shrimp

2 pounds large or jumbo
    shrimp
1 cup flour
1 cup milk
2 eggs
1 teaspoon salt
1 cup breadcrumbs
Vegetable oil

Clean and devein shrimp. Split shrimp down back if desired. Mix flour, milk, eggs and salt together. Dip shrimp in mixture. Roll in breadcrumbs. Deep fry 5-6 shrimp in oil in electric wok until golden brown. Drain on paper towel.
Yield: 8 servings.

Serve with sweet and sour sauce or tartar sauce (page 155).

Shrimp and Wild Rice Casserole

1 (10 ¾ ounce) can cream of
  mushroom soup
⅓ cup mayonnaise
⅓ cup milk
Few drops of red pepper
  sauce
½ cup thinly sliced onions
¼ cup thinly sliced bell pepper
¼ cup butter
1 pound medium size shrimp,
  boiled and shelled
2 cups cooked long grain wild
  rice
Vegetable cooking spray
½ cup buttered breadcrumbs

Combine soup, mayonnaise, milk and red pepper sauce. Sauté onion and bell pepper in butter until soft. Mix with soup mixture, rice and shrimp. Pour into a 13x9 inch baking dish treated with spray. Sprinkle with buttered breadcrumbs. Bake in oven at 350° for 30 minutes.
Yield: 8 servings.

Carol's Shrimp Casserole

¼ cup chopped onion
2 tablespoons butter
2 tablespoons flour
½ teaspoon salt
Dash pepper
1 cup light cream
½ teaspoon worcestershire
  sauce
1 (3 ounce) can sliced mushrooms, drained
2 cups medium, cleaned and
  cooked shrimp
2 cups hot cooked rice
½ cup grated sharp Cheddar
  cheese
½ cup butter cracker crumbs

Cook onion in butter until tender, but not brown. Blend in flour. Add salt and pepper. Gradually stir in cream and worcestershire. Cook, stirring until thick. Add mushrooms and shrimp. Heat. Place rice in greased 1½ quart casserole. Add shrimp mixture. Top with cheese. Border with cracker crumbs. Bake at 350° for 20 minutes.
Yield: 4 servings.

Sesame Shrimp and Asparagus

1½ pounds asparagus (fresh or frozen)
1 tablespoon sesame seed
⅓ cup salad or peanut oil
2 small onions, sliced very thin
1½ pounds large shrimp, shelled and deveined
4 teaspoons soy sauce
1¼ teaspoons salt (optional)

Break off tough ends of asparagus and discard. Cut asparagus into 2 inch pieces. Set aside. In wok or 12 inch skillet at 375°, toast sesame seed until golden, stirring occasionally. Remove sesame seed to small bowl. Set aside. In wok at 400° add oil. Cook, stirring frequently, asparagus, onions and shrimp until shrimp are pink and vegetables are tender crisp. Stir in sesame seed, soy sauce and salt until mixed.
Yield: 6 servings.

Serve with rice for a wonderful ladies luncheon menu.

Shrimp in Wine Sauce

Have all ingredients measured and ready. This cooks quickly and should be served immediately.

1 pound large raw shrimp, shelled and deveined
¼ cup flour
¼ cup olive or salad oil
2 teaspoons canned tomato paste
2 tablespoons warm water
1 teaspoon salt
½ teaspoon pepper
Dash cayenne pepper
¼ cup dry white wine
1 tablespoons snipped parsley
1 scallion, snipped
Lemon wedges

Coat shrimp with flour. Sauté shrimp until golden in hot oil. Pour excess oil into saucepan. Add tomato paste, water, salt, pepper and cayenne. Cook over low heat 5 minutes. Add wine to shrimp in skillet. Cook, uncovered, over low heat 3 minutes. Pour sauce over shrimp. Sprinkle with parsley and scallions. Cook 5 minutes. Serve with lemon wedges.
Yield: 2 servings.

Crabmeat au Gratin

1 stalk celery, finely chopped
1 cup finely chopped onion
½ cup margarine or butter
½ cup flour
1 (12 ounce) can evaporated
  milk
2 egg yolks
1 teaspoon salt
½ teaspoon red pepper
¼ teaspoon black pepper
1 pound white crabmeat,
  picked and shredded
½ pound Cheddar cheese,
  grated

Sauté onion and celery in butter until onions are wilted. Blend flour into mixture. Add milk gradually, stirring constantly. Add egg yolks, salt, red and black pepper. Cook 5 minutes. Put crabmeat in a mixing bowl. Pour cooked sauce over crabmeat. Blend well. Transfer into lightly greased 11x7 inch baking dish. Top with Cheddar cheese. Bake at 375° for 10-15 minutes until light brown.
Yield: 6 servings.

Y-Bor City Stuffed Crab

4 day old hamburger buns or
  ½ loaf day old French bread
3 eggs
½ cup milk
½ cup butter
1 cup chopped green onions
½ cup chopped celery
2 cloves garlic, minced
½ cup chopped bell pepper
½ teaspoon worcestershire
  sauce
1 pound white crabmeat,
  picked and shredded
Salt, pepper and cayenne to
  taste
1 cup evaporated milk
¼ cup chives
¼ cup parsley
Breadcrumbs
Artificial crab shells

Soak bread or buns in egg and milk mixture until saturated. In skillet, sauté onions, celery, garlic and green pepper in butter until wilted. Add worcestershire and crabmeat. Season to taste with salt, black pepper and cayenne. Stir in evaporated milk. Cook over medium heat 15 minutes, stirring constantly. Add chives and parsley. Add bread mixture and mix well. Stuff artificial crab shells with mixture. Sprinkle tops of stuffed crabs with breadcrumbs. Bake at 375° for 10 minutes or until well brown.
Yield: 12 crab shells.

Freezes well.

Sunday Night Crabmeat Casserole

2 (6½ ounce) cans crabmeat
1 cup milk
1½ cups mayonnaise
6 hard boiled eggs, finely
    chopped
1 tablespoon chopped parsley
Salt and pepper to taste
1 cup breadcrumbs
1 tablespoon butter or marga-
    rine
Sliced water chestnuts, op-
    tional

Combine all ingredients, excluding breadcrumbs and butter. Pour into greased casserole dish. Set aside. Melt butter in skillet over medium heat. Add breadcrumbs, stirring until crisp. Top casserole with breadcrumbs. Bake at 350° for 40 minutes.
Yield: 4 servings.

Oysters Pierre

½ pound fresh mushrooms,
    thinly sliced
½ cup butter or margarine
3 tablespoons flour
3 small garlic cloves, minced
3 tablespoons finely chopped
    green onion
3 tablespoons minced parsley
¼ teaspoon cayenne pepper
1 teaspoon salt
½ cup dry sherry
4 dozen small oysters, well
    drained
½ cup breadcrumbs
Minced parsley

Sauté mushrooms in 2 tablespoons butter. Set aside. In heavy skillet, melt 4 tablespoons butter. Add flour. Cook on low heat, stirring constantly, until light brown. Add garlic, green onions and parsley. Cook 5 minutes. Add cayenne, salt and sherry. Add oysters and mushrooms. Simmer 5 minutes. Transfer mixture to individual ramekins. Top with breadcrumbs. Dot with remaining butter. Bake at 350° for 15 minutes, until bubbly. Sprinkle with minced parsley for garnish.
Yield: 6 servings.

*The state grass of Texas is sideoats grama
(Bouteloua curtipendula).*

Ernie's Hot Coquille

12 tablespoons butter
6 tablespoons flour
2 teaspoons salt
¼ teaspoon white pepper
3 cups light cream
1 pound scallops
½ cup finely chopped onion
1 cup sliced mushrooms
1 pound shrimp, cooked and
* shelled*
¼ cup sherry
1 pound crabmeat
6 tablespoons finely ground
* breadcrumbs*

Melt 9 tablespoons butter in saucepan. Add flour and cook over low heat for several minutes. Season with salt and pepper. Gradually add cream. Cook sauce, stirring constantly until it bubbles. Simmer 5 minutes. In a skillet, sauté scallops and onions in 3 tablepsoons of butter until onions are golden brown. Remove scallops and onions. In same skillet, sauté sliced mushrooms for 3 minutes. Combine mushrooms, scallops, onions and cream sauce. Stir in shrimp, crabmeat, and sherry. Place in 11x7 inch baking dish. Sprinkle with breadcrumbs. Bake at 400° for 10 minutes.
Yield: 10 servings.

Crawfish Étouffée Fettucine

1½ cups butter
3 medium onions, chopped
3 stalks celery, chopped
2 bell peppers, chopped
¼ cup flour
3 tablespoons chopped pars-
* ley*
2-3 pounds crawfish tails,
* peeled*
1 pint half and half cream
1 pound processed cheese,
* cubed*
2 tablespoons chopped jala-
* peño peppers*
3 garlic cloves, crushed
Salt and pepper to taste
1 (16 ounce) package fettuc-
* ine noodles*
Parmesan cheese to taste

Melt butter in large heavy saucepan. Add onions, celery, and bell pepper. Cook 10 minutes until clear. Add flour, blending well. Cover and cook 15 minutes, stirring occasionally. Add parsley and crawfish tails. Cover and cook 20 minutes, stirring often. Add cream, cheese, jalapeños, and garlic. Mix well. Add salt and pepper. Cook covered on low heat 20 minutes, stirring occasionally. Cook noodles according to package directions. Drain. Add sauce. Mix thoroughly. Pour into a 3 quart buttered baking dish. Sprinkle with Parmesan cheese. Bake at 350° for 12 minutes.
Yield: 12 servings.

"One Skillet" Breakfast

½ cup chopped green pepper
4-5 slices bacon, diced
½ cup chopped onion
⅓ cup mayonnaise or salad dressing
¼ cup milk
8 eggs, slightly beaten
2 tablespoons chopped pimiento

Combine green pepper, bacon and onion in skillet. Cook until bacon is crisp and onion and pepper are tender. Drain off excess fat. Combine mayonnise with milk. Add eggs and pimiento. Pour this mixture over bacon-vegetable mixture. Cook slowly, stirring occasionally until eggs are done. Yield: 4 servings.

Breakfast Pizza

1 pound bulk sausage
1 (8 ounce) can crescent rolls
1 cup frozen hash brown potatoes, thawed
2 cups grated Cheddar cheese
3 eggs
¼ cup milk
½ teaspoon salt
¼ teaspoon black pepper

Crumble sausage in frying pan. Cook and drain. Press crescent rolls onto greased pizza pan to make crust. Place sausage on crust. Layer hash browns, then cheese. Mix eggs, milk, salt, and pepper. Pour over sausage. Bake at 325° for 20-25 minutes. Yield: 6 servings.

Great for teenagers.

Breakfast Sausage Casserole

Must be made ahead. Keeps for several days.

16 slices bread, buttered
1 pound bulk pork sausage, cooked and drained
1½ cups shredded Cheddar cheese
6 eggs, beaten
2 cups half and half cream
1 teaspoon salt
Dash pepper

Layer buttered bread slices in a greased 13x9 inch baking dish. Top with cooked sausage. Sprinkle with cheese. Combine eggs, cream, salt and pepper. Pour over cheese. Cover casserole and chill overnight. Remove from refrigerator 15 minutes before baking. Bake uncovered casserole at 350° for 30-45 minutes, until set. Cut into squares. Yield: 8-10 servings.

Sausage Squares

1 pound bulk sausage
½ cup chopped onion
¼ cup grated Parmesan
   cheese
½ cup grated Swiss cheese
1 egg, beaten
¼ teaspoon hot pepper sauce
1¼ teaspoons salt
2 tablespoons chopped parsley
2 cups baking mix
⅔ cup milk
¼ cup mayonnaise
1 egg yolk, beaten

Cook sausage and onion until brown. Drain off fat. Add cheeses, beaten egg, pepper sauce, salt and parsley. Make dough by adding milk and mayonnaise to baking mix. Spread ½ of dough over bottom of a well greased 8 inch square pan. Cover with sausage mixture. Spread remaining dough over sausage mixture. Brush top with beaten egg yolk. Bake at 400° for 25-30 minutes. Cut into squares. Serve hot for breakfast or brunch. Yield: 16 squares.

May be made ahead of time and frozen.

Royal Breakfast Casserole

6 slices buttered bread
1 pound hot sausage, cooked
   and drained
6 large eggs, beaten
1 pint half and half cream
1 teaspoon mustard
1 teaspoon salt
4 cups grated Cheddar cheese

Layer buttered bread slices in a 13x9 inch baking dish. Top with cooked sausage. Beat eggs, cream, mustard, and salt together. Pour egg mixture over all. Top with Cheddar cheese. Bake at 350° for 30 minutes. Yield: 12 servings.

Egg mixture may be mixed together the night before. Great for New Year's Eve Breakfast or overnight guests.

Look for the lovely rain lilies a few days after a thunder-storm. The bulbs lie dormant in the soil until added moisture brings forth their dainty blooms.

24-Hour Wine and Cheese Omelet

1 large loaf day old French or
   Italian bread, broken into
   small pieces
6 tablespoons butter, melted
¾ pound Swiss cheese, shredded
½ pound Monterey Jack
   cheese, shredded
9 thin slices Genoa salami
   (¼-½ pound), coarsely
   chopped
16 eggs
3¼ cups milk
½ cup dry white wine
4 large whole green onions,
   minced
1 tablespoon spicy mustard
¼ teaspoon ground pepper
⅛ teaspoon red pepper
1½ cups sour cream
⅔-1 cup freshly grated Parmesan cheese

Butter two 13x9 inch baking dishes. Spread bread pieces over bottom and drizzle with butter. Sprinkle with Swiss and Monterey Jack cheeses and salami. Beat together eggs, milk, wine, green onions, mustard, and peppers until mixture is foamy. Pour egg mixture over cheese. Cover dishes with foil. Refrigerate overnight. Remove from refrigerator 30 minutes before baking. Bake, covered at 325° for 1 hour. Uncover, spread with sour cream and sprinkle with Parmesan. Bake uncovered until lightly browned, 10 minutes.
Yield: 20 servings.

Great for Brunch or Midnight Breakfast. Serve with salad or fruit and rolls.

Hamburger Quiche

½ pound ground beef
½ cup mayonnaise
½ cup milk
2 eggs
1 tablespoon cornstarch
½ pound Cheddar cheese,
   grated
½ cup chopped onion
Salt and pepper to taste
1 (9 inch) unbaked pie shell

Brown ground beef. Drain and set aside. Beat mayonnaise, milk, eggs and cornstarch together. Stir in cheese, onion, meat, salt and pepper. Pour into pie shell. Bake at 350° for 35-45 minutes.
Yield: 4 servings.

May be wrapped in foil and frozen after baking. Thaw. Warm in a low oven. This is a quiche kids love.

Vegetable-Sausage Quiche

1 pound bulk hot sausage
1 (10 ounce) package frozen
 broccoli or spinach
1 cup whipping cream
8 ounces processed cheese
1 cup grated Cheddar cheese
4 eggs
2 (9 inch) unbaked pie shells
1 cup grated mozzarella
 cheese

Crumble sausage in pan. Cook and drain. Cook broccoli or spinach and drain. Heat cream in top of double boiler until hot. Add Cheddar cheese and processed cheese to cream. Stir until melted. Beat 4 eggs. Add to cream. Let cool. Layer in pie shell: sausage, vegetable, cream/cheese mixture. Top with mozzarella cheese. Bake at 350° for 30-40 minutes.
Yield: 2 quiches.

Asparagus & Ham Quiche

1 (9 inch) unbaked pie shell
1 cup grated Swiss cheese
1 ounce grated Gruyère cheese
8-12 spears cooked asparagus
8-12 slices boiled ham
3 eggs
1⅓ cups half and half cream
½ teaspoon salt
Pinch of cayenne pepper
Nutmeg, freshly ground

Sprinkle base of pie shell with ¼ of the grated cheeses. Wrap each spear of asparagus with a slice of ham. Arrange these in a circle in the unbaked pie shell. Sprinkle remainder of cheese over ham and base of pie shell.

Beat eggs slightly. Add half and half, salt, cayenne, and nutmeg. Mix well. Pour into prepared pie shell. Bake at 375° for 35-45 minutes, until a knife comes out clean from the center of mixture. Remove from oven. Cool 7-10 minutes before serving.
Yield: 6-8 servings.

Great luncheon dish.

Cheese and Pepper Soufflé

1 teaspoon butter
1 (12 ounce) jar jalapeño
  peppers
1 pound sharp Cheddar
  cheese, grated
1 pound Monterey Jack
  cheese, grated
6 eggs
1 (12 ounce) can evaporated
  milk

Wash, split, and remove seeds from peppers. Drain on paper towel. Butter a 13x9 inch baking dish. Place one scant layer of mixed grated cheese on bottom of dish. Layer the peppers and remaining cheese. Beat eggs and milk. Pour over mixture in dish. Bake at 350° for 40-45 minutes. Cool. Cut into bite-size squares.
Yield: 48 squares.

Great for brunch.

Chilies Rellenos

1 (7 ounce) can whole green
  chilies
½ pound Monterey Jack
  cheese, grated
½ pound Cheddar cheese,
  grated
3 eggs
2¼ cups milk
1 cup baking mix
Seasoned salt

Preheat oven to 325°. Split chilies, rinse, and remove seeds. Dry and arrange on bottom of 11x8 inch baking dish. Sprinkle grated cheeses on top of chilies. Beat eggs, blending in milk and baking mix. Pour over cheese and chilies. Sprinkle with seasoned salt. Bake 50-55 minutes.
Yield: 8 servings.

Good for Breakfast, Brunch or Lunch.

Phlox cuspidata

Mexican Quiche

8 eggs, beaten
½ cup flour
1 teaspoon baking powder
2 cups cottage cheese
½ pound Cheddar cheese, grated
½ pound Monterey Jack cheese, grated
¼ cup melted butter
1 (7 ounce) can chopped green chiles, drained

Combine all ingredients in a large bowl. Mix well. Pour into a greased 13x9 baking dish. Bake at 350° for 1 hour.
Yield: 8 servings.

May be made ahead. Reheat before serving.

Electric Blender Soufflé

1 tablespoon butter, softened
6 eggs
¼ cup grated Parmesan cheese
½ teaspoon mustard
½ pound sharp Cheddar cheese
11 ounces cream cheese

Butter soufflé dish. Blend eggs, Parmesan cheese and mustard in an electric blender. Cut Cheddar cheese into squares. Add to mixture while blending. Cut cream cheese into pieces. Add while blending. Continue blending at high speed five seconds. Pour into soufflé dish. Bake at 350° for 50 minutes.
Yield: 8 servings.

Overnight Brunch Casserole

Must be made ahead.

½ cup chopped green onion
½ cup chopped green pepper
2 tablespoons butter or margarine
8 eggs
3 cups chopped cooked ham
3 cups milk
2 cups grated Cheddar cheese
1⅓ cup quick cooking oats plus oat bran
¼ cup chopped mushrooms

Sauté onion and green pepper in butter until tender. Beat eggs. Add all remaining ingredients. Mix well. Pour into a greased 13x9 inch baking dish. Refrigerate overnight. Bake uncovered at 325° for 45 minutes.
Yield: 12 servings.

Apple-Cheese Breakfast Casserole

Must be made ahead.

1 (21 ounce) can apple pie filling
1 teaspoon cinnamon
6 slices bread
2 tablespoons butter, melted
4 eggs
½ cup milk
½ teaspoon salt
¼ teaspoon nutmeg
1 cup grated Cheddar cheese

Combine pie filling with cinnamon. Set aside. Cut bread into 1 inch cubes. Brush sides and bottom of a 12 inch pie plate with melted butter. Spread bread cubes in bottom of dish. Drizzle with remaining butter. Beat eggs with milk, salt and nutmeg. Pour eggs and milk mixture over cubes. Spoon pie filling over cubes. Top with grated cheese. Cover and refrigerate overnight. Bake uncovered at 375° for 30 minutes.
Yield: 8 servings.

Ruellia nudiflora

Wild petunia - *Ruellia nudiflora*
Here's an excellent perennial for wildflower gardens. With adequate water, wild petunia's purple flowers will bloom from spring to fall. Each day, new blossoms open as the old ones wither. Found commonly in the Hill Country, wild petunia grows up to 2 feet tall.

Strawberry Jello Cake

1 (16½ ounce) white cake mix
1 (3 ounce) box strawberry
   gelatin
½ cup oil
½ cup cold water
4 eggs
½ (10 ounce) box frozen
   strawberries, thawed

Mix together cake mix and jello. Add oil and water. Add eggs, one at a time. Add strawberries. Pour into 2 (9 inch) pans, lined with waxed paper. Bake at 350° for 20-25 minutes.

Mix at medium speed until fluffy. Ice cooled cake.
Yield: 20 servings.

Icing:
1 (16 ounce) box powdered
   sugar, sifted
½ cup margarine, softened
½ (10 ounce) box frozen
   strawberries, thawed

Boston Cream Cake

Cake:
3 eggs, beaten
1 cup sugar
1 cup flour
1 teaspoon baking powder
2 tablespoons milk

Mix all ingredients well. Pour into 2 (9 inch) greased and floured cake pans. Bake at 375° for 25 minutes. Cool. Slice horizontally through center to yield 4 thin cake layers.

Filling:
2 cups milk
1 cup sugar
½ cup flour
2 eggs
1 tablespoon butter
1½ teaspoons vanilla
Whipped cream
Fresh strawberries, optional
Melted chocolate, optional
Chocolate curls, optional

Bring milk to boil. Mix sugar and flour. Break eggs into bowl. Add sugar and flour mixture. Stir mixture into milk as it begins to boil. Add butter. Stir until thickened. Add vanilla and cool. Spread filling between layers. Reassemble layers to make one 4 layered cake. Frost with whipped cream. Decorate with fresh strawberries, melted chocolate, or chocolate curls.
Yield: 12 servings.

Christmas Breakfast Cake

Cake:
1 (8 ounce) package cream
   cheese
1 cup butter or margarine
1½ cups sugar
1½ teaspoons vanilla
4 eggs
2¼ cups flour
1½ teaspoons baking powder
½ cup chopped pecans
¾ cup chopped maraschino
   cherries
½ cup finely chopped pecans

Glaze:
1½ cups powdered sugar
2 tablespoons milk
Whole cherries, optional
Whole pecans, optional

Blend cream cheese, butter or margarine, sugar and vanilla. Add eggs, one at a time, mixing ingredients after each egg. Add 2 cups flour and baking powder. Combine remaining flour with nuts. Fold into batter. Fold in cherries. Grease tube pan. Sprinkle pan with finely chopped nuts. Pour in batter. Bake at 325° for 1 hour 20 minutes. Cool 5 minutes before removing cake from pan.

Mix powdered sugar and milk in small bowl. Glaze while cake is still warm. Garnish with cherries and pecans.
Yield: 12 servings.

This keeps well in refrigerator for a few days and makes a nice Christmas gift for a friend or neighbor.

Some seeds need special treatment before they will germinate. Bluebonnets, for instance, have a hard seed coat which must be scarified, or broken down. Others need a cold, moist period, or statification in order to germinate.

Tropical Dream Cake

Cake:
2 cups sugar
1 cup cooking oil
3 eggs
1 (8 ounce) can crushed
  pineapple
1½ teaspoons vanilla
2 cups flour
1 cup whole wheat flour
1 teaspoon salt
1 teaspoon baking soda
1 teaspoon baking powder
1 teaspoon cinnamon
2 cups diced bananas

Glaze:
1¾ cups sifted powdered
  sugar
2-3 tablespoons orange juice

Beat sugar and oil. Add eggs one at a time. Blend in undrained pineapple and vanilla. Stir together flours, salt, baking soda, baking powder and cinnamon. Blend into pineapple mixture. Stir in bananas. Pour into greased bundt pan. Bake at 350° for 60-70 minutes. Cool 10 minutes before removing cake from pan.

Mix powdered sugar and orange juice. Drizzle cooled cake with glaze.
Yield: 15-20 servings.

Helianthus annuus

Italian Cream Cake

Cake:
1 cup buttermilk
1 teaspoon baking soda
5 eggs, separated
2 cups sugar
½ cup margarine
½ cup shortening
2 cups sifted flour
1 teaspoon vanilla
1 cup chopped pecans
1 (4 ounce) can coconut

Icing:
1 (8 ounce) package cream
   cheese, softened
½ cup margarine, softened
1 (16 ounce) box powdered
   sugar
1 teaspoon vanilla

Preheat oven to 325°. Combine soda and buttermilk. Let stand a few minutes. Beat egg whites until stiff. Cream sugar, margarine and shortening. Add egg yolks, one at a time, beating after each addition. Add buttermilk alternately with flour to creamed mixture. Stir in vanilla. Fold in egg whites. Gently stir in pecans and coconut. Pour into 3 (9 inch) greased and floured pans. Bake at 325° for 25 minutes, until cake tests done.

Cream cheese and margarine. Add vanilla. Beat in powdered sugar a little at a time until mixture is of spreading consistency.
Yield: 20 servings.

Freezes well.

Banana Crunch Cake

5 tablespoons butter or margarine
1 (16.5 ounce) box coconut
   pecan or coconut almond
   frosting mix
1 cup rolled oats
1 cup sour cream
4 eggs
2 large bananas, mashed
1 (18.5 ounce) yellow cake
   mix

Preheat oven to 350°. Grease and flour a 10 inch tube pan. Melt butter. Stir in frosting mix and oats until crumbly. Set aside. Blend sour cream, eggs, and bananas in large bowl. Blend in cake mix. Beat 2 minutes. Pour 2 cups batter into prepared pan. Sprinkle with 1 cup crumb mixture. Bake 50-60 minutes until toothpick inserted in center comes out clean. Cool in pan 15 minutes. Remove from pan. Turn cake so crumb mixture is on top.
Yield: 15-20 servings.

Perfect for Brunch or Breakfast.

Banana Split Cake

Crust:
2 cups crushed graham crackers
½ cup butter, softened

Filling:
1 (3 ounce) package cream cheese, softened
2 cups powdered sugar
4 bananas, sliced
1 (8 ounce) can crushed pineapple, drained
1 (8 ounce) carton frozen whipped topping, thawed
1 (5.5 ounce) can chocolate syrup
1 (6 ounce) jar maraschino cherries, sliced
1 cup chopped nuts
Fresh strawberries

Mix crackers and butter together. Press into 13x9 inch pan to form crust. Bake at 400° for 5 minutes. Cool 30 minutes.

Mix cream cheese and sugar together. Spread over crust. Layer remaining ingredients. Refrigerate 2 hours or until firm.
Yield: 12 servings.

Wonderful summertime dessert.

Peachy Lemon Cake

1 (18.5 ounce) deluxe lemon cake mix

Icing:
1 (16.5 ounce) can vanilla cream frosting mix
¼ teaspoon ground ginger
½ teaspoon rum extract
1⅓ cups frozen sliced peaches, thawed and drained or 3 medium ripe peaches, peeled, pitted and sliced

Prepare cake as directed on package for 2 (8x1½ inch) round layer pans.

Prepare vanilla cream frosting mix as directed on package. Add ginger and rum extract. Spread half of frosting on one cake layer. Arrange peach slices on frosting. Add second layer. Top with frosting and peaches. Refrigerate until served.
Yield: 20 servings.

Candy Apple Cake

2 cups sugar
1½ cups oil
3 eggs
3 cups flour
1 teaspoon salt
1 teaspoon baking soda
¾ teaspoon cinnamon
¼ teaspoon nutmeg
1 teaspoon vanilla
1 tablespoon lemon juice
3 cups chopped apples
1½ cups chopped pecans or
   walnuts

Icing:
½ cup brown sugar, packed
2 tablespoons cream
¼ cup butter

Mix sugar, oil and eggs. Sift flour. Add salt, soda and spices. Add to oil mixture. Add flavorings, apples and nuts. Pour into greased bundt pan. Bake at 350° for 1 hour.

Boil ingredients 2½ minutes, stirring constantly. Pour over warm cake.
Yield: 15-20 servings.

Freezes well. Good cake to take to a family with small children - a nice change from a pound cake.

Applesauce Cake

2½ cups cake flour
2 cups sugar
1½ teaspoons baking soda
1½ teaspoons salt
¼ teaspoon baking powder
¾ teaspoon cinnamon
½ teaspoon cloves
½ teaspoon allspice
1½ cups applesauce
½ cup water
½ cup oil
2 eggs
1 cup raisins
½ cup chopped walnuts
Powdered sugar

Beat first 12 ingredients together. Add raisins and walnuts. Pour into a 13x9 inch greased and floured pan. Bake at 350° for 30 minutes. Cool. Sprinkle with powdered sugar.
Yield: 16-20 servings.

May be frozen. When adding raisins, toss lightly with flour so they do not sink to bottom of cake.

Fabulous Carrot Cake

2 cups sugar
2 cups flour
2 teaspoons baking soda
2 teaspoons cinnamon
4 eggs, beaten
1 (8 ounce) can crushed
    pineapple
1½ cups salad oil
2 teaspoons vanilla
1 teaspoon salt
1 cup flaked coconut
2 cups grated carrots
1 cup chopped pecans

Frosting:
6 ounces cream cheese,
    softened
1 (16 ounce) box powdered
    sugar
½ cup butter, softened
1 teaspoon lemon juice
Dash salt

Sift together sugar, flour, baking soda and cinnamon. In a separate bowl, mix eggs, crushed pineapple including juice, oil, vanilla, salt, coconut, carrots and pecans. Add dry ingredients to liquid mixture. Line 3 (8 inch) pans with waxed paper. Bake at 350° for 35-40 minutes. Cool on rack for 30 minutes.

Combine all ingredients. Frost cake when cool.
Yield: 20 servings.

Coconut Cake

1 (18.5 ounce) white cake mix
¼ cup oil
1 cup sour cream
1 (15 ounce) can cream of
    coconut
3 eggs

Icing:
1 (16 ounce) box powdered
    sugar
1 (8 ounce) package cream
    cheese, softened
1 teaspoon vanilla
1 tablespoon milk
1 cup grated coconut

Mix ingredients in order given. Bake in a greased and floured 13x9 inch pan. Bake at 325° for 50 minutes. May be baked in 2 (8 inch) pans for 40 minutes.

Beat first 4 ingredients until fluffy. Sprinkle coconut on top.
Yield: 24 squares.

Bundt Crunch Cake

Crust:
½ cup butter, melted
⅓ cup sugar
1 cup chopped pecans
2 cups crushed vanilla wafers

Filling:
1 cup butter, softened
2 cups sugar
4 eggs
1 cup milk
1½ teaspoons vanilla
2⅔ cups flour
½ teaspoon salt
1½ teaspoons baking powder
1 teaspoon butter flavoring

Mix all ingredients. Press onto bottom and sides of well greased bundt pan. (Two loaf pans may also be used if desired.)

Cream butter and sugar until light and fluffy. Add eggs and beat. Combine milk and vanilla with beaten eggs. Mix remaining dry ingredients. Add to batter alternately with dry ingredients, starting and ending with dry ingredients. Add butter flavoring. Pour into crust. Bake at 325° for 1-1 hour 15 minutes, until done. Turn out on rack to cool.
Yield: 15-20 servings.

Amaretto Bundt Cake

Cake:
½ cup ground pecans
2 (7 ounce) packages almond paste
1 deluxe yellow cake mix
1 (3¾ ounces) package instant vanilla pudding mix
4 eggs
½ cup vegetable oil
½ cup Amaretto liqueur
½ cup water

Glaze:
½ cup butter
½ cup sugar
¼ cup Amaretto liqueur
¼ cup water

Lightly grease bundt cake pan. Sprinkle ground pecans evenly over the bottom. Crumble almond paste in food processor with steel blade. Blend with cake mix and instant pudding mix in a large bowl. Add eggs, oil, Amaretto and water. Beat 4 minutes until mixture is well blended. Pour into pan. Bake at 350° for 1 hour. Cool 10 minutes.

Melt butter in microwave on high 1 minute in a 4 cup measure. Add sugar, Amaretto and water. Bring to boil on high 2 minutes. Stir once. Make slits in top of cake. Pour glaze over cake in pan. Let stand several hours. Invert on a serving dish.
Yield: 15-20 servings.

Coconut Pound Cake

3 cups sugar
½ cup butter, softened
⅔ cup shortening
5 eggs
3 cups flour
1 teaspoon baking powder
½ teaspoon salt
1 cup milk
1 cup flaked coconut
1½ teaspoons vanilla

Cream sugar, butter and shortening. Add eggs, one at a time, beating after each addition. Sift flour, baking powder and salt. Add to creamed mixture alternately with milk. Stir in coconut and vanilla. Pour into bundt pan. Bake at 325° for 1½ hours.
Yield: 15-20 servings.

7-Up Pound Cake

Vegetable cooking spray
1 cup margarine, softened
½ cup shortening
3 cups sugar
5 eggs
3 cups flour
6 ounces lemon-lime carbon-
    ated drink
1 teaspoon vanilla
1 teaspoon almond flavoring
1 teaspoon butter flavoring

Spray bundt pan with vegetable cooking spray. Cream margarine, shortening and sugar. Add remaining ingredients. Pour into prepared pan. Bake at 325° for 1 hour.
Yield: 15-20 servings.

Freezes well.

Sisyrinchium sagittiferum

Rum Cake

This cake gets better with time. Prepare a day ahead.

1 (18.5 ounce) package butter
   recipe cake mix
1 (3 ounce) package instant
   vanilla pudding mix
½ cup oil
½ cup rum
½ cup water
4 eggs
1½ cups chopped pecans

Icing:
1 cup sugar
¼ cup water
¼ cup butter
¼ cup rum

Preheat oven to 350°. Grease and flour an angel food cake pan or bundt cake pan. Mix first 6 ingredients for 4 minutes. Sprinkle chopped pecans on bottom of pan. Pour cake batter over pecans. Bake at 350° for 50 minutes.

Boil all ingredients together. Pour over hot cake while in pan. Let stand 30 minutes. Invert cake.
Yield: 10-12 servings.

Lillie Mae's Lemon Pound Cake

1½ cups butter, softened
1 (8 ounce) package cream
   cheese, softened
3 cups sugar
6 eggs
3 cups flour
1½ teaspoons vanilla
1 teaspoon lemon extract

Preheat oven to 350°. Grease and flour a tube cake pan. Cream butter and cream cheese. Add sugar. Add eggs one at a time. Add flour, vanilla and lemon extract. Blend until smooth. Bake 1 hour and 20 minutes.
Yield: 15-20 servings.

M-M-Mocha Cake

4 squares unsweetened
  chocolate
½ cup hot water
½ cup sugar
2 cups cake flour, sifted
1 teaspoon baking soda
1 teaspoon salt
½ cup butter or margarine,
  softened
1¼ cups sugar
1 teaspoon vanilla
3 eggs
⅔ cup milk

Filling:
3 cups heavy cream, chilled
1½ cups powdered sugar,
  sifted
½ cup unsweetened cocoa,
  sifted
⅛ teaspoon salt
2 teaspoons instant coffee

Decoration:
½ square semi-sweet chocolate, melted
14 whole unblanched almonds

Combine chocolate and hot water in double boiler. Stir constantly over hot water to melt chocolate. Add ½ cup sugar. Cook, stirring 2 minutes to dissolve. Remove from hot water. Cool to lukewarm. Sift flour with soda and salt. Beat butter until fluffy at medium speed in a large mixing bowl. Gradually beat in 1¼ cups sugar. Add vanilla. Add eggs, one at a time and beat after each addition. Add flour mixture, alternately with milk. Blend in chocolate. Pour into 2 (9 inch) greased and floured pans. Bake at 350° for 25 minutes until surface springs back. (Do not overbake.) Cool 10 minutes. Invert layers. Cool on racks.

Combine cream, sugar, cocoa, salt and coffee in medium bowl. Refrigerate 30 minutes. Beat until stiff. Refrigerate again. Split layers in half to make four. Place layer, cut side up, on plate. Spread with ⅔ cup mocha filling. Repeat twice. Top with last layer, cut side down. Turn 1¼ cups filling into pastry bag with #2 star tip. Frost remaining top and sides of cake smoothly. With pastry bag, make a swirl around top of cake and make a small circle the same inside. Go around base of cake the same way.

Dip almonds in chocolate covering half of almond. Arrange on cake.

Yield: 20-25 servings.

The white area of the "banner" petals of bluebonnets indicate to pollinators that the pollen is good. Once the flower has been pollinated or gets old, the white spot turns red.

Fudge Cake

Cake:
1 cup butter
4 tablespoons cocoa
2 cups sugar
4 eggs
1⅓ cups flour
2 teaspoons vanilla
4 cups chopped nuts
35 marshmallows

Icing:
½ cup butter
¼ cup milk
¼ cup cocoa
1 (16 ounce) box powdered
* sugar*
1 teaspoon vanilla

Line 13x9 inch pan with waxed paper. Melt butter and cocoa. Cool. Mix sugar and eggs. Add butter and cocoa. Add flour and mix. Add vanilla and nuts. Pour into prepared pan. Bake at 350° for 30-45 minutes. While cake bakes, cut 35 marshmallows in half. Place cut side of marshmallows on hot cake. Cool.

Melt butter. Add milk and cocoa. Stir in powdered sugar and vanilla. Pour over cooled cake.
Yield: 16-20 servings.

Peanut Butter Cake

Cake:
1 (18.5 ounce) box golden
* vanilla pudding recipe cake*
* mix*
⅓ cup peanut butter

Icing:
½ cup evaporated milk
1 cup sugar
½ cup butter
½ cup semi-sweet chocolate
* chips*
⅓ cup peanut butter

Prepare cake mix as directed on box. Add peanut butter. Bake in 13x9 inch cake pan.

Boil milk, sugar, and butter for 3 minutes. Immediately add the chocolate chips and peanut butter. Take from heat and beat quickly. Pour on cake.
Yield: 24 servings.

Freezes well.

Cheesecake

Must be made ahead.

Crust:
1 ¾ cups graham cracker
   crumbs
¼ cup sugar
⅓ cup butter

Filling:
9 ounces cream cheese
4 eggs
1 ½ teaspoons vanilla
¾ cup sugar

Topping:
1 pint sour cream
½ cup sugar
1 ½ teaspoons vanilla
Fresh strawberries, optional

Add sugar and butter to graham cracker crumbs. Press crust into bottom of springform pan. Bake at 375° for 8 minutes.

Beat cream cheese until soft. Add eggs one at a time, mixing well after each addition. Add vanilla and sugar. Pour over crust. Bake at 325° for 55 minutes.

Mix sour cream, sugar and vanilla. Pour over cake. Bake at 325° for 5 minutes. Top with fresh strawberries if desired. Refrigerate cake at least 9 hours.
Yield: 20-25 servings.

Award Winning Cheesecake

Crust:
2 cups graham cracker
  crumbs
½ teaspoon cinnamon
1 tablespoon sugar
4 tablespoons butter, melted

Filling:
¾ cup sugar
3 eggs
3 (8 ounce) packages cream
  cheese, softened
1 teaspoon vanilla
1 teaspoon lemon juice
3 cups sour cream
¼ cup butter, melted

Combine crust ingredients (saving 1 cup of crumbs to sprinkle on top of cake). Press into a 9 inch springform pan. Bake at 350° for 8 minutes. Cool.

Beat sugar and eggs. Add cream cheese, vanilla, lemon juice and sour cream. Beat well. Add melted butter and beat.

Pour filling over crust. Sprinkle top with remaining crumb mixture. Bake at 350° for 60 minutes. Turn oven off, open door, and leave cake in to cool 1 ½ hours. Refrigerate.
Yield: 20-25 servings.

New York Cheesecake

Must be made ahead.

5 (8 ounce) packages cream
  cheese, softened
1¾ cups sugar
3 tablespoons flour
1 teaspoon vanilla
Juice of one lemon
5 whole eggs plus 2 egg yolks
¼ cup whipping cream
1 (16 ounce) can pie filling,
  any flavor

Mix first 5 ingredients until smooth. Add whole eggs, one at a time, egg yolks and whipping cream. Bake in a greased angel food cake pan at 500° for 10 minutes. Reduce heat to 225°. Bake 1 hour and 20 minutes. Cool. Remove from pan and top with pie filling. Refrigerate at least 4 hours.
Yield: 15-20 servings.

Chocolate Cheesecake

Must be made ahead.

Crust:
1 (8 ounce) box chocolate
  wafers, crushed
½ cup margarine, melted
¼ teaspoon cinnamon

Filling:
1 (12 ounce) package chocolate chips, melted
4 (8 ounce) packages cream
  cheese, softened
2 cups sugar
4 eggs
1 tablespoon cocoa
2 teaspoons vanilla
2 cups sour cream

Combine crushed wafers, margarine and cinnamon. Press into a 10-inch springform pan. Chill crust.

Beat cream cheese until fluffy and smooth. Gradually beat in sugar and eggs, one at a time, beating after each addition. Add melted chocolate chips, cocoa and vanilla. Blend well. Stir in sour cream. Pour filling into crust. Bake at 350° for 1 hour and 10 minutes. Cool to room temperature. Chill 5 hours.
Yield: 20-25 servings.

Freezes well. Extremely rich.

Peanut Butter Cheesecake

Must be made ahead.

Crust:
1 (12 ounce) box vanilla
    wafers
½ cup sugar
2 tablespoons butter, melted

Filling:
2 (8 ounce) packages cream
    cheese, softened
1½ cups sugar
1 (6 ounce) jar creamy pea-
    nut butter
5 eggs
½ cup sour cream
2 teaspoons fresh lemon juice
1 cup chocolate chips

Topping:
1 cup sour cream
¾ cup chocolate chips, melted
½ cup sugar

Combine ingredients in food processor. Press mixture onto bottom and sides of a springform pan.

Combine all ingredients except chocolate chips in food processor and blend until smooth. Add chocolate chips and mix off and on for 10 seconds. Spread filling on crust. Bake at 350° for 70-80 minutes, until center of filling is firm. Let stand at room temperature for 15 minutes.

Blend all ingredients. Spread over cheese-cake. Bake for 10 additional minutes. Let cool. Refregerate 3 hours before serving. Yield: 8-10 servings.

Almond Bars

1 box Coconut Almond or
    Coconut Pecan frosting mix
1 cup flour
½ cup butter or margarine,
    melted
2 teaspoons almond extract
1 cup powdered sugar
½ teaspoon almond extract
2-3 tablespoons milk

Preheat oven to 400°. Grease 13x9 inch baking pan. Combine frosting mix, flour, butter, and 2 teaspoons almond extract. Press into pan. Bake 10-12 minutes. Combine sugar, ½ teaspoon almond extract and enough milk to make icing. Drizzle over bars while still warm. Cut into bars while warm. Yield: 2 dozen.

Karen's Lemon Squares

Crust:
2 cups flour
1 cup butter, softened
½ cup powdered sugar

Topping:
4 eggs
2 cups sugar
Dash salt
Juice of 2 lemons
¼ cup flour
1 teaspoon baking powder
Powdered sugar

Preheat oven to 350°. Mix crust ingredients and press into a 13x9 inch baking pan. Bake 20 minutes.

Mix eggs, sugar, salt and lemon juice. Blend in flour and baking powder. Pour mixture over hot crust. Bake 25 minutes. Cool. Cut into squares. Sprinkle with powdered sugar. Yield: 24 squares.

Butterscotch Cheesecake Bars

⅓ cup butter or margarine
1 (12 ounce) package
  butterscotch morsels
2 cups graham cracker crumbs
1 cup chopped pecans
1 (8 ounce) package cream
  cheese, softened
1 (14 ounce) can sweetened
  condensed milk
1 teaspoon vanilla
1 egg

Preheat oven to 350°. Melt butter and butterscotch in a medium saucepan. Stir in crumbs and nuts. Press half of the mixture into bottom of a greased 13x9 inch baking pan. Beat cream cheese until fluffy. Beat in milk, vanilla and egg. Mix well. Pour into prepared pan. Top with remaining crumb mixture. Bake 25-30 minutes (until toothpick inserted near center comes out clean). Cool to room temperature. Chill before cutting into bars. Store in refrigerator.
Yield: 30 bars.

Pumpkin Cheesecake Bars

Layer 1:
1 (16 ounce) package pound
   cake mix
1 egg
2 tablespoons margarine,
   melted
2 teaspoons pumpkin pie
   spice

Layer 2:
1 (8 ounce) package cream
   cheese, softened
1 (14 ounce) can sweetened
   condensed milk
1 (16 ounce) can pumpkin
2 eggs
½ teaspoon salt
2 teaspoons pumpkin pie
   spice
1 cup chopped nuts

Preheat oven to 350°. In a large mixing bowl, on low speed of mixer, combine Layer 1 ingredients until crumbly. Press into bottom of 15x10 inch jelly roll pan.

Beat cream cheese until fluffy in a large mixing bowl. Gradually beat in remaining ingredients, excluding nuts. Mix well. Pour over crust. Top with nuts. Bake 35 minutes. Cover and chill. Cut into bars. Store in refrigerator.
Yield: 48 bars.

Great treats for Halloween! Freeze well after cooking.

Chess Bars

Crust:
1 egg, slightly beaten
1 (18.25 ounce) package
   yellow butter recipe cake
   mix
½ cup butter, softened

Topping:
1 (8 ounce) package cream
   cheese, softened
3 eggs
1 teaspoon vanilla
1 (16 ounce) box powdered
   sugar

Preheat oven to 350°. Combine crust ingredients. Press mixture into a 13x9 inch baking pan.

Beat cream cheese with eggs and vanilla. Blend in powdered sugar, beating until smooth. Pour over crust. Bake at 350° for 10 minutes. Reduce heat to 325°. Bake 30 minutes. The cheese mixture blends into crust. (Do not burn.) Cut into bars.
Yield: 24 bars.

Freeze well.

Chocolate Buttersweets

Cookie:
1 cup butter or margarine, softened
1 cup powdered sugar
½ teaspoon salt
1 teaspoon vanilla
2½ cups flour

Creamy Nut Filling:
1 (3 ounce) package cream cheese, softened
1 cup sifted powdered sugar
2 tablespoons flour
1 teaspoon lemon flavoring
½ cup chopped walnuts
¼ cup flaked coconut

Chocolate Frosting:
1 cup semi-sweet chocolate morsels
4 tablespoons butter or margarine
4 tablespoons water
1 cup sifted powdered sugar

Cream butter and sugar until light and fluffy. Add salt and vanilla, beating well. Gradually stir in flour, mixing until well blended. Shape dough into 1 inch balls. Place on ungreased cookie sheet. Press a hole in the center of each ball, using top of a thimble dipped in flour. Bake at 350° for 12-15 minutes, until lightly browned.

Combine cream cheese, powdered sugar, flour and lemon flavoring. Beat until smooth. Stir in walnuts and coconut. While cookies are still warm, fill center of each with 1 teaspoon filling.

Combine chocolate, butter and water in small saucepan. Stir until completely melted over low heat. Remove from heat. Stir in powdered sugar. Beat until smooth. (If frosting is too thick, blend in a few more drops of water.) Frost cooled cookies.
Yield: 4 dozen.

Oenothera missouriensis

Snowballs

¾ *cup butter, softened*
1 *teaspoon vanilla*
1 *tablespoon water*
⅛ *teaspoon salt*
⅓ *cup sugar*
2 *cups less 4 tablespoons*
  flour
1 *(16 ounce) package semi-*
  sweet chocolate chips
1 *cup finely ground pecans*
Powdered sugar

Preheat oven to 300°. Combine butter, vanilla, water, salt and sugar. Stir in flour and chips. Add pecans and mix. Form into 1 inch balls. Bake on an ungreased cookie sheet 30 minutes. Roll cookies in powdered sugar while still warm.
Yield: 4 dozen.

Snowcapped Chocolate Cookies

½ *cup shortening*
4 *ounces unsweetened choco-*
  late
2 *cups sugar*
2 *teaspoons vanilla*
4 *eggs*
2 *cups flour*
2 *teaspoons baking powder*
⅛ *teaspoon salt*
½ *cup chopped nuts*
Powdered sugar

Melt chocolate and shortening. Add sugar and vanilla. Mix well. Add eggs, beating well after each egg. Sift flour, baking powder and salt together. Add to chocolate mixture along with nuts. Chill dough until balls can be formed. Bake at 350° for 12-15 minutes. Roll in powdered sugar.
Yield: 4 dozen.

Bees can see only four main colors: yellow-orange, blue, blue-green, and ultraviolet. They are red "colorblind". Hummingbirds, on the other hand, usually find red flowers most attractive.

Peppermint Tea Party Brownies

Cake:
½ cup butter
2 (1 ounce) squares un-
   sweetened chocolate
2 eggs
1 cup sugar
½ cup sifted flour
⅛ teaspoon salt
½ cup chopped nuts
¼ teaspoon peppermint
   extract

Icing:
1 cup sifted powdered sugar
2 tablespoons butter, softened
Food coloring (green or red)
1 tablespoon cream
¾ teaspoon peppermint
   extract

Glaze:
1 (1 ounce) square semi-
   sweet chocolate
1 tablespoon butter

Melt butter and chocolate together. Beat 2 eggs until light and lemon-colored. Add to chocolate mixture. Add sugar and mix well. Add flour, salt, nuts, and extract. Pour into 11x7 inch pan. Bake at 350° for 20 minutes. Cool.

Mix all ingredients until spreading consistency. Spread over entire cake layer. Refrigerate until set.

Melt chocolate and butter. Spread over icing layer. Refrigerate. Cut into bars. Let stand out 10-15 minutes before serving.
Yield: 3 dozen.

May be doubled and stored in freezer until ready to serve. (Layer with wax paper.) Use a jelly roll pan when doubling.

Thelesperma filifolium

Best Chocolate Brownies Ever

½ cup butter or margarine
2 (1 ounce) squares un-
    sweetened chocolate
2 eggs
1 cup sugar
⅔ cup flour
1 teaspoon vanilla
½ cup chopped nuts, optional

Melt butter and chocolate. Cool slightly. Beat eggs and sugar together. Add chocolate mixture. Beat. Add flour and vanilla. Beat. Bake at 325° for 25 minutes in a greased 10x7 inch pan.
Yield: 8 servings.

May be frozen and/or frosted.

Turtle Caramel Brownies

1 (14 ounce) package cara-
    mels
⅓ cup evaporated milk
1 (18.25 ounce) box German
    chocolate cake mix
¾ cup butter, melted
1 cup chopped pecans
⅓ cup evaporated milk
1 (6 ounce) package choco-
    late chips

Preheat oven to 350°. Melt caramels and ⅓ cup evaporated milk in a heavy saucepan. Use low heat, stirring often. Keep warm. In a large bowl, mix remaining ingredients except chocolate chips. Press half the dough into a lightly greased and floured 13x9 inch pan. Bake for 6 minutes. Sprinkle with chocolate chips. Spread caramel mixture over chips. Using a spatula, spread remaining dough evenly over caramel. Bake 15-20 minutes more. Cool completely before cutting.
Yield: 3 dozen.

Tastes like chocolate turtle candy. Delicious!

Oatmeal Chocolate Chip Cookies

1 cup butter or margarine,
softened
1 cup brown sugar, packed
1 cup sugar
2 eggs
1 teaspoon vanilla
2 cups flour
1 teaspoon baking soda
½ teaspoon salt
½ teaspoon baking powder
2 cups oatmeal
1 (12 ounce) package chocolate chips
½ cup chopped nuts

Cream together butter, sugars, eggs, and vanilla until fluffy. Sift flour, soda, salt and baking powder together. Stir into butter mixture. Add oatmeal, chocolate chips, and nuts. Drop by teaspoon onto cookie sheet. Bake at 350° for 10-12 minutes.
Yield: 8 dozen.

Freezes well.

Snickerdoodles

½ cup butter or margarine
½ cup shortening
1½ cups sugar
2 eggs
2¾ cups flour
2 teaspoons cream of tartar
1 teaspoon baking soda
¼ teaspoon salt
2 tablespoons sugar
2 teaspoons cinnamon

Cream butter, shortening and sugar together. Add eggs and beat. Add remaining ingredients, excluding sugar and cinnamon. Beat together. Form into ¾ inch balls. Roll into sugar and cinnamon mixture. Place on ungreased cookie sheet. Bake at 400° for 8-10 minutes.
Yield: 5 dozen.

For a variation, 1 (12 ounce) package white chocolate bits and ½ cup macadamia nuts may be used. May be frozen.

Peanut Blossoms

½ cup shortening
½ cup peanut butter
½ cup brown sugar, packed
1 egg
2 tablespoons milk
1 teaspoon vanilla
1¾ cups flour
1 teaspoon baking soda
½ teaspoon salt
Sugar
48 chocolate kisses or mini-
   ature peanut butter cups

Cream together shortening and peanut butter. Add brown sugar. Mix well. Add egg, milk, and vanilla. Beat well. Blend in flour, soda, and salt, mixing thoroughly. Shape into 1 inch balls. Roll in sugar. Place on lightly greased cookie sheet. Bake at 350° for 5 minutes. Remove from oven. Press kisses or peanut butter cups in center of cookie until edges crack. Return to oven and bake 2-5 minutes longer.
Yield: 4 dozen.

Freezes well.

Heide's Christmas Cookies

2 cups brown sugar, packed
1 pound butter, softened
8 eggs, slightly beaten
6 tablespoons milk
6 cups flour
6 teaspoons baking soda
2 teaspoons cinnamon
2 teaspoons nutmeg
2 teaspoons cloves
1 teaspoon salt
2 jiggers whiskey
1 teaspoon butter flavoring
1 pound candied red cherries
1 pound candied pineapple,
   green and yellow
1½ pounds white raisins
11 cups (3 pounds) broken
   pecan halves

Cream together brown sugar and butter. Add eggs and milk. Sift together 4½ cups flour, soda, cinnamon, nutmeg, cloves, and salt. Add half of sifted ingredients to creamed mixture. Blend well. Add whiskey, butter flavoring and remaining sifted ingredients, blending well. Cut candied fruit on floured cutting board. Coat with remaining 1½ cups flour. (For ease, place fruit and flour in covered bowl and shake to coat.) In large bowl, mix flour-coated fruit, raisins, and pecans together. Add creamed mixture and blend. Store dough in cool place overnight for flavors to blend. Drop mixture by rounded teaspoonfuls onto ungreased cookie sheet. Bake at 250° for 15 minutes.
Yield: 20 dozen.

A wonderful gift for friends at Christmas. May easily be cut in half. May be frozen after baking.

Sand Tarts

½ pound butter or margarine,
* softened*
½ cup sifted powdered sugar
2 cups sifted cake flour
1 cup chopped pecans
1 teaspoon vanilla
Powdered sugar

Cream butter and powdered sugar. Add flour, nuts and vanilla. Shape into balls or crescents. Bake on a greased cookie sheet at 325° for 20 minutes. Roll in powdered sugar while warm. Yield: 4 dozen.

Ice Box Cookies

8 ounces butter or margarine,
* softened*
1 (16 ounce) box brown
* sugar*
2 eggs
½ teaspoon salt
1 teaspoon baking soda
3½ cups sifted flour
1 teaspoon vanilla
1 cup chopped nuts

Cream butter and sugar together. Add eggs, mixing well. Sift salt and soda with flour. Gradually add to mixture. Add vanilla and nuts. Drop by teaspoon on cookie sheet. Bake at 350° for 10 minutes.
Yield: 7 dozen.

Dough may be rolled into a quarter-size log, covered with foil, and stored in freezer. Slice what is needed and bake. Great for emergencies!

Sharon's "Special" Strawberry Pie

Crust:
3 egg whites, beaten
1 cup sugar
1 teaspoon vanilla
½ cup crushed soda crackers
¼ teaspoon baking powder
½ cup chopped pecans

Filling:
1 quart sliced, sweetened
* strawberries*
1 (8 ounce) carton frozen
* whipped topping, thawed*

Grease a 10 inch pie plate. Beat egg whites to peaks. Add sugar and vanilla. Beat until stiff. Combine cracker crumbs, nuts and baking powder. Fold into egg whites gently. Spread into greased pie plate forming crust. Bake at 325° for 30 minutes. Cool.

Combine strawberries and whipped topping. Spread into cooled crust. Refrigerate.
Yield: 8-10 servings.

French Lemon Pie

4 eggs
1 cup light corn syrup
1 teaspoon grated lemon peel
⅓ cup lemon juice
2 tablespoons melted butter
½ cup sugar
2 tablespoons flour
1 (9 inch) unbaked pie crust
½ cup whipping cream

Beat eggs well. Add corn syrup, lemon peel, lemon juice, and melted butter. Combine sugar and flour. Stir into egg mixture. Pour into unbaked pie crust. Bake at 350° for 50 minutes. Chill. To serve, whip cream and spoon onto pie.
Yield: 8-10 servings.

French Silk Pie

½ cup butter
¾ cup sugar
1 teaspoon vanilla
1-2 squares bitter chocolate
2 eggs
1 baked pie crust
1 cup heavy cream, whipped
Shaved chocolate

Cream together butter, sugar and vanilla. Melt one square of the chocolate over hot water. Cool and add to the creamed mixture. Add one egg and beat five minutes. Add second egg and beat five minutes. Pour into baked pie crust. Cover with whipped cream and shaved chocolate. Refrigerate.
Yield: 8-10 servings.

Freezes well. After frozen, store in plastic bag. May be served frozen or after it has set at room temperature for several minutes.

The passionflower *(Passiflora incarnata)* has a rich history of folklore. Its flower parts supposedly symbolize each phase of Christ's suffering on the cross.

Mom's Apple Betty

5 large apples — Jonathan or
  Granny Smith
½ cup sugar
4 tablespoons water
¾ cup brown sugar, packed
1 cup flour
¾ cup butter or margarine
Cinnamon

Peel, core and chop apples into bite-size pieces. Line bottom of pie plate with apples. Pour sugar and water over apples. Mix brown sugar, flour and butter. Sprinkle this mixture over apples. Top with cinnamon. Bake at 350° for 45 minutes.
Yield: 8-10 servings.

Pumpkin-Apple Pie

⅓ cup brown sugar, packed
1 tablespoon cornstarch
1 tablespoon cinnamon
¼ teaspoon salt
⅓ cup water
2 tablespoons butter
3 cups sliced apples
1 egg
⅓ cup sugar
¾ cup pumpkin
¼ teaspoon salt
¼ teaspoon ginger
½ teaspoon cinnamon
⅛ teaspoon cloves
¾ cup evaporated milk
1 (9 inch) unbaked pie crust

Combine first four ingredients in a saucepan. Stir in water and butter. Bring to boil, add apples and cook for 4 minutes over medium heat. Set aside. Beat egg in separate bowl. Add remaining ingredients and blend well. Spoon apple mixture into pie crust. Carefully spoon pumpkin layer over apples. Bake at 375° for 50-55 minutes.
Yield: 8-10 servings.

Something different for holiday pumpkin pies.

Beth's Chocolate Cream Pie

1 cup sugar
4 tablespoons flour
Dash salt
1½ cups milk
2 eggs
1 square unsweetened chocolate
2 tablespoons butter
½ teaspoon vanilla
1 baked pie crust

Meringue:
1 tablespoon water
3 egg whites
Dash salt
¼ teaspoon cream of tartar
½ teaspoon vanilla
6 tablespoons sugar

Mix sugar, flour and salt in a double boiler. Stir in milk. Bring mixture to almost boiling (about 12 minutes). Separate 2 eggs and beat yolks. Add a little milk to the yolks and pour into hot mixture, stirring constantly. Add chocolate, stirring until melted. Remove from heat. Add butter and vanilla. Pour into baked pie crust and top with meringue.

Combine water, egg whites, salt, and cream of tartar. Beat with electric mixer on high until soft peaks form. Add ½ teaspoon vanilla. Add sugar, 2 tablespoons at a time, beating until completely dissolved after each addition. Beat until stiff peaks form. Spread on pie filling. Bake at 325° for 20 minutes, until lightly browned.
Yield: 8-10 servings.

Janell's Buttermilk Pie

½ cup pecans
1 unbaked pie crust
½ cup butter
1½ cups sugar
2 teaspoons vanilla
3 eggs
3 tablespoons flour
½ teaspoon salt
1 cup buttermilk

Chop pecans. Sprinkle into pie crust. Make custard mixture by creaming butter and sugar. Add vanilla and eggs. Beat. Combine flour and salt with above mixture. Add buttermilk, blending well. Pour over pecans. Bake at 300° for 1½ hours.
Yield: 8-10 servings.

Dan's Kentucky Pie

½ cup melted butter
1 cup sugar
1 cup white corn syrup
4 eggs
1 tablespoon bourbon
½ cup chocolate chips
1 cup pecan halves
1 unbaked pie crust
Whipped cream for garnish

Mix the ingredients together. Pour into an unbaked pie crust. Bake at 350° for 45 minutes. Cool and garnish pie pieces with whipped cream.
Yield: 8-10 servings.

The Best Pecan Pie

Crust:
3 cups flour
1½ teaspoons salt
1¼ cups shortening
10 tablespoons ice water

Mix flour and salt. Cut in shortening. Sprinkle with ice water. Mix. Refrigerate dough at least 15 minutes. Roll cold dough out on floured surface.
Yield: 2 (9 inch) crusts.

Filling:
1 cup dark corn syrup
¾ cup sugar
3 eggs, beaten
3 tablespoons butter, melted
1 teaspoon vanilla
1 cup broken pecan pieces

Preheat oven to 350°. Mix all ingredients. Pour into unbaked pie crust. Bake 45 minutes.
Yield: 8-10 servings.

Fudge Pecan Pie

2 eggs
1 cup sugar
1 cup white corn syrup
2 tablespoons margarine
2 squares unsweetened
  chocolate
1 teaspoon vanilla
1 cup pecans
1 (8 inch) unbaked pie crust

Beat eggs by hand. Add sugar and corn syrup. Melt margarine with chocolate. Add to egg mixture. Fold in vanilla and pecans. Pour into unbaked pie crust. Bake at 350° for 1 hour.
Yield: 8-10 servings.

Crunchy Peanut Butter Pie

Crust:
½ cup margarine
1 cup flour
½ cup finely chopped roasted
  peanuts

Filling:
1 (3 ounce) package cream
  cheese, softened to room
  temperature
1 cup powdered sugar
½ cup crunchy peanut butter
½ cup milk
1 (8 ounce) carton whipped
  topping, thawed

Cut margarine into flour until crumbly mixture forms. Stir in nuts. Press mixture evenly into a 9 inch pie plate. Bake at 350° for 20 minutes. Cool.

Beat cream cheese, sugar and peanut butter. Add milk gradually. Fold in whipped topping. Pile mixture into cooled pie crust. Freeze until firm.
Yield: 8-10 servings.

May be made ahead and frozen.

Peanut Butter Pie

Crust:
1½ cups crushed chocolate
   creme sandwich cookies
¼ cup melted butter

Filling:
1 (8 ounce) package cream
   cheese, softened
½ cup sugar
1 cup peanut butter, smooth
   or crunchy
1 (8 ounce) container frozen
   whipped topping, thawed
Hot fudge sauce

Combine cookies and butter. Press into a 9 inch pie plate or an 8 inch springform pan.

Beat cream cheese, sugar and peanut butter together. Beat in the thawed whipped topping, slowly. Pour into prepared pie crust. Chill pie overnight. Top with hot fudge sauce to serve.
Yield: 6-8 servings.

A favorite dessert served at a popular restaurant in Oregon. Always a best seller.

Brandy Alexander Pie

1 (14 ounce) can sweetened
   condensed milk
1 cup whipping cream,
   whipped
2 tablespoons cream de cacao
2 tablespoons brandy
1 (9 inch) graham cracker
   crust
Shaved chocolate

Combine milk, whipped cream, cream de cacao and brandy. Pour into graham cracker crust and freeze for 4-6 hours. Garnish with shaved chocolate.
Yield: 8-10 servings.

Chocolate cookie crust may be substituted.

Chocolate Mousse Pie

Chocolate Leaves:
8 ounces semi-sweet chocolate
**1 tablespoon vegetable short-
  ening**
Camellia or other waxy leaves

Crust:
**3 cups chocolate wafer
  crumbs**
½ cup melted unsalted butter

Filling:
1 pound semi-sweet chocolate
2 eggs
4 egg yolks
2 cups whipping cream
**6 tablespoons powdered
  sugar**
**4 egg whites, room tempera-
  ture**

Icing:
2 cups whipping cream
Sugar

Melt chocolate and shortening in top of double boiler. Using a spoon, coat underside of leaves. Chill or freeze until firm.

Combine crumbs and butter. Press on bottom and completely up sides of 10 inch springform pan. Refrigerate 30 minutes (or chill in freezer).

Soften chocolate in top of double boiler over simmering water. Let cool to lukewarm (95°). Add whole eggs and mix well. Add yolks and mix until thoroughly blended. Whip cream with powdered sugar until soft peaks form. Beat egg whites until stiff but not dry. Stir a little of the cream and whites into chocolate mixture to lighten. Fold in remaining cream and whites until completely incorporated. Turn into crust and chill at least 6 hours or overnight.

Whip cream with sugar to taste until quite stiff. Loosen crust on all sides using sharp knife. Remove springform. Spread all but about ½ cup cream over top of mousse. Pipe remaining cream into rosettes in center of pie. Separate chocolate from leaves, starting at stem end of leaf. Arrange in overlapping pattern around rosettes.
Yield: 10-12 servings.

May be prepared ahead and frozen. Thaw overnight in refrigerator.

Crustless Chocolate Fudge Pie

2 large eggs
1 cup sugar
½ cup flour
1 teaspoon vanilla
½ cup margarine
1 square unsweetened choco-
*   late*
½ cup pecans

Mix together eggs, sugar, flour and vanilla. Melt margarine and chocolate. Add to first mixture, stirring well. Pour mixture into a buttered 8 inch pie plate. Top with pecans or mix pecans into batter. Bake at 350° for 25 minutes.
Yield: 6-8 servings.

Eclair Dessert

Must be made ahead.

Filling:
2 (3 ounce) packages instant
*   French vanilla pudding*
3 cups milk
1 (8 ounce) carton frozen
*   whipped topping, thawed*

Crust:
1 (16 ounce) box graham
*   crackers*

Topping:
2 ounces unsweetened choco-
*   late*
3 tablespoons butter
2 tablespoons white corn
*   syrup*
3 tablespoons milk
1½-2 cups powdered sugar,
*   sifted*

Mix vanilla pudding and milk until thickened. Add whipped topping.

Line a 13x9 inch pan with whole graham crackers. Pour half of the filling over crackers. Cover filling with another layer of whole graham crackers. Add remaining pudding mixture. Add another layer of whole graham crackers over pudding mixture.

Melt chocolate and butter. Add syrup and milk. Mix in powdered sugar. Pour topping over graham crackers. Set several hours.
Yield: 16 servings.

Candy Bar Pie

1⅓ cups grated coconut
2 tablespoons melted butter
1 teaspoon instant coffee
2 tablespoons water
1 (7½ ounce) milk chocolate
    candy bar with almonds,
    broken
4 cups frozen whipped top-
    ping, thawed
Chocolate curls, optional
Slivered toasted almonds,
    optional

Combine coconut and butter. Press into an 8 inch pie plate. Bake at 325° for 10 minutes, until coconut is golden. Cool thoroughly. In small saucepan, dissolve coffee in water. Add chocolate bar. Stir chocolate mixture over low heat until melted. Cool. Fold in whipped dessert topping. Pile into coconut crust. Garnish with chocolate curls or slivered toasted almonds. Chill in freezer several hours or overnight. (Will not freeze solid.)
Yield: 8-10 servings.

Cherry Delight

Must be made ahead.

Crust:
1½ cups crushed graham
    crackers
¼ cup sugar
¼ cup margarine, softened
1 teaspoon cinnamon

Filling:
1 (8 ounce) package cream
    cheese, softened
1 cup powdered sugar
½ pint whipping cream
1 teaspoon powdered sugar
1 teaspoon vanilla
1 (16 ounce) can cherry pie
    filling

Mix ingredients. Press into a 9x9 inch pan. Bake at 350° for 5 minutes. Cool.

Whip cream cheese with 1 cup powdered sugar until fluffy. Spread over crust. Whip cream, sugar and vanilla. Spread over cream cheese. Top with cherry pie filling. Chill at least 8 hours.
Yield: 12 servings.

Delight your own taste with other prepared pie fillings such as pineapple, blueberry, etc.

Strawberry Forgotten Torte

Filling:
6 egg whites, room temperature
¼ teaspoon salt
½ teaspoon cream of tartar
1½ cups sugar
1 teaspoon vanilla

Topping:
½ pint whipping cream
2 (10 ounce) packages frozen strawberries

Preheat oven to 450°. Butter bottom of a 9 inch angel food cake pan. Beat egg whites until peaks form. Add salt and cream of tartar. Beat until stiff. Add sugar gradually. Beat until stiff. Fold in vanilla. Spread evenly in buttered pan. Place cake in oven. Close door. Turn off heat at once. Let stand overnight. (Do not open oven door.) Next morning, remove from oven. Loosen edges and turn out on plate.

Frost with stiffly beaten whipping cream. Chill until serving time. Serve with strawberries on top.
Yield: 10-12 servings.

Raspberry Squares

1½ cups flour
½ teaspoon salt
½ teaspoon baking soda
1 cup brown sugar, packed
⅔ cup oatmeal
1⅓ cups chopped pecans
¾ cup margarine, melted
¾ cup raspberry jam

Sift flour, salt and soda together. Add brown sugar, oatmeal and pecans. Mix. Add margarine, blending with fork. Press half of mixture into bottom of 12x9 inch pan. Spread jam over mixture. Cover jam with remaining mixture. Bake at 350° for 25-30 minutes. Cut into squares when cool.
Yield: 30-35 squares.

May be made a day ahead and kept in refrigerator.

Stained Glass Pizza

1 (14 ounce) can apricot
  halves
1 (12 ounce) can pineapple
  chunks
1 (8 ounce) package cream
  cheese, softened
2 tablespoons butter, softened
1 cup baking mix
½ cup sugar
¼ teaspoon grated lemon peel
2 tablespoons cornstarch
¼ teaspoon salt
¼ cup lemon juice
1 pint strawberries, halved
⅔ cup green grapes (or fruit
  in season)
Mint

Drain all canned fruits separately. Retain syrup. Mix 3 ounces cream cheese, butter, and baking mix until it forms a ball. Grease a 12 inch pizza pan. Spread dough on pan as for a pizza. Bake at 425° for 8 minutes until golden brown. Cream remainder of cream cheese with 2 tablespoons apricot juice. Add ¼ cup sugar and lemon peel. Spread on cooled crust. Line pizza with fruits — apricots, strawberries, and grapes. Center with pineapple chunks. Place several strawberries and a sprig of mint in the middle.

Glaze:

Mix ¼ cup sugar, cornstarch, salt, 1 cup apricot syrup, ½ cup pineapple syrup and ¼ cup lemon juice in a small saucepan. Heat until thick. Pour over fruit. Cover with plastic wrap and refrigerate.
Yield: 10-12 servings.

Looks pretty on a party table. Slice like a pizza.

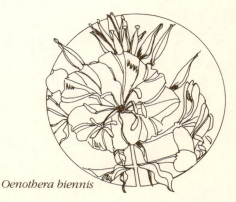

Oenothera biennis

Chocolate Chip/Cream Cheese Cupcakes

Filling:
1 cup water
5 tablespoons oil
1 teaspoon vanilla
1 tablespoon cider vinegar
1½ cups flour
1 cup sugar
¼ cup cocoa
1 teaspoon baking soda
½ teaspoon salt

Topping:
**1 (8 ounce) package cream
  cheese, softened**
1 egg
⅓ cup sugar
**1 (6 ounce) package choco-
  late chips**

Mix first 4 ingredients. Add to next 5 ingredients. Mix well. Fill cupcake papers half full.

Beat cream cheese, egg and sugar. Fold in chocolate chips. Pour a heaping tablespoon of topping on each cupcake. Bake at 350° for 25 minutes.
Yield: 12 cupcakes.

Super for a ladies luncheon or a birthday party.

Pecan Tassies

Filling:
⅔ cup brown sugar, packed
1 tablespoon margarine
1 egg, beaten
1 teaspoon vanilla
1 cup chopped pecans

Crust:
**1 (3 ounce) package cream
  cheese, softened**
½ cup margarine, softened
1 cup flour

Cream brown sugar and margarine. Add egg, vanilla and nuts.

Cream cheese and margarine. Add flour. Mix well. Chill 1 hour. Form into 12 balls. Press into small muffin tins. Add filling. Bake at 325° for 25 minutes.
Yield: 12 tassies.

Must be made ahead.

Coffee Nut Tortoni

Must be made ahead.

1 cup heavy cream
¼ cup sugar
1 tablespoon instant coffee
1 teaspoon vanilla
Few drops almond flavoring
1 egg white
2 tablespoons sugar
¼ cup finely chopped al-
**   monds**
¼ cup toasted coconut,
**   crumbled**

Whip the cream. Fold in ¼ cup sugar, coffee and flavorings. Beat egg whites until soft peaks form. Add 2 tablespoons sugar gradually. Beat until stiff peaks form. Mix almonds and coconut together. Fold egg white and half the nut mixture into whipped cream mixture. Spoon into 6 small soufflé cups or paper baking cups set in a muffin pan. Sprinkle remaining nut mixture on top. Freeze until firm.
Yield: 6-8 servings.

This is a light, pretty dessert. Store in freezer for that special occasion.

White Chocolate Pretzels

1 (24 ounce) package almond
**   bark**
1 (12 ounce) package pret-
**   zels**
Red and green sprinkles,
**   optional**

Melt almond bark according to package directions. Dip pretzels into melted mixture. Place on a cookie sheet covered with wax paper. Sprinkle with red and green sprinkles. Place in freezer 30 minutes to harden. (These may be dipped on one side or both, either in white or dark chocolate.)
Yield: 12 ounces.

Nice for a Christmas hostess gift.

Corn Crunch

½ cup butter
1 cup light brown sugar,
    packed
¼ cup honey
1 teaspoon vanilla
3 quarts popped popcorn
1 cup nuts (almonds and
    peanuts)

Melt butter in 1 quart saucepan over low heat. Stir in brown sugar and honey over medium heat, stirring constantly. Bring to boil. Boil gently for 5 minutes without stirring. Remove from heat. Stir in vanilla. Pour over popped corn and nuts. Bake at 250° for 1 hour, stirring every 15 minutes. Pour onto waxed paper to cool. Store in tightly covered container.
Yield: 3 quarts

Caramel Corn

1 cup butter
2 cups brown sugar, packed
½ cup corn syrup
1 teaspoon salt
½ teaspoon baking soda
1 teaspoon vanilla
6 quarts popped popcorn

Melt butter in extra large saucepan. Stir in brown sugar, corn syrup and salt. Bring to boil, stirring constantly. Boil 5 minutes without stirring. Remove from heat. Stir in vanilla and soda (mixture will foam up). Place popcorn in large aluminum roast pan. Coat popcorn with syrup mixture. Stir. Bake at 250° for 1-1½ hours, stirring every 15 minutes. When consistency changes, bake 15 minutes longer.
Yield: 6 quarts.

Store in airtight container. Makes a wonderful gift item, especially for children.

Asclepias tuberosa

Coconut Balls

Must be made ahead.

½ cup margarine, melted
1 pound shredded coconut
1 (14 ounce) can sweetened
  condensed milk
1 (16 ounce) box powdered
  sugar
1 (16 ounce) jar maraschino
  cherries
3 cups chopped pecans
2 (8 ounce) chocolate candy
  bars
1 (12 ounce) package semi-
  sweet chocolate chips
¾ bar paraffin wax

Combine first 6 ingredients. Stir until well mixed. Form into 1 inch balls. Refrigerate overnight on cookie sheets. Melt remaining ingredients in a double boiler. Dip balls into chocolate mixture, keeping chocolate mixture warm. Place on cooling rack.
Yield: 100 plus.

Freezes well.

Baked Fudge

4 eggs
2 cups sugar
½ cup flour
½ cup cocoa
1 cup butter or margarine,
  melted
1 cup chopped pecans
1¾ teaspoons vanilla
¼ teaspoon salt
Whipped cream

Beat eggs until lemon colored. Add dry ingredients. Mix until well blended. Add melted butter and stir in remaining ingredients excluding whipped cream. Pour into a 12x8 inch pan. Set pan in larger pan of water. Bake at 325° for 45-50 minutes until set like custard. Serve warm with whipped cream.
Yield: 12 servings.

Super delicious for chocolate lovers!

Millionaires

Base:
1½ pounds caramels
2 tablespoons water
2 tablespoons margarine
3 cups chopped pecans
Vegetable shortening spray

Topping:
1 (9 ounce) chocolate bar
⅓ bar paraffin wax

Combine caramels, water and margarine. Melt in double boiler or microwave, stirring occasionally. Add pecans and stir. Drop by teaspoons onto waxed paper sprayed with vegetable shortening.

Combine chocolate and paraffin. Melt in double boiler, stirring occasionally until smooth. Using a toothpick or tongs, dip caramel patties in melted chocolate. Drop onto waxed paper while dipping. Keep double boiler on low burner. (This keeps chocolate at nice consistency. It is helpful to put caramel patties in freezer for a few minutes before dipping. Dip them while cold.)
Yield: 4 dozen.

Millionaires store nicely in the refrigerator or freezer.

Butterscotch Goodies

2 (6 ounce) packages butter-
scotch morsels
½ cup peanut butter
1 cup peanuts
1 cup high protein crispy
cereal flakes
1 (3 ounce) can Chinese
noodles

Melt butterscotch morsels and peanut butter in a double boiler. Turn heat off. Add peanuts, cereal and noodles. Stir until thoroughly coated. Drop by teaspoons onto lightly buttered waxed paper. Candy will harden in 1-2 hours.
Yield: 40-44 goodies.

Freezes well. Makes a nice do-ahead Christmas goodie.

Centaurium beyrichii

Mountain pinks - *Centaurium beyrichii*
Nestled on rocky limestone slopes, these tiny plants have pink flowers which form natural bouquets. Only 4" to 12" tall, mountain pinks are easy to overlook. They range from North to Central Texas, reseeding each year. Members of the Gentian family, mountain pinks share similar characteristics with Texas bluebells.

Meat Marinade

1 (46 ounce) can pineapple
  juice
1 cup red wine
1 cup sugar
1 cup soy sauce
1 teaspoon flavor enhancer
1 teaspoon garlic powder

Mix ingredients well. Pour over meat and
marinate 2 hours or longer.
Yield: Enough for 3 pounds meat.

Good for beef or chicken.

Gourmet Seasoned Salt

1½ cups salt
2 teaspoons crumbled thyme
  leaves
2 teaspoons ground marjo-
  ram
2 teaspoons garlic salt
3 tablespoons paprika
2 teaspoons curry powder
4 teaspoons dry mustard
1 teaspoon onion powder

Mix all ingredients. Pour into airtight jars.
Yield: 1¾ cups.

Good on vegetables, meats and popcorn.

Engelmannia pinnatifida

Cumberland Sauce

5 shallots, finely chopped
Zest and juice of 1 orange
(cut peel without white
membrane into julienne
strips)
Zest and juice of 1 lemon
½ cup currant jelly
½ cup Port wine
1 teaspoon spicy mustard
Dash of ground ginger
Dash of ground red pepper

Combine shallots, citrus peel and juice in small saucepan. Place over low heat. Simmer 10 minutes, stirring frequently. Add remaining ingredients. Simmer 10 minutes, stirring occasionally. Serve at room temperature. Yield: 1 cup.

May be prepared up to 2 weeks in advance and refrigerated.

Chef's Cheese Sauce for Baked Potatoes

½ cup sour cream
4 tablespoons butter or mar-
garine, softened
1 cup shredded sharp Ched-
dar cheese
2 tablespoons chopped green
onion

Combine all ingredients. Beat until light and fluffy. Yield: 4 servings.

May be made ahead of time.

Spicy Peach Spread

8 cups sliced peaches,
crushed or blended
4 cups sugar
¼ teaspoon salt
1 teaspoon cinnamon
½ teaspoon ginger
½ teaspoon allspice
¼ teaspoon ground cloves

Mix peaches, sugar and salt in large kettle. Boil rapidly, stirring constantly to prevent scorching. As sauce becomes thick, lower heat to reduce spattering. Add cinnamon, ginger, allspice, and cloves. Continue cooking until sauce is thick enough to almost flake off the spoon. Pour into hot sterilized jars to within ½ inch of top. Seal. Yield: 4 pints.

Sherrie's Sweet Pickles

1 (gallon) jar whole sour
  pickles
1 (5 pound) bag sugar
½ cup pickling spices
10 sticks cinnamon, may be
  broken
2 cloves garlic

Drain pickles. Cut into chunks and rinse with cool water. Put chunks into large container. Cover with sugar and other seasonings. Mix thoroughly. Put pickle mixture into gallon jar plus one quart jar. Let sit at room temperature for 3 days, turning jar occasionally. After sugar has melted, refrigerate and enjoy.
Yield: A ton of pickle chunks.

Makes a wonderful gift in a decorated jar.

Lois' Hot-Sweet Pickles

1 gallon sliced hamburger dill
  pickles
1 (5 pound) bag sugar
1 (2 ounce) jar hot pepper
  sauce

Drain juice from pickles. Layer pickles, sugar, and pepper sauce in several layers in a gallon jar. Turn the jar each day for 7 days (stand on end 1 day, upright the next, etc.). Seal into Mason Jars. Keep chilled after opening.
Yield: 8 pints.

A wonderful "new neighbor" gift. Best when served cold.

Coreopsis lanceolata

Pickled Mushrooms

Must be made ahead.

3 pounds small mushrooms
1 cup wine vinegar
1 cup corn oil
3 green onions, chopped
1 tablespoon salt
3 tablespoons sugar
6 teaspoons parsley flakes
Black pepper to taste

Combine oil and vinegar. Boil 3 minutes. Mix remaining ingredients and place in 5 (6 ounce) jars. Cool before refrigerating. Serve after 2 days.
Yield: 5 (6 ounce) jars.

Cranberry Fluff

1 pound whole cranberries
1 pound marshmallows
1 cup sugar
1 (20 ounce) can crushed
  pineapple, drained
1 pint frozen whipped topping, thawed
½ cup chopped nuts, optional

Grind cranberries and marshmallows in grinder. Add sugar and let stand 1 hour. Add pineapple, whipped topping, and nuts. Store in refrigerator.
Yield: 10 servings.

Freezes well. It wouldn't be Thanksgiving without it!

Hot Pineapple Bake

½ cup sugar
1 tablespoon flour
2 eggs, beaten
1 (16 ounce) can crushed
  pineapple
3-4 slices white bread
4 tablespoons butter

Combine sugar, flour, eggs and pineapple. Place in a buttered 8x8 inch baking dish. Trim crust from bread. Cut bread into cubes. Place on top. Dot with butter Bake at 400° for 20 minutes until lightly browned.
Yield: 4-6 servings.

Wonderful served with ham.

Zippy Cranberry Relish

Must be made ahead.

1 pound fresh cranberries
1 (12 ounce) can crushed
**   pineapple**
⅓ cup grated orange peel
½ teaspoon ground cinnamon
½ teaspoon powdered ginger
1 ounce sweet vermouth

Prepare cranberries according to package directions for whole cranberry sauce. Add drained pineapple, orange peel, cinnamon, powdered ginger, and sweet vermouth. Chill for at least 24 hours.
Yield: 8 servings.

Good for holidays.

Chunky Pimiento Cheese

2 pounds processed cheese,
**   diced**
½ pound sharp Cheddar
**   cheese, diced**
Salad dressing
¼ cup sweet pickle relish
2 (8 ounce) jars diced pimien-
**   tos**
¾ teaspoon garlic salt

Mix cheeses with electric mixer or food processor adding salad dressing until desired consistency is reached. Add pickle relish, pimientos, and garlic salt. Mix. Store in an airtight container in refrigerator until served.
Yield: 2½ pounds.

Makes wonderful sandwiches.

Crab Sandwiches

6 slices American cheese
12 slices bread
1 (6½ ounce) can crabmeat
3 eggs
2 cups milk
Salt and pepper

Grease 13x9 inch baking dish. Remove crusts from bread. Place 6 slices bread in dish. Put 1 slice of cheese on each slice of bread. Top with crabmeat and remaining slices of bread. Mix eggs, milk, salt and pepper. Pour over sandwiches and refrigerate 1 hour or more. Bake at 350° 40 minutes, until lightly browned.
Yield: 6 servings.

Cucumber Sandwiches

1 large unpeeled cucumber
6 green onions (bulb and
about 1 inch green)
1 (8 ounce) package cream
cheese, softened
2 tablespoons mayonnaise
48 small party rolls

Using blender, briefly blend cucumber and onion (mixture should not be mushy). Drain mixture in colander for at least ½ hour. Combine this mixture with cream cheese and mayonnaise. Spread both sides of rolls with a small amount of mayonnaise (to prevent sogginess). Add cucumber mix.
Yield: 48 finger sandwiches.

May be prepared ahead of time and stored in an airtight container.

Vegetable Sandwiches

1 (8 ounce) package cream
cheese, softened
1 tablespoon lemon juice
¼ cup chopped celery
¾ cup grated carrot
¼ cup finely chopped green
pepper
¼ cup chopped cucumber
¼ cup grated onion
1½ tablespoons mayonnaise

Combine all ingredients. Chill 2 hours. Remove crust from whole wheat bread. Spread bread with mixture. Cut sandwiches in halves or fourths.
Yield: 24 servings.

May be refrigerated for several days.

Swiss Tuna Grill

1 (6½ ounce) can tuna,
drained
½ cup (2 ounces) shredded
Swiss cheese
½ cup chopped celery
2 tablespoons chopped onion
¼ cup mayonnaise
¼ cup sour cream
Dash pepper
Butter
10-12 slices bread

Mix all ingredients, except butter and bread. Spread desired amount of tuna mixture between 2 slices of bread. Butter both sides of sandwich. Broil until golden brown, less than 5 minutes per side.
Yield: 4-6 sandwiches.

Serve with fresh fruit, chips and pickles for a light and easy summer supper.

Homemade Granola

1 cup safflower oil
1 cup honey
2 teaspoons vanilla
1 teaspoon salt
6-8 ounces slivered almonds
1 cup sesame seeds
1½ (18 ounce) boxes old-
    fashioned oatmeal
2 cups wheat germ
2 cups bran cereal
1 cup shredded coconut

Heat oil, honey, vanilla, salt, almonds, and sesame seeds over low heat until well mixed. Mix oatmeal, wheat germ, bran cereal, and coconut in large bowl. Pour heated liquid mixture over dry mixture. Mix well. Divide mixture between 2 ungreased cookie sheets. Bake at 300° until browned (approximately 30 minutes). Stir every 10 minutes during baking. (Mixture burns easily.) Store in air-tight container. Use as a cereal.
Yield: 24 servings.

Freezes well.

Pepper Jelly

1 cup ground bell pepper
6 cups sugar
1½ cups white vinegar
¼ cup hot pepper
1 (6 ounce) bottle fruit pectin

Combine all ingredients except fruit pectin. Bring to a boil. Boil two minutes. Remove from heat. Let stand 5 minutes. Add fruit pectin. Put in sterile jars. Seal with vacuum lid or paraffin.
Yield: 2 pints.

Hot Mustard

1 cup dry mustard
1 cup apple cider vinegar
1 cup brown sugar
1 egg

Combine dry mustard and vinegar. Let stand two hours. Add brown sugar and egg. Simmer in double boiler until thick. Refrigerate.
Yield: 3 cups.

Great on ham or ham sandwiches.

Cheese 'n Chive Butter

1 cup butter, softened
1½ cups shredded Cheddar
  cheese
2 tablespoons chopped chives
¼ teaspoon garlic powder
¼ teaspoon hot pepper sauce

Beat butter until light and fluffy. Add remaining ingredients. Mix well. Cover and chill. Yield: 1⅔ cups.

Serve at room temperature on hot bread, vegetables or baked potatoes.

Mild Barbecue Sauce

1 (10¾ ounce) can onion
  soup
1 (10¾ ounce) can tomato
  soup
2 tablespoons cornstarch
2 cloves garlic, minced
¼ cup vinegar
3 tablespoons brown sugar
1 tablespoon worcestershire
  sauce

Mix all ingredients in a medium sized bowl. Stores well in refrigerator. Yield: 2½ cups.

Christmas Aroma

Not for drinking — just for smelling.

2 cups sugar
2 cups water
1 cup pineapple juice
1 cup orange juice
½ cup lemon juice
25 whole cloves
2 cinnamon sticks

Boil sugar and water for 2 minutes. Add remaining ingredients. Simmer over very low heat. More water may be added as needed.

A holiday must!

Callirhoe involucrata

Winecup - *Callirhoe involucrata*
Winecup is a delicate, prostrate perennial, usually 6" to 12", found on sandy soils in open woods and scrublands. The burgundy flowers bloom in early spring throughout Texas. Winecup is a member of the Mallow family, along with such flowers as the hibiscus, and crop species like cotton and okra.

"Wine is the child of sun and earth, but cannot come into existence without the help of work. It needs the collaboration of art and patience, of time and care. It needs a long wait in the dark before arriving at that triumph of flavour which is a source of wonder to the brain as much as to the palate …"

P. Claudel

Capture the bouquet of Texas wines as you read this exclusive section written by noted wine expert, Sarah Jane English.

Pairing Wines With Foods

A colleague once told me that nothing learned is ever lost. Her example was cutting out paper figures in the second grade. At the time, we were seated at a table cutting and pasting copy. Obviously, the time was before personal computers.

In behalf of my little story, I wonder if you remember the school exams that asked you to compare and contrast ideas, things or whatever? If my colleague's theory holds true, you'll remember comparing and contrasting. It's the same with food and wine. They're either alike or different. Certain foods go with certain wines because they're comparable. Other combinations may have an affinity because of stark contrasts. The one that comes to mind that I like is peanut butter and Champagne.

Your particular preference for flavors and textures, and the degree of exactness is personal. According to Dr. Morley Kare, University of Pennsylvania Professor of Physiology, part of your preferences are determined when you are conceived: they are genetic.

The nice thing about pairing wines with foods is that there are no absolutes. Matching wine and food is an art, not a science. Individual tastes govern selections and they should rule the decision. Having said that, I would like to point out that chemistry shows why certain combinations of flavors go well together. Those combinations, however, can be altered by adding one significant ingredient. That's why suggesting broad categories such as a Texas white wine with Gulf Coast fish are not always effective. There are too many styles of white wines and too many ways to prepare fish. A more acceptable generalized rule is that delicate foods need delicate wines and heartier foods need heftier wines. In addition, there are also textures and weights to consider and whether items compliment one another.

Let's consider Texas quail. Quails are inherently sweet meats. They also can carry other flavors. For example, quail that is grilled would have a smoky character. Many Texas chefs believe that choosing one wood over another, say a pecan rather than a mesquite, can alter the smoked flavor. In any event, sweet meat with a smoky flavor goes well with a sweet Llano Estacado or Ste. Genevieve Chenin Blanc or Fall Creek Emerald Riesling. A crisply roasted quail filled with herbal stuffing would be better served with a crisp La Escarbada Sauvignon Blanc or a Slaughter-Leftwich

Sauvignon Blanc. Marinating the bird in a berry/wine marinade adds fruity flavors that would better match a fruity Sanchez Creek Chambourcin or a Pheasant Ridge Proprietor's Reserve.

In any event, wine selections are influenced by the cooking methods, sauces, stuffings or marinades used. Of course, there are some people who are going to drink red wine with everything because they like only red wines. The same is true of white wine drinkers. That's fine. I don't believe wine and food pairings should ever be too precise.

Chemically, wine contains more than several hundred organic compounds with estimates ranging up to 2000. They combine to give flavors and odors to wine. Olfactory, by the way, is responsible for 85% or more of what you taste in wine. Of all the constituents, acidity has prime significance. Acid is probably the most important consideration in determining which wines go with which foods. For some reason, crisp acid works with food. Wines with crisp acids highlight the flavors in foods.

There are some don'ts. Don't try to use wines high in alcohol with food. Big, robust cabernet sauvignons are difficult to match with food. The exception, of course, is fortified wines like Val Verde Tawny Port or La Buena Vida Port with Stilton or sweet wines like Sauternes with foie gras. High alcohol, unless balanced by sweetneses, kills flavors.

Low alcohol, acidity and texture combine in some wines to make them the best food choices: beaujolais and other light fruity red wines, or rieslings and chenin blancs and table whites for the white wine.

Foods that are prepared as sweet dishes are very difficult to match with wines, for example, duck with sweetened and spicy fruit sauces. Likewise, dishes that are too hot with spices make wine pairing difficult. In the case of Mexican dishes, I prefer a sparkling wine (Moyer Texas Sparkling, Llano Estacado or Wimberley Valley) or a riesling (Llano Estacado, La Escabarda, Messina Hof, Schoppaul Hill, Oberhellmann). Sparkling wines clean and refresh the palate. Sweet riesling calms the heat of spices.

There are also misconceptions. Serving the wine used to prepare a dish does not guarantee a good match. Also, the spiciest wine – gewurztraminer is an example – does not necessarily go well with the spiciest food.

Remember, suggested pairings of food and wine are not culinary imperatives but merely suggestions. There are no certainties in this art form. With that in mind, I offer some suggestions.

Foods prepared with abundant butter, and mild, gently flavored foods are the easiest to pair with wine. Butter give a dish mellowness that has a smooth effect on a dish. Chicken cooked simply in butter will go with almost any wine. The same is true for fresh, young veal. Both have understated flavors that makes versatile pairings possible.

For those reasons, chicken and veal are easier to pair with wine than lamb, venison, wild boar, exotic game or other highly flavored dishes – or even shellfish or fish. In all cases, the simpler the preparation, the easier the pairing.

Consider the similarity of characteristics between food and wine: age and freshness, the fruitiness, spices, smoothness, herbs, light or heavy, whether smoked, butteriness, degrees of complexity in both wine and food and so forth. For example, prepare a lightly flavored, medium textured fish in butter, lemon and garlic and serve with a lightly flavored, medium bodied Slaughter-Leftwich Sauvignon Blanc, Fall Creek Sauvignon Blanc, La Escarbada Sauvignon Blanc or Teysha Fume Blanc. Generaly, the wine is lean (not rich), has a nice crispness and enough flavor to take the garlic and butter and yet is the same weight as the fish. Venison or other game prepared with herbs and spices or even just grilled – depending on the age and strong flavors of the meat–calls for a red wine flavored with toasty, smoky aromas and hearty, earthy nuances to compliment the dish. Cypress Valley 1984 Barbera is perfect. Fall creek Carnelian is also a good match. The Texas cabernet sauvignon wines from any of the wineries that produce them – Pheasant Ridge, Oberhellman, Messina Hof, Wimberly Valley, Llano Estacado, Fall Creek, Sanchez Creek, Slaughter-Leftwich, Preston Trail, Teysha–are good matches.

A tightly textured, strong cabernet sauvignon can offset the strong flavor of some lamb. A crisp chardonnay or sauvignon blanc can cut through the oiliness in many fishes. If a wine does not go with fish, and generally red wines do not, it often makes it taste metallic. Chenin blancs and rieslings are good with light, poached fish dishes.

Sometimes food and wine are balanced by letting the flavors and characteristics of each one come through separately but without fighting each other. Very dry white wines, like those from La Escarbada, or even sparkling wines, like those from Moyer, Llano Estacado, Wimberly Valley and La Buena Vida, often work well with smoked fish.

The more difficult foods to match include fresh tomatoes and asparagus, fresh citrus fruits, spicy condiments, oregano, coriander and ginger. If any of these items dominates, it may be best to serve a high acid sparkling wine as a palate cleanser or plain water. In such cases where they are lightly included, choose a simple, uncomplicated wine that is not too fruity or packed with too many flavors: chenin blancs, table whites, or wines that refresh without distracting from the food.

Wines should not be served with salads dressed with vinaigrette. Use a cream or cheese dressing. Often the crisp fresh greens in salads make wines seem dull. Within a course or even among several courses, usually there is a logical progression of flavors and the wines should be considered. As wine warms, it too develops and changes flavors. If several wines and courses are served, they should progress together: lighter wines and dishes before heavier ones. Fruity and nutty flavors often offer interesting contracts.

To further help you in pairing wines with foods, the following list gives an idea about the characteristics in foods we use with meats, fish and fowl (the major consideration in selecting a wine for a one-wine meal). Match wines with similar or contrasting characteristics.

wild rice – nutty, earthy, a neutral food

pablano sauce – spicy, vegetative, acid

garlic – strong, pungent, sharp, distinctive

parsley – green herbal, mild, fresh

black pepper – strong, hot, sharp, spicy

onions – sweet, sour, strong

mustard – strong, hot, acid, pungent

mushroom – earthy, musty, a neutral food

grilling – smoky, sweet, spicy

apple – sweet, acid, fruity

sage – distinctive, herbal, dusty, pungent

lemon – sharp, acid, citrus, sour

rosemary – herbal, floral

bacon – sweet, pungent, oily, strong

dill – herbal, floral

cucumber – vegetative, acid, pungent

curry – distinctive, sharp, perfumy

coconut – sweet, nutty, rich, creamy

almond – nutty, rich, crunchy

butter – rich, fatty, mellow, smooth

hot pepper – acid, pungent, sharp, distinctive

cream and cheese – rich, fatty, smooth, pungent or sweet

spinach – greenness, acid, vegetative, sharp, tannic

fennel – licorice, sharp, bitter, pungent

eggplant – sharp, acid, smooth, bitter

potato – mild, textured, a neutral food

carrot – sweet, textured

pecans – tannic, sweet, textured

The main acids in wine are tartaric and malic, and they are less sour than acetic (vinegar) and citric acids (lemon, etc.). Generally, younger wines have higher acids than older ones. Both cream and wine have lactic acid. Wines undergoing secondary fermentation have more lactic acid and blend with cream (chardonnay, some sauvignon blanc). Most reds undergo malo-lactic fermentation.

A Simple Explanation of Wine

A very simple explanation of wine is that grapes ferment naturally to make wine. During the process, yeasts help convert the grape sugar to alcohol and carbonic acid gas (which escapes). The fermentation can be stopped before all the sugar is converted. Such wines have residual sugar and varying degrees of sweetness. When the sugar is totally converted, the wines are dry.

White wines can be sweet or dry, light or medium bodied. The sweeter products (usually chenin blancs, rieslings, colombard, blush wines, some gewurztraminers and proprietary wines) go with Mexican foods and other highly seasoned foods. The dryer products go especially well with seafoods, fowl, rabbit and veal (usually sauvignon blanc and chardonnay), but sauces and seasonings make a difference. Texas red wines are generally more full bodied and dry, and go well with beef, lamb and game (cabernet sauvignon, ruby cabernet, zinfandel, barbera). Carnelian and chambourcin are dry, medium bodied red wines. Sparkling wines are suitable for most dishes and occasions. The acidity in dry sparkling wine helps clean the palate. Texas also produces dessert wines (muscat canelli, late harvest riesling and muscadine) and Port. Your knowledgeable wine merchant can help you with the available selections.

Texas Wineries

Most of these wineries were bonded after 1980. The vines are young and the wine will improve as the vines age. Production is often small and the supply limited, so not all wines are equally easy to find throughout the state.

Alamo Farms Vineyards and Winery (1988)

Bieganowski Cellars (1988)

Bluebonnet Hill Winery (1985)

Chateau Montgolfier Vineyards (1982)

Cordier Estates, Inc./Ste. Genevieve Wines (1987)

Cypress Valley Winery (1982)

Fall Creek Vineyards (1979)

Guadalupe Valley Winery (1975)

La Buena Vida Vineyards (1976)

La Escarbada XIT Winery (1985)

Llano Estacado Winery (1976)

Messina Hof Wine Cellars (1983)

Moyer Texas Sparkling Wines (1987)

Oberhellmann Vineyards (1982)

Padernales Vineyards (1986)

Pheasant Ridge Winery (1982)

Piney Woods Country Wines (1987)

Preston Trail Winery (1986)

Sanchez Creek Vineyard (1979)

St. Lawrence Winery (1988)

Sister Creek Winery (1988)

Slaughter -Leftwich Vineyards (1988)

Tejas Vineyard (1986)

Teysha Cellars (1988)

Val Verde Winery (1883)

Wimberley Valley Wines (1983)

In Summary

Given these suggestions and a list of characteristics in many of the foods we eat, it bears repeating: your particular preference for flavors and textures remains personal, as does your preference in pairing wines with foods. In any event, wine in moderation can have healthful benefits. Also, moderate amounts of wine enhance not only the food, but the joy of the evening and the well-being of the diners. So share Texas wines with your friends and among yourselves, and experience the "next big thing from Texas!"

CONTRIBUTORS

The Cookbook Committee of Cypress Woodlands Junior Forum wishes to thank all of the many contributors and testers who have been very supportive in the creation of WILD ABOUT TEXAS. It is our sincere hope that no one has been mistakenly omitted.

Jane Abston
Susan Adkins
Pam Ahern
Denise Alford
Camille Anderson
Caroline Anderson
Jimmie Ruth Arceneaux
Patti Arnold
Lynn Bacon
Charlotte Baker
Nancy Battle
Marjorie Baylis
Ruth Becker
Susan Biggs
Kay Black
Cheryl Blaize
Beverly Bland
Cathy Blank
Norma Blenderman
Kathie Blinn
Susan Boss
Janiece Boyd
Karen Braden
Nancy Brandimarte
Sharon Brandt
Linda Brewer
Dena Britton
Gay Brown
Irma Bujnoch
Margo Cagney
Kathy Carson
Bernadette Carty
Kathy Chaffin
Kathy Chenowith
Gerry Christensen
Florra Clarke

Betty Clem
Sue Coffey
Susan Cofran
Peggy Jo Coker
Marsha Connally
Nancy Cook
Nancy Copeland
Suzanne Craig
Kay Crocker
Rosalie Cross
Margie Crump
Eileen Cummins
Marilyn Curtis
Jan Dean
Beth Deakins
Lynn Deyo
Frances Dodier
Mary Doerfler
Peggy Dollens
Karen Donelson
Mary Lynn Dozier
Sheron Drew
Margaret Dunagan
Connie Dyer
Peggy Edwards
Mary Ellington
Suzanne Ellis
Elizabeth Erwin
Linda Estrada
Joan Evans
Cherrill Farnsworth
Gloria Fawcett
Nancy Fenton
Patsy Fielder
JoAnn Finn
Jimmie Sue Francis

Andrea Garrity
Edna Gilbert
Pam Gilbert
Mary Giles
Susan Gisondi
Alana Glass
Charla Glass
Carole Goodman
Kalyn Green
Mike Greenwood
Gayle Guthrie
Celia Haas
Mary Hahn
Becky Halbardier
Margaret Hamilton
Lynda Hart
Candy Hawthorne
Bonnie Heimlich
Wendy Henley
Diane Henson
Kay Higgins
Carole Hill
Martha Hill
Suzanne Hill
Judy Hillegeist
Dana Hines
Leslie Hix
Sandy Hopkins
Cathy Howard
Jeanie Hubbard
Tony Jansky
Patsy Jenkins
Sharon Johnson
Madalyn Jones
Louise Jowdy
Martha Ann Kappel

Charlotte Kelly
Sharon Kephart
Sue Kikis
Ellen Kindred
Connie Klepper
Janet Knight
Sonia Koudelka
Shelia Little-Kribbs
Sherrita Krus
Gayle Lambert
JoAnn Lawrenz
Sharon Leigh
Peggy Lesch
Clara Lewis
Karen Lewis
Sherry Lindley
Nancy Lohmeier
Genevieve Loria
Jeannette Loverdi
Sherri Lowe
Cindy MacKay
Betty Mahlmann
Judy Manka
Jackie Marcotte
Jean Marshall
Nancy Maxwell
Londa May
Becky McDermott
Mary Ann McIlvain
Winkle McKinley
Dawn McNeill
Susan McPhail
Cheryl McWilliams
Virginia Medford
Debbie Melroy
Judy Merrill
Brenda Moody
Debbie Moody
Judy Moores
Charlene Moriarty
Ann Morris

Linda Mulherin
Diane Murray
Helen Meyers
Carol Newell
Janet Newkirk
Susanne O'Connell
Ann Payne
Betty Pease
Nancy Petrucciani
Ann Pettey
Mamie Polk
Vicki Potts
Ann Prince
Maria Pyle
Jennifer Reilly
Georgan Reitmeier
Karen Rice
Gail Rickey
Rhonda Riffle
Jackie Riley
Beverly Robb
Claudette Rodgers
Antonia Roesler
Kim Rootes
Pat Rose
Laura Rowe
Susan Ryder
Diane Sanford
Cynthia Sauer
Bonnie Savage
Barbara Schlattman
Susan Sellers
Lorene Servos
Mary Lee Shawver
Sherrie Sherertz
Barbara Shuford
Irene Skor
Barbara Sleet
Carrie Smith
Nancy Speaks
Connie Jo Sperry

Blaine Stacy
Jimmye Stafford
Pat Stahl
Pam Stewart
Margaret Sullivan
Mary Summers
Barbie Swartz
Carol Tabor
Dede Tarrance
Cheryl Thiltgen
Loretta Tidwell
Margie Tillotson
Sue Treece
Donna Vadala
Diane VanDuzer
Vicki Villarreal
Jan Wade
Judy Waisath
Mimi Walsh
Nancy Walter
Nancy Warwick
Jolyne Wassell
Kitty Watkins
Janey West
Sarah Jane West
Daisy White
Jane White
Linda Williams
Pat Williams
Sandy Williams
Bunny Wilson
Nancy Wilson
Lynette Windsor
Mary Wood
Charlotte Woodrow
Kathy Woolverton
Kandice Wright
Barbara Young
Carolyn Young
Kim Young
Michelle Zapalac

Also Special Thanks to Charles Dunagan, Tony Hill, Charles Jansky, Sheryn Jones, Fred Kappel, John Krus, Bob Lindley, Paul Strobel, John White and the many friends and supporters of Cypress Woodlands Junior Forum.

NOTES

NOTES

Cypress-Woodlands Junior Forum Inc.
P.O. Box 90020
Department 242
Houston, Texas 77290
1-713-580-4970

Please send me _____copies of *Wild About Texas* @ $17.95 each _____
Postage and handling   @   2.50 each _____
Gift wrap   @   2.00 each _____
                                              Total Enclosed _____

Name _____

Address _____

City _____ State _____ Zip _____

Make checks payable to *Wild About Texas*.
All proceeds will be used for community projects and programs.

Cypress-Woodlands Junior Forum Inc.
P.O. Box 90020
Department 242
Houston, Texas 77290
1-713-580-4970

Please send me _____copies of *Wild About Texas* @ $17.95 each _____
Postage and handling   @   2.50 each _____
Gift wrap   @   2.00 each _____
                                              Total Enclosed _____

Name _____

Address _____

City _____ State _____ Zip _____

Make checks payable to *Wild About Texas*.
All proceeds will be used for community projects and programs.

Cypress-Woodlands Junior Forum Inc.
P.O. Box 90020
Department 242
Houston, Texas 77290
1-713-580-4970

Please send me _____copies of *Wild About Texas* @ $17.95 each _____
Postage and handling   @   2.50 each _____
Gift wrap   @   2.00 each _____
                                              Total Enclosed _____

Name _____

Address _____

City _____ State _____ Zip _____

Make checks payable to *Wild About Texas*.
All proceeds will be used for community projects and programs.

If you would like to see *Wild About Texas* in your area, please send the names and addresses of your local gift or book stores.

If you would like to see *Wild About Texas* in your area, please send the names and addresses of your local gift or book stores.

If you would like to see *Wild About Texas* in your area, please send the names and addresses of your local gift or book stores.